Methodology and History of Economics

This edited volume provides an in-depth exploration into the influential work of Wade Hands, examining the changing relationship between methodology and the history of economics in connection with contemporary developments in economics.

The papers in this volume fall into four parts, each devoted to an important theme in Wade Hands' work. The first part explores the influence and scope of *Reflection without Rules*, capturing the rich debate that the book generated about what guides methodological and philosophical thinking in economics. The second part examines Hands' research on Paul Samuelson's economics and the methodological dimensions of Samuelson's thinking. Part three looks to Hands' long-standing interest in the philosophical foundations of pragmatist thinking. The final part addresses his more recent research in the methodological import of the emergence of behavioural economics. Together, the contributors show how Hands' insights in complexity theory, identity, and stratification are key to understanding a reconfigured economic methodology. They also reveal how his willingness to draw from multiple academic disciplines gives us a platform for interrogating mainstream economics and provides the basis for a humane yet scientific alternative.

This unique volume will be essential reading for advanced students and researchers across social economics, history of economic thought, economic methodology, political economy, and philosophy of social science.

Bruce Caldwell is a Research Professor of Economics and the Director of the Center for the History of Political Economy at Duke University. He is the author of *Beyond Positivism: Economic Methodology in the 20th Century*, first published in 1982. For the past three decades, his research has focused on the multi-faceted writings of the Nobel prize-winning economist and social theorist Friedrich A. Hayek.

John Davis, Professor Emeritus of Economics, Marquette University and University of Amsterdam, is author of *The Theory of the Individual in Economics* (2003). He is also the editor of the Routledge Advances in Social Economics series. Davis' research has focused on the philosophy and methodology of economics, identity and economics, and healthcare economics.

Uskali Mäki is a Philosophy Professor at the University of Helsinki and a Visiting Professor at Nankai University, China. He is a former editor of the *Journal of Economic Methodology* (1995–2005). His current research is mainly on the philosophy of economics and other social sciences, on models, scientific realism, interdisciplinarity, and social aspects of science.

Esther-Mirjam Sent is Professor of Economic Theory and Policy at Radboud University in the Netherlands. Sent is co-editor of the *Journal of Institutional Economics*. Her research explores behavioral economics, experimental economics, and economic policy, as well as the history and philosophy of economic science.

Routledge INEM Advances in Economic Methodology

Series Editor: Esther–Mirjam Sent
University of Nijmegen, The Netherlands

The field of economic methodology has expanded rapidly during the last few decades. This expansion has occurred in part because of changes within the discipline of economics, in part because of changes in the prevailing philosophical conception of scientific knowledge, and also because of various transformations within the wider society. Research in economic methodology now reflects not only developments in contemporary economic theory, the history of economic thought, and the philosophy of science; but it also reflects developments in science studies, historical epistemology, and social theorizing more generally. The field of economic methodology still includes the search for rules for the proper conduct of economic science, but it also covers a vast array of other subjects and accommodates a variety of different approaches to those subjects.

The objective of this series is to provide a forum for the publication of significant works in the growing field of economic methodology. Since the series defines methodology quite broadly, it will publish books on a wide range of different methodological subjects. The series is also open to a variety of different types of works: original research monographs, edited collections, as well as republication of significant earlier contributions to the methodological literature. The International Network for Economic Methodology (INEM) is proud to sponsor this important series of contributions to the methodological literature.

The Positive and the Normative in Economic Thought
Edited by Sina Badiei and Agnès Grivaux

Methodology and History of Economics
Reflections with and without Rules
Edited by Bruce Caldwell, John Davis, Uskali Mäki and Esther-Mirjam Sent

For more information about this series, please visit: www.routledge.com/ Routledge-INEM-Advances-in-Economic-Methodology/book-series/ SE0630

Methodology and History of Economics

Essays in Honour of D. Wade Hands

Reflections with and without Rules

Edited by Bruce Caldwell, John Davis, Uskali Mäki, and Esther-Mirjam Sent

Routledge
Taylor & Francis Group

LONDON AND NEW YORK

First published 2023
by Routledge
4 Park Square, Milton Park, Abingdon, Oxon OX14 4RN

and by Routledge
605 Third Avenue, New York, NY 10158

Routledge is an imprint of the Taylor & Francis Group, an informa business

British Library Cataloguing-in-Publication Data
A catalogue record for this book is available from the British Library

Library of Congress Cataloging-in-Publication Data
A catalog record has been requested for this book

ISBN: 978-1-032-20946-3 (hbk)
ISBN: 978-1-032-20949-4 (pbk)
ISBN: 978-1-003-26605-1 (ebk)

DOI: 10.4324/9781003266051

Typeset in Bembo
by KnowledgeWorks Global Ltd.

Contents

Contributors

Marcel Boumans, Utrecht University, The Netherlands

Bruce Caldwell, Duke University, USA

John B. Davis, University of Amsterdam, The Netherlands; and Marquette University, USA

Sheila Dow, University of Stirling, United Kingdom; and University of Victoria, Canada

Daniel M. Hausman, Rutgers University, USA

Kevin Hoover, Duke University, USA

Robert Leonard, University of Quebec at Montreal, Canada

Uskali Mäki, University of Helsinki, Finland

Caterina Marchionni, University of Helsinki, Finland

Steven G. Medema, Duke University, USA

Mary Morgan, London School of Economics, United Kingdom

Don Ross, University College Cork, Ireland; University of Cape Town, South Africa; and Georgia State University, USA

Malcolm Rutherford, University of Victoria, Canada

Esther–Mirjam Sent, Radboud University, The Netherlands

Jack Vromen, Erasmus University Rotterdam, The Netherlands

Wade Hands as an Historian and Philosopher of Economics

Bruce Caldwell, John B. Davis, Uskali Mäki, and Esther-Mirjam Sent

This volume recognizes, highlights, and honors Wade Hands' remarkable contributions to the history and philosophy of economics and his standing as a pre-eminent member of the community of scholars who investigate these themes. We begin by personally introducing Wade through our own encounters and interactions with him going back many years.

> I first learned of Wade and his work when in January 1982 he sent me a copy of a paper reviewing Mark Blaug's contributions to economic methodology that was forthcoming in *Philosophy of the Social Sciences*. Accompanying it was a note that read in part "Since this journal is probably not read by most economists, I decided to send copies to those in the profession who I felt might find it of interest. Your work on methodology puts you on this (rather short) list." I have no idea how he got my name but I am certainly glad that he did. I have been lucky to count him as a friend for forty years. He was right that we were a vanishingly small group at the time. It is in no small part due to Wade's continued contributions to the field, as a scholar and an editor, that it has grown into what it is today.
>
> *Bruce Caldwell*

> One of the best things that happened to me in my professional life was being co-editor with Wade of the *Journal of Economic Methodology* from 2005 to 2020. Editing a journal is very rule-driven but it also involves a continuous need to exercise judgment. Wade was one of the most reasonable people I've ever worked with, and also had keen insight into the value of the research that came to the *Journal*. When we began we inherited a field that had largely traveled well-trodden paths but was suddenly rapidly changing, virtually exploding with new ideas. Wade's openness to new research topics never failed to demonstrate both great insight into their potential and also a generosity to researchers taking chances. He's an instinctive pluralist, and has a deep understanding of the questions our subject produces.
>
> *John Davis*

DOI: 10.4324/9781003266051-1

Wade has been a luxury companion on our long journey since the beginnings of economic methodology as a field. At the 1984 HES conference in Pittsburgh where we first met, he rescued me from an aggressive discussant on my early F53 paper. In 1993, on our long walk (with Bruce too) along the hot Atlantic beach in North Carolina, we conceived Wade's blockbuster *Reflection without Rules* (sorry about the title…). In 2001 he visited EIPE in Rotterdam, teaching a magnificent course for our students based on his *Reflection* that was to appear later that year. In the next decade, Wade spent several periods as visiting professor at TINT in Helsinki, interacting with our large community of philosophers of economics and other social sciences. And much more in between these highlights, not forgetting countless dinners, intensive and inspiring as can be. It has been an immensely rewarding friendship and extended intellectual adventure.

Uskali Mäki

I first became acquainted with the work of Wade through Philip Mirowski, who first served on my dissertation committee and next became my colleague. The two of them acted as my mentors during my early career. And whenever colleagues tried to attack Phil by pointing their arrows at me, Wade would always come to my rescue. Because he used a special font type in his referee reports, I could tell who the constructive critic of some of my submissions was. Indeed, Wade manages to combine creativity and compassion, eloquence and empathy. This is a rare combination. As a result, it is with extra gratitude that I look back on my interactions with Wade.

Esther-Mirjam Sent

D. Wade Hands

D. Wade Hands retired in June 2021 as a Distinguished Professor of Economics at the University of Puget Sound, where he had begun as an Assistant Professor in 1980. He did his PhD in economics at University of Indiana, where among those who influenced him was the noted philosopher and historian of science H. Scott Gordon.

Wade has also been a Visiting Professor at the University of Helsinki in the "Trends and Tensions in Intellectual Integration" Group, at the GRESE Institute University of Paris 1, a Visiting Scholar at Erasmus University Institute for Philosophy and Economics in Rotterdam, and in the Departments of Economics at the University of Notre Dame and Duke University.

Among the prizes, awards, and honors he has received are:

• the History of Economics Society 2004 Joseph J. Spengler Book Prize for the best book in the history of economics for his *Reflection Without Rules: Economic Methodology and Contemporary Science Theory*

- a 2005 National Science Foundation STS Research Award for "Agreement on Demand: Studies in the History of Demand Theory 1930-1950"
- the 2018 Best Article Award from the European Society for the History of Economic Thought for "The Individual and the Market: Paul Samuelson on (Homothetic) Santa Claus Economics" (that appeared in *The European Journal of the History of Economic Thought* in 2016)
- the 2018 Warren Samuels Prize for Interdisciplinary Research in the History of Economic Thought and Methodology and Emerald Literati Award for "Hypothetical Pattern Explanations in Economic Science: Hayek's Explanation of the Principle and Pattern Prediction Meets Contemporary Philosophy of Science" (that appeared in *Research in the History of Economic Thought and Methodology* 36A, 2018, 37–57
- a 2011 grant from the Institute for New Economic Thinking for "Paul Samuelson and the Keynesian Golden Age"
- a 2011 grant from the Institute for New Economic Thinking for an International Workshop on "The Methodology, Systemic Risk, and the Economics Profession" (with J. Davis)
- a 2014 grant from the Institute for New Economic Thinking for "Agents and Markets: The Representative Agent in Mid- versus Late-Twentieth Century Economics"
- and over the years a number of University of Puget Sound research grants.

Wade is a past President of the History of Economics Society, has held numerous positions in history of economics societies and the International Network for Economic Method, has done summer teaching at the Duke Center for the History of Political Economy, and been on multiple PhD committees or acted as an external thesis examiner.

Wade was co-editor of *Journal of Economic Methodology* from 2005 to 2020 during which time he gave new direction to the field of economic methodology, was on many journal editorial boards, and continued to review papers for a large number of journals.

He has published over 100 scholarly journal papers, book chapters, comments, introductions, and book reviews. Among the nearly dozen books he has authored or co-edited, four especially stand out: his monumental, influential *Reflection Without Rules: Economic Methodology and Contemporary Science Theory* (2001), *The Handbook of Economic Methodology* (Davis, Hands, and Mäki, 1998), *Agreement on Demand: Consumer Theory in the Twentieth Century* (Hands and Mirowski, 2006), and *The Elgar Companion to Recent Economic Methodology* (Davis and Hands, 2011). These books stand out as important contributions to the history and methodology of economics in themselves, but they also point us to Wade's larger body of publications with their many themes and to the development in his thinking over his career.

Wade Hands as a scholar and researcher

Wade began publishing immediately upon arriving at Puget Sound. His early publications include technical papers (e.g., 1981, 1982, 1983) reflecting his teaching and expertise in mathematical economics (see 1991 [1994]), and this research has continued throughout his career. His main interest, however, was the on-going methodological debates over growth of economic knowledge, especially as drew on Karl Popper about whom he became a recognized expert (1985a, 1988, 1991a, 1991b, 1992, 1993a, 1997b, 1998, 2013b) and also on Imre Lakatos (1985b, 1990b, 1993a). From this he turned increasingly to the evolution of economic methodology itself and in particular to its relationships to new currents in philosophy of science thinking (1994a, 1994b, 1995, 1997a, 1997b, 1997c).

This early period of Wade's research was bookended by two papers with variations of the same title "Thirteen Theses on Progress in Economic Methodology" (1990c, 2001a), in which he took stock of the state of the field at the end of the 1980s and then showed where it stood ten years later. In between these papers, he was a co-editor of the Elgar *Handbook of Economic Methodology* (1998) that gave the first comprehensive survey of the state of methodological thinking in economics with over 100 contributors and some 150 entries. This was then followed by the publication of his very influential *Reflection without Rules* book (2001b) – a definitive synthesis at the Millennium of the state of the field combined with a review and appraisal of the relation of methodological thinking in economics to contemporary science theory as he called it, comprising both philosophy and sociology of science.

The premise of the book was how economic methodology had in a number of new ways gone beyond the logical empiricist, "received view" in philosophy of science whose dominance in the philosophy of science had started waning from the 1950s already and was gradually replaced by many other perspectives to science. The expression the book used to capture this was its idea of many new "turns" in methodological thinking: the naturalistic turn, the sociological turn, the pragmatic turn, the economic turn. It treated psychology, cognitivism, evolutionary biology, philosophy of mind, sociology, feminism, and realism as newly central to the field. This went well beyond how most methodologists had envisioned the field, and made him a natural choice as a new editor of the *Journal of Economic Methodology* to continue the directions it had taken.

Reflection was important both in that it showed there were unappreciated philosophical and theoretical resources to methodological thinking about economics, and also in that it showed this thinking dealt with social science types of problems neglected by many philosophers of science. The book also heralded the emergence of the methodology of economics as a distinct, new field of research in economics, one no longer simply a borrowing from existing philosophy of science, and one moreover with a complex relationship to economics itself.

After *Reflection*, though these themes remained ones Wade continued to write on, he increasingly examined methodological thinking of central figures in the history of economics, including Harold Hotelling (1998), Frank Knight (2006), Milton Friedman (2003, 2009a), Lionel Robbins (2009b), Paul Samuelson (2014b, 2016, 2019b), and Friedrich Hayek (2018). He also published a number of papers examining and evaluating the state of standard economic theory in a time when economics itself was undergoing change (2010a, 2010b, 2013a, 2017a, 2017b, 2017c, 2019a). In both instances, he showed that methodological thinking on the part of economists, including highly regarded individuals, was less clear and well thought out than the profession had commonly assumed, and thus in need of deeper elucidation.

If in the past influential economists had from time to time made various methodological claims and pronouncements, it had now become clear that methodology was a more difficult subject than many economists had assumed. This was different from how research in the history of economics impacted economics. In that case, since history mostly concerned the past, most economists felt free to ignore it. In contrast, methodology remained an on-going issue in economics, and indeed became more so with the development of new research approaches and as economics began to draw more from other disciplines.

A later focus in Wade's research was the role of normative thinking in economics (2012, 2013c). Since Robbins, taking economics to be a value-free science had long been a pillar of standard economics, but the philosophical underpinnings of this notion had gone largely unexamined. Wade contributed to opening up a new discussion of the place of normativity in economics, particularly in his chapter "The Positive-Normative Dichotomy and Economics" in Elsevier's *Philosophy of Economics. Handbook of the Philosophy of Science* (2012). He then extended this investigation into the role normative thinking plays in behavioral economics, especially in connection with the challenge libertarian paternalism poses to traditional welfarism (2014a, 2020, 2021a).

Indeed, one of the impressive features of Wade's research history is the wide array of subjects it addresses. The breadth of subjects he has investigated stands out compared to how many researchers focus on just a few subjects they know especially well. Among other things, Wade has had a tremendous ability to focus on often unappreciated fundamental problems in economic explanation. To give a sense of this, we highlight three of these.

One such subject concerns his analysis of the problem of self-defeating and self-fulfilling public prediction and its long history in philosophy of science and in social science (1990a). Prediction is often seen as one of the main goals of economics in its attempt to be the most quantitative of the social sciences and make policy recommendations. During the mathematization of economics and the introduction of probability theory into economics in the 1920s, prediction was seen as an indication of objectivity. As a first approximation, economists abstracted from such difficulties as infinite regress and reflexivity by assuming that people believe and expect whatever the facts are. In that way theorists need not worry about what those beliefs and expectations are. However, once one goes beyond this first approximation, the difficulties loom large. In his 1990 paper, Wade shows that Emil Grunberg, Franco Modigliani, and Herbert Simon were precursors to the general concept of rational expectations.

Another subject involves the symmetry that Wade observed between economics and philosophy of science in their trying to understand the interests of economic agents and scientists (1994b). He notes that while economists do not normally use the term "interests," they do in fact explain economic behavior on the basis of the "interests" of the agents involved. Likewise, scientists make intentional choices on the basis of their beliefs and desires. However, philosophers of science who attempt to explore this symmetry encounter the problem that the standard model of microbehavior has almost no implications for macrobehavior (1995).

Then there are papers that Wade wrote along with Philip Mirowski (Hands and Mirowski, 1998, Mirowski and Hands, 1998). They argue that neoclassical economics owes its strength to its persistent inability to enforce any monolithic orthodoxy. In particular, they outline three approaches to neoclassical demand theory, associated with the University of Chicago Economics Department (in particular Milton Friedman and George Stigler), the Cowles Commission at the University of Chicago (especially Kenneth Arrow and Gerard Debreu), and the Massachusetts Institute of Technology (most notably Paul Samuelson).

There are many other subjects Wade has brought to light that have influenced others thinking in methodology and the philosophy and history of economics. The contributors to this volume have taken up a number of them. We turn to them for a further look at Wade's contributions.

The chapters in this volume

The chapters in this volume fall into four parts, each devoted to an important theme in Wade's work: the influence and scope of his *Reflection Without Rules*, his research on the methodological dimensions of Paul Samuelson's thinking, his long-standing interest in the philosophical foundations of pragmatist thinking, and his recent examination of methodological reasoning in behavioral economics.

Reflection with and without rules

We characterize this section as "reflection with and without rules" to capture the rich debate Wade's *Reflections* book has generated about what guides methodological and philosophical thinking in economics. What are the rules? When do they apply? What else underlies methodological and philosophical thinking in economics?

First, in her "Insider, Outsider, Stranger, Resident Field-Worker? Reflections on Wade Hands' Authorial Stance in *Reflection Without Rules*" (2001), Mary Morgan frames her discussion of the book in terms of the uniquely multi-sided authorial stance he occupies in the book. The book explained the changing contours of philosophy of science to economists and used his philosophical gaze to unpack the changes in economists' interests over the parallel period. Rereading now, it seems he played the "insider" and "outsider" in both communities: implying either a considerable intellectual balancing act, or possibly a shifting "standpoint" – or maybe something a little different. Morgan concludes that the best way to conceive Wade's authorial knowledge is as an insider from economics, undertaking "resident field work" in philosophy to bring it back for the economics community.

Marcel Boumans, in his "Reflections without Rules: Reflections about Rules after Twenty Years," follows with a discussion of how Wade's *Reflection* book has affected change in methodology and economic philosophy since its publication. He argues that the book appeared at a time when the intense debates about the rules of proper science had come to an end. This ending was not a closure; it did not mean that any consensus was reached, except the commonly shared view that the rules of the Received View were passé. It was mainly a "turn" or a "move away." Like in the dominant economic view of the 1990s, undisturbed emerging systems were considered to be good, so the only ethical rule was no rules at all. Boumans admits that it is not clear whether Hand's *Reflections* draws the same conclusions, though it touches on this conception – what Boumans calls an Austrian view – as the book's title seems to suggest. But the relevant question for Boumans is whether this view still bears relevance after a decade of major crises. According to the authors of the Dahlem report (Colander et al., 2009), it does not anymore, and Boumans agrees. We need an ethical code in particular when economic knowledge can do harm. But the nature of these rules are different than those of the positivists: (1) know what you know and (2) be honest about it. Philosophy and history of science and science studies therefore still have an important role to play, these are the fields that can help to map out what we know, what the often implicit rules are of how we gain that knowledge, and in what sense we can trust it. These can never be universal rules but have to be situated locally and historically and sociologically contextualized.

Caterina Marchionni's chapter, "Social aspects of economics modelling," reviews issues that lie at the intersection of sociology of science and economic methodology, an area of inquiry Wade has been keen to promote. In particular, it first examines how shared norms about what counts as a good economic explanation shape the kind of models economists build. She argues that adherence to such norms is what keeps the field together and allows for knowledge production. Yet, it also tends to systematically obscure some aspects of the phenomena and hence create blind spots. Second, the chapter discusses the wider effects economic models have on society due to the phenomenon known as performativity. It suggests that if, and when, economic models are performative, then the blind spots end up affecting not only our understanding of economic phenomena but also our social institutions. This possibility calls for an ethical perspective on economic modelling alongside the epistemic and social ones.

The methodological dimensions and implications of Paul Samuelson's economics

The second section of the volume examines Wade's work on Paul Samuelson's economics. Samuelson played an enormous role in defining postwar economics, but comparatively little research has examined its methodological dimensions and implications. Wade has been a leader in this regard, and his careful analyses of Samuelson's thinking have influenced and inspired others.

Sheila Dow in her "Unification and Pluralism in Economics" points to how recently Wade has drawn attention to the explanatory pluralism present in Samuelson's *Foundations* (Samuelson, 1947) alongside its derivational unification (Hands, 2019b, 2021b). Her purpose is to pursue this analysis in relation to the unificationist and pluralist discourses in economics. A consideration of Samuelson's philosophy of science suggests the presence of a degree of pluralism in other domains than explanation. But a broader discussion of the meanings of, and justifications for, both unification and pluralism indicates that derivational unification limits the admissibility of, and scope for, pluralism in other domains. This analysis is then applied to current debates over the future direction of mainstream macroeconomics.

Steven G. Medema's "In Search of Santa Claus: Samuelson, Stigler, and Coase Theorem Worlds" adds another perspective. He notes that Samuelson was fond of labeling mathematical models with extremely strong and empirically unrealistic assumptions, "Santa Claus" economics. But there was one economic result that, in Samuelson's view, could not be captured even in a Santa Claus world: the Coase theorem, an object of his repeated derision. His friend George Stigler, though, had no such problems and, indeed, was perhaps the biggest cheerleader for the theorem. Medema examines their respective treatments of the Coase theorem in an effort to explain their contrasting positions. In doing so, he suggests that their views on appropriate degrees of abstraction – and perhaps the limits of their theoretical imaginations – were conditioned in part by the results to which that abstraction led.

Don Ross follows with his "Neo-Samuelsonian methodology, normative economics, and the quantitative intentional stance." He argues that Wade's 2013 paper critically consolidated a new and growing approach to revealed preference interpretations and methods, which he called "Contemporary Revealed Preference Theory" (CRPT). Wade recognized that CRPT is folded into a more comprehensive philosophy of economics due to Ross, which Ross dubs "Neo-Samuelsonian Philosophy of Economics" (NSEP). Hands calls this "the elephant in the room" where his criticisms of CRPT as an account of normative economics are concerned. Ross now addresses Hands' criticisms of CRPT using the full resources of Neo-Samuelsonian Philosophy of Economics (NSPE). This leads to substantial reconsideration of normative economics, with respect to both assessments of general rationality in economic agents, and emphasis on welfare improvement in applied policy work. Main conclusions are that (1) economists are not properly in the business of assessing general rationality, a topic best left to a philosophical tradition descended from Aristotle; (2) the borrowing of theoretical structures from the foundations of microeconomics in the project of philosophical decision theory encourages the idea that there should be a rigorous bridge between economists' interest in technical choice consistency and philosophers' interest in general rationality, but NSPE implies that this approach to bridge building is misguided; (3) economics is a policy science, but the policy domains to which it aims to be relevant are public and corporate, not personal; and (4) NSPE provides clearer insight than alternative philosophies of economics as to why economists concentrate on welfare, rather than well-being, as their primary normative target.

The philosophical foundations of pragmatism

The third section of the book addresses Wade's long-standing interest in pragmatism, including his attention to John Dewey who influenced institutionalist economics.

Kevin Hoover in "Models, Truth, and Analytic Inference in Economics" begins with the paradoxical nature of economic models. A popular view of models among economists and philosophers alike is that all models are false, but some are useful. Models are frequently treated as convenient fictions, idealizations, stories about credible worlds, or "near enough" to the truth. But such understandings pose serious questions, among them: if models are false, how is it that they are so useful? how can they have any bearing on what is actually the case in the world? how can we evaluate them empirically? how can we develop them for greater precision? for understanding how models related to the world, how they can successfully support scientific investigation? This chapter argues that these and related questions reflect a fundamental confusion: models are, in fact, useful only to the degree that they are instruments for stating truth. The confusion arises from a failure to understand how models relate to the world analogically. Analogies are fundamentally incomplete and perspectival, so that the truths that state are necessarily piecemeal, but models may nonetheless be apt. A critical distinction is drawn between accuracy and precision in modeling. Modeling is related to Charles Peirce's *analytical inference*. And the application of analytical inference in economics is illustrated with a historical case-study of Lawrence Klein's early econometric models of the US economy.

In "Institutional Economics and John Dewey's Instrumentalism" Malcolm Rutherford returns us to the roots of American pragmatism. Previous discussions concerning the relationship between John Dewey's pragmatic instrumentalism and institutional economics have focused on Clarence Ayres and on issues of valuation. This chapter gives attention to the actual conduct of economic investigations by institutionalists such as Wesley Mitchell, Walton Hamilton, and John R. Commons. It is argued that many aspects of Dewey's instrumentalism are clearly displayed in the problem centered, investigational, and experimental methods employed by institutionalists, and in their commitment to problem-solving through social control. While the standard criticisms of institutionalist methodology are found to be misplaced, some serious difficulties with the application of Dewey's experimentalism to social science are located.

In "*Metanoia*: E. F. Schumacher's Rejection of *Homo Oeconomicus*, 1950–1972" Robert Leonard looks to a less familiar source of methodological thinking about economics. Until roughly 1950, the Anglo-German economist E. F. Schumacher (1911–1977) was a conventional Fabian economist, inspired by Keynes and thoroughly committed to modern economic growth and development. By 1970, however, he had rejected much of this and, with his authorship of *Small is Beautiful* (1973), was about to become a symbolic figure in the counter-cultural and environmental movement of the 1970s. Drawing on both published and archival sources, this article traces that change in Schumacher. Specifically, we portray his changing attitude to economics and the economy as the consequence of a deeper transformation of the *self*, stimulated by his engagement with esoteric and religious influences, such as Gurdjieff-Ouspensky, Buddhism, and Christianity. Our point of entry to this story is a 1972 talk on the method of economics, given by the "new" Schumacher at the invitation of his old wartime colleague and Fabian comrade, Joan Robinson.

Methodological reasoning in behavioral economics

A fourth, more recent subject of Wade's research is the methodological import of the emergence of behavioral economics.

Daniel M. Hausman reviews a central concern of Wade's work in his "Hands On Nudging" – a comment on Wade's recent essay, "Libertarian Paternalism: Taking Econs Seriously" (2020). In that essay, Wade refines the criticism offered by Infante, Lecouteux, and Sugden (2016) of libertarian paternalism and "nudging." That criticism is more carefully articulated to depict libertarian paternalism as directed to individuals who possess a set of preferences that satisfy the standard axioms, but whose choices fail to reveal their preferences because of psychological failings. Since most people, in contrast, make up "on the fly" many of their preferences, libertarian paternalism does not apply to most cases of problematic preferences. This chapter goes on to argue that rather than neutralizing the errors caused by psychological foibles, nudges are among the factors causing preferences, which are only a fallible indicator of well-being.

In his "Does the inclusion of social preferences in economic models challenge the positive – normative distinction?" Jack Vromen combines the subject of behavioral economics with another of Wade's long-standing concerns: normative economics. He begins by noting that Wade has argued that the inclusion of social preferences in economic models challenges the positive-normative distinction in economics (Hands, 2008). However, Vromen argues that this need not be the case. In their social preference models, behavioral economists can simply treat the social preferences that individuals (allegedly) have as relevant facts about some individuals for developing models with greater explanatory power than the "standard self-interest-only model." If behavioral economists simply left it with that, their analyses would fall squarely in the "positive analysis" category. But behavioral economists typically move beyond this by also treating the existence of social preferences favorably for their welfare-enhancing effects. Vromen argues that not even this needs to push their analyses into the "normative analysis" category. For even though their welfare evaluations inevitably involve normative welfare criteria (that they often do not make explicit), these normative welfare criteria need not necessarily reflect their own moral values. If instead these normative welfare criteria reflect the moral values of others (such as those of the individuals whose welfares are at stake, or of "standard" economists), then on Mongin's (2006) authoritative criterion their welfare analyses might be (and in fact actually are) called instances of positive welfare economics. The paper concludes by arguing that while staying within the confines of "positive analysis" is a logical (or conceptual) possibility for behavioral economists who recognize and welcome the existence of social preferences, it remains to be seen whether doing so is also psychologically possible and also whether it is a good idea to try to do so.

References

Colander, David, Michael Goldberg, Armin Haas, Katarina Juselius, Alan Kirman, Thomas Lux, and Brigitte Sloth (2009). "The Financial Crisis and the Systemic Failure of the Economics Profession," *Critical Review*, 21 (2–3), 249–267.

Davis, John, D. Wade Hands, and Uskali Mäki, eds. (1998) *The Handbook of Economic Methodology*, Cheltenham: Edward Elgar.

Davis, John and D. Wade Hands, eds. (2011) *The Elgar Companion to Recent Economic Methodology*, Cheltenham: Edward Elgar.

Hands, D. Wade (1981) "A Note on Global Hicksian Stability Conditions," *Economics Letters*, 8, 221–226.

Hands, D. Wade (1982) "A Comment on 'A Generalization of the Gross Substitute System'," *Economic Studies Quarterly*, 33, 277–280.

Hands, D. Wade (1983) "Stability in a Discrete Time Model of the Walrasian Tatonnement," *Journal of Economic Dynamics and Control*, 6, 399–411.

Hands, D. Wade (1985a) "Karl Popper and Economic Methodology: A New Look," *Economics and Philosophy*, 1, 83–99.

Hands, D. Wade (1985b) "Second Thoughts on Lakatos," *History of Political Economy*, 17, 1–16.

Hands, D. Wade (1988) "Ad Hocness in Economics and Popperian Philosophy," in *The Popperian Legacy in Economics and Beyond*, N. de Marchi (ed.), Cambridge, UK: Cambridge University Press, 121–137.

Hands, D. Wade (1990a) "Grunberg and Modigliani, Public Predictions and the New Classical Macroeconomics," *Research in the History of Economic Thought and Methodology*, 7, 207–223.

Hands, D. Wade (1990b) "Second Thoughts on 'Second Thoughts:' Reconsidering the Lakatosian Progress of The General Theory," *Review of Political Economy*, 2, 67–81.

Hands, D. Wade (1990c) "Thirteen Theses on Progress in Economic Methodology," *Finnish Economic Papers*, 3, 72–76.

Hands, D. Wade (1991a) "Popper, the Rationality Principle and Economic Explanation," in *Economics, Culture and Education: Essays in Honor of Mark Blaug*, G. K. Shaw (ed.), Cheltenham: Edward Elgar, 108–119.

Hands, D. Wade (1991b) "The Problem of Excess Content: Economics, Novelty and a Long Popperian Tale," in *Appraising Economic Theories: Studies in the Methodology of Research Programs*, M. Blaug and N. de Marchi (eds.), Cheltenham: Edward Elgar, 58–75.

Hands, D. Wade (1992) "Falsification, Situational Analysis and Scientific Research Programs: The Popperian Tradition in Economic Methodology," in *Post-Popperian Methodology of Economics: Recovering Practice*, N. de Marchi (ed.), Philadelphia: Kluwer Academic Publishing, 19–53.

Hands, D. Wade (1993a) "Popper and Lakatos in Economic Methodology," in *Rationality, Institutions and Economic Methodology*, Bo Gustafsson, Christian Knudsen, and Uskali Mäki (eds.), London: Routledge, 61–75.

Hands, D. Wade (1994a) "Blurred Boundaries: Recent Changes in the Relationship Between Economics and the Philosophy of Natural Science," *Studies in History and Philosophy of Science*, 25, 751–772.

Hands, D. Wade (1994b) "The Sociology of Scientific Knowledge and Economics: Some Thoughts on the Possibilities," in *New Directions in Economic Methodology*, R. Backhouse (ed.), London: Routledge, 75–106.

Hands, D. Wade (1995) "Social Epistemology Meets the Invisible Hand: Kitcher on the Advancement of Science," *Dialogue*, 34, 605–621.

Hands, D. Wade (1997a) "Caveat Emptor: Economics and Contemporary Philosophy of Science," *Philosophy of Science*, 64 (Proceedings), S107–S116.

Hands, D. Wade (1997b) "Conjectures and Reputations: The Sociology of Scientific Knowledge and the History of Economic Thought," *History of Political Economy*, 29, 695–739.

Hands, D. Wade (1997c) "Empirical Realism as Meta-Method: Tony Lawson on Neoclassical Economics," *Ekonomia*, 1, 39–53.

Hands, D. Wade (1998) "Ad Hocness in Economics and Popperian Philosophy," in *The Popperian Legacy in Economics and Beyond*, N. de Marchi (ed.), Cambridge, UK: Cambridge University Press, 121–137.

Hands, D. Wade (2001a) "Economic Methodology is Dead – Long Live Economic Methodology: Thirteen Theses on the New Economic Methodology," *Journal of Economic Methodology*, 8, 49–63.

Hands, D. Wade (2001b) *Reflection Without Rules: Economic Methodology and Contemporary Science Theory*, Cambridge, UK: Cambridge University Press.

Hands, D. Wade (2003) "Did Milton Friedman's Methodology License the Formalist Revolution?," *Journal of Economic Methodology*, 10, 507–520.

Hands, D. Wade (2006) "Frank Knight and Pragmatism," *The European Journal of the History of Economic Thought*, 13, 571–605.

Hands, D. Wade (2008) "Philosophy and Economics," in *The New Palgrave Dictionary of Economics*, 2nd ed., S. E. Durlauf and L. E. Blume, eds., London: Palgrave, 410–420.

Hands, D. Wade (2009a) "Did Milton Friedman's Positive Methodology License the Formalist Revolution?," in *The Methodology of Positive Economics: Reflections on the Milton Friedman Legacy*, U. Mäki (ed.), Cambridge: Cambridge University Press, 143–164.

Hands, D. Wade (2009b) "Effective Tension in Robbins's Economic Methodology," *Economica*, 76, 831–844.

Hands, D. Wade (2010a) "The Phase Diagram Technique for Analyzing the Stability of Multiple-Market Equilibrium" in *Famous Figures and Diagrams in Economics*, M. Blaug and P. Lloyd (eds.), Cheltenham: Edward Elgar, 280–285.

Hands, D. Wade (2010b) "Stabilizing Consumer Choice: The Role of 'True Dynamic Stability' and Related Concepts in the History of Consumer Choice Theory," *The European Journal of the History of Economic Thought*, 17, 313–343.

Hands, D. Wade (2012) "The Positive-Normative Dichotomy and Economics," in Philosophy of Economics, U. Mäki (ed.), Vol. 13 of D. Gabbay, P. Thagard, and J. Woods (eds.), *Handbook of the Philosophy of Science*. Amsterdam: Elsevier, 219–239.

Hands, D. Wade (2013a) "Foundations of Contemporary Revealed Preference Theory," *Erkenntnis*, 78, 1081–1108.

Hands, D. Wade (2013b) "GP08 is the New F53: Gul and Pesendorfer's Methodological Essay from the Viewpoint of Blaug's Popperian Methodology," in *Mark Blaug: Rebel with Many Causes*, M. Boumans and M. Klaes (eds.), Cheltenham: Edward Elgar, 245–265.

Hands, D. Wade (2013c) "Mark Blaug on the Normativity of Welfare Economics," *Erasmus Journal for Philosophy and Economics*, 6, 1–25.

Hands, D. Wade (2014a) "Normative Ecological Rationality: Normative Rationality in the Fast-and-Frugal-Heuristics Research Program," *Journal of Economics Methodology*, 21, 396–410.

Hands, D. Wade (2014b) "Paul Samuelson and Revealed Preference Theory," *History of Political Economy*, 46, 85–116.

Hands, D. Wade (2016) "The Individual and the Market: Paul Samuelson on (Homothetic) Santa Claus Economics," *The European Journal of the History of Economic Thought*, 23: 425–452.

Hands, D. Wade (2017a) "Conundrums of the Representative Agent," *Cambridge Journal of Economics*, 41, 1685–1704.

Hands, D. Wade (2017b) "Revealed Preference, Afriat's Theorem, and Falsifiability: A Review Essay on *Revealed Preference Theory* by Christopher P. Chambers and Federico Echenique," *OEconomia*, 7–3, 409–438.

Hands, D. Wade (2017c) "The Road to Rationalization: A History of 'Where the Empirical Lives' (or Has Lived) in Consumer Choice Theory," *The European Journal of the History of Economic Thought*, 24, 555–588.

Hands, D. Wade (2018) "Hypothetical Pattern Explanations in Economic Science: Hayek's Explanation of the Principle and Pattern Prediction Meets Contemporary Philosophy of Science," *Research in the History of Economic Thought and Methodology*, 36A, 37–57.

Hands, D. Wade (2019a) "Economic Methodology in the Twenty-First Century (So Far): Some Post-*Reflection* Reflections," *Review of Economic Philosophy*, 20, 221–252.

Hands, D. Wade (2019b) "Re-Examining Samuelson's Operationalist Methodology," in *Paul Samuelson: Master of Modern Economics*, R. Anderson, W. A. Barnett, and R. A. Cord (eds.), London: Palgrave Macmillan, 39–67.

Hands, D. Wade (2020) "Libertarian Paternalism: Taking Econs Seriously," *International Review of Economics*, 67, 419–441.

Hands, D. Wade (2021a) "Libertarian Paternalism: Making Rational Fools," *Review of Behavioral Economics*, 8, 305–326.

Hands, D. Wade (2021b) "The Many Faces of Unification and Pluralism in Economics: The Case of Paul Samuelson's *Foundations of Economic Analysis*," *Studies in History and Philosophy of Science Part A*, 88, 209–219.

Hands, D. Wade and Philip Mirowski (1998) "Harold Hotelling and the Neoclassical Dream," in *Economics and Methodology: Crossing Boundaries*, R. Backhouse, D. Hausman, U. Mäki, and A. Salanti (eds.), Macmillan and St. Martin's, 322–397.

Hands, D. Wade and Philip Mirowski, eds. (2006) *Agreement on Demand: Consumer Theory in the Twentieth Century*, Durham, NC: Duke University Press.

Infante, Gerardo, Guilhem Lecouteux, and Robert Sugden (2016) "Preference Purification and the Inner Rational Agent: A Critique of the Conventional Wisdom of Behavioural Welfare Economics," *Journal of Economic Methodology*, 23, 1–25.

Mirowski, Philip and D. Wade Hands (1998) "A Paradox of Budgets: The Postwar Stabilization of American Neoclassical Demand Theory", in Mary S. Morgan and Malcolm Rutherford (eds.), *From Interwar Pluralism to Postwar Neoclassicism*, Annual Supplement to Volume 30, History of Political Economy. Durham: Duke University Press, 260–292.

Mongin, Philippe (2006) "Value Judgments and Value Neutrality in Economics," *Economica*, 73, 257–286.

Samuelson, Paul A. (1947) *Foundations of Economic Analysis*. Cambridge: Harvard University Press.

Part I

Reflection with and without rules

1   Insider, Outsider, Stranger, Resident Field-Worker?

Reflections on Wade Hands' Authorial Stance in *Reflection without Rules*

Mary S. Morgan

Introduction

In his magnum opus *Reflection Without Rules* (2001) (hereafter *RWR*), Wade Hands declared the death of the legend that mid-20th-century philosophers provided rules for scientists on the latter's correct prosecution of science and so their search for true knowledge. The distance of 20 years firmly supports that disenchantment; we *can* put those legends well behind us, though, as Wade showed us, with the death of those -isms, we have gained new ones.

RWR depends on both insider and outsider perspectives by economists, philosophers, sociologists, and historians. In the period when Wade was writing, history of economics and philosophy of economics were two marginal sub-fields, mainly practiced inside economics, not outside. A few of these insider scholars (including Wade and myself) were also part of the mainstream philosophy of science (PoS) and/or history of science (HoS) communities, though few in those latter communities showed any interest in economics (or indeed, in social sciences). This has now changed radically: a number of scholars from the HoS and PoS communities work on economics, and economics has become a science of study for them; but many scholars working on history of economics and some in philosophy of economics continue to remain inside economics departments and hardly ever go to those broader HoS and PoS meetings or publish in their journals. This perhaps accounts for our insider mentality, and our narrow focus on history of 'economic thought' (i.e. on theorising) and 'economic methodology' (until recently, largely an examination of theorising).[1]

So what about Wade? Which communities did/does he belong to in order to make his *reflections*? Wade had an initial training in economics and a career in economics to become Distinguished Professor of Economics. At the same time, Wade is one of the few economic methodologists who also publishes, writes referee reports, and participates in the PoS community. He is certainly an 'insider' in economics, but how does he play the role of explaining philosophy to the economists? Does he pretend to be a 'stranger' from the PoS community, in the sense defined by Georg Simmel (1908): as one who comes from the outside but stays in their new community. This label is not

DOI: 10.4324/9781003266051-3

immediately apt for Wade, given his initial field-training and insider status. But there is something important here about the role of 'the stranger' that does apply to Wade. For Simmel, the stranger, by virtue of being so, carries an "objective attitude" and is more open to making assessments that are both "practically and theoretically" freer of local, insider, customary beliefs. The stranger can both observe close-up and remain remote, at the same time.[2] So while Wade may appear solely an insider in economics, he managed to play the stranger's hand to advantage in *RWR*. How did this work?

Insider Knowledge and the Search for 'Truth'

Time-distance reinforces the original enchantment in reading Wade's early chapters on 19th-century British economist-philosophers: Mill, Senior, and Cairnes; and on the later 19th-/early 20th-century US institutionalist/ pragmatist combination: Veblen, Ayres, Peirce, and Dewey. These critical examples of how philosophers-cum-social scientists wrote about their engagement with their dual subject areas exhibit the benefits of their dual citizenship. The 19th-century British protagonists in Wade's account were insiders jointly in philosophy and economics. As philosophers, they were writing about what kind of science economics was, and as economists, about how to think about economics and how to do it. (If there were a second edition of *RWR*, I would suggest to add Jevons explicitly in this group as both the philosopher and economist, for his work and insights on both fronts would bridge from the classical economists into modern technocratic and mathematical economics.) Arguably, late 19th-century US philosophers were also joint insiders, for, as Wade points out, the pragmatist movement was as important in social sciences as in philosophy. This kind of double engagement was mostly lost in 20th-century writings in both economics and philosophy, until, perhaps (or perhaps not) the 'economics turn' in philosophy in the late 20th century, where we can again see scholars like Wade making contributions in both fields.

Wade's engagement with the search for scientific knowledge in the 20th-century reveals that his insider interests are more closely concerned with modern economic theorising than with applied modes of economics, such as econometrics, or experimental economics. (These choices mark Wade's own 'standpoint' in later terms.) Such theoretical work has usually depended on the 20th-century base definition of economics as the efficient use of scarce resources, a framing which has missed out much of relevance in economists' discussion of knowledge and its evolution. In particular, such work has largely ignored the linkages among economic growth, distribution, and the change in technological knowledge in modes of production. While Wade notably goes back to the important insights of Veblen and Ayres into technology, it might also have been rewarding for his discussion of the late 20th-century economists' interests to have broadened his account back into the classical economics work on innovation, machines, and the division of human labour in Smith,

Ricardo, and of course Marx. Similarly, 19th-century economists were as much concerned with the historical evolution of the economy and society as biologists were with evolution in the natural world. Indeed, the arch 19th-century evolutionist, Herbert Spencer's extended theory of evolution – from the development of single-celled organisms through to the human body through to the organisation of society – was based on continual processes of specialisation and the division of labour. Spencer is strangely forgotten by most modern scholars, though his reputation at the time was greater than Darwin's, whose own evolutionary theory has found favour in a branch of economics, nicely epitomised in Nelson and Winter's (1982) seminal economic analysis on how evolving firms carry their knowledge in 'routines' – as relevant to public as to private institutions.

Post *RWR*, there has been a surge in literature on the relations between the growth of scientific and technical knowledge; these have come from a range of social science backgrounds, including of course economics, but perhaps even more strongly focussed in management fields and sociology. At the same time, another insider community in economics has reframed the characteristics of knowledge away from philosophers' worries about 'truth' by focussing instead on the essential characteristics of knowledge being its 'reliability and usefulness' (O'Brien, 2013): the knowledge that grows out of science into technologies. In the last few years, economic history (which had grown almost as marginal as the history of economics within economics departments) has come right back into the fold of mainstream economics. Economic historians have produced an ongoing and considerable literature on the relationship between the scientific revolution and the industrial revolution (though this remains a hotly debated big story[3]). Wade touches on aspects of scientific knowledge production (citing particularly the economic historian Paul David as a collaborator with Partha Dasgupta), but this more recent argument – one that reframes the notion of scientific knowledge – is perhaps more germain to his agenda. We can leave aside the 'usefulness' adjective as something essential for technology and focus on the quality of 'reliability', which speaks more closely to our broader sense of scientific knowledge.

So, while the picture of science from the philosophers of legend had scientists searching for Truth, the economic historians now see scientists as searching for reliable knowledge, reliability being the key to claiming something as knowledge. This looks to be a more prosaic achievement, but the proof of the pudding is in the eating: do the sciences produce knowledge that you can reliably use, and for economists, this surely means reliable in action, not just in policy, but in any economics-based action by any actors in any field. It might well be that economists will find this newer characterisation of knowledge consistent with their modern preference, for example, in providing model-based analysis of productivity, should be; using experimental findings for poverty programmes; developing behavioural nudges in pandemics; and so forth. That is, they will find (and perhaps already do) narrower but satisfactory claims of reliability more useful than sparse claims to 'Truth'.

The Outsider Role and the Standpoints of Strangers

The mid-20th-century legend makers were, in Wade's account, mostly outsiders: strict philosophers, missionaries carrying their written rules for Truth-making into science. Part of that missionary stance, to the insiders, lay in their outsider picture of Science as one monolithic rock: there is one notion of science (based largely on physics) and one right way of doing it. One missing track from Wade's account of the collapse of the legends in the PoS is those (insider) philosophers of science who gave up on there being one science and saw instead a number of scientifically acceptable ways ('styles of thinking' or 'reasoning') of how scientists do their work to get to know things. This was not a recognition of there being so-called special sciences, i.e. disciplinary labels such as chemistry and biology. Rather it was a different cut that focussed on how science could be, and was being, done in different ways across the full range of sciences. Following the account of their long historical development (recorded by Crombie's monumental work, 1988), Hacking (1992) developed his philosophical analysis of these six ways of 'reasoning': mathematical proof on the basis of axioms, experimental exploration, hypothetical construction of models by analogy, taxonomic work, statistical thinking, and historical genetic development. To this list, Forrester (1996) added a seventh style: case studies (and there may well be more). Since then, the recipes in the list have hybridised, so that many specific scientific endeavours are hard to classify (e.g. do simulations of mathematical models use an experimental- or model-based form of reasoning?); combination recipes are easily found everywhere in the sciences.

According to this newer 1990s PoS approach, each mode or way or genre of doing science has developed a rational basis (scientific-artisanal rules) for accessing reliable knowledge, each of which could be appreciated as paths to knowledge, but there are no overall philosophical rules (of logic or reasoning) that overarch them all. So philosophers of science can give them all individually a tick for knowledge-finding rules but offer no imperialising rules from philosophy that get to Truth. In effect, this move created a list of 'middle-level-m' methodological recipes of how those ways of doing science (should) work, and what kind of knowledge scientists gained (pluses and minuses) from each mode of engagement with their scientific materials. This 'naturalist' turn suggested or entailed the recognition and assessment that there were good 'middle-m' practice rules that could bear on the very 'small-m' aspects of doing science, i.e. the methods applicable for any particular 'middle-m' mode of doing science. At the time, this move was seen, within the PoS community, as part of the ending of the legend debates, and proved a liberating move for philosophers as outsiders to venture inside the science spaces (alongside the sociologists, cognitive scientists, etc.).

In *RWR*, Wade makes much of a broader 'naturalist turn' across scholars in different fields who study science, not just away from the philosophical legends, but towards more radical 'outsider' positions on which to stand, to understand and judge how science makes (rather than finds) knowledge: 'standpoint' accounts. His account of these naturalist turn literatures suggests these standpoints could be, and have been, based on a number of other disciplines focussed on how knowledge is acquired – sociology, cognitive psychology, evolutionary biology, economics, plus standpoint variants of philosophy: feminist philosophy, and social epistemology. In this argument, all these 'standpoints' are 'stranger-outsider' positions that potentially help us understand the development of reliable scientific knowledge. This naturalist turn has surely engendered many insights from these standpoints, though, of course, with hindsight, we can also see the danger of substituting other outside disciplinary reflections and rules for the insider disciplinary understandings of scientists, just as the philosophers of science of the legend had done – while the stranger-outsider has an objective stance, they judge science according to their own field knowledge rather than that of the science they are studying. This leads to some peculiar outcomes. One of strangest of these was the infinite regress found when a sociology of scientific knowledge (SSK) outsider position was taken to judge the same SSK programme (Ashmore, 1989). Another was evident in the economics of economic knowledge: as Wade noticed, Kitcher (the outsider from philosophy) used game theory to explore that topic and found the same "explaining everything/explaining nothing" syndrome that the insider John Sutton (1990) had already found in using game theory to investigate firm behaviour in industrial economics.

Some standpoint accounts, perhaps particularly the philosophical ones, have missed the important point that science is not just a matter of thinking, or even of labelling, but of doing, both in small- and large-scale work. Perhaps there is no science that does not involve some forms of technical work: in collecting, gathering, cleaning data; organising categorisations, interventions, and analyses; and making inferences and deducing outcomes. Doing science involves a whole set of processes of "representing and intervening", to use the title of one important nail in the end of the legend debates that Wade notes: Ian Hacking's experimental realist argument (1983) about electrons, if you can spray them, they are real (even though you cannot see them). It is to the advantage of the sociological and SSK standpoints that they have indeed taken this issue – that science involves intervention in the world – seriously, and their focus on how science is practised has embedded them in studying the activities of science.

Since *RWR* (and following the Crombie-Hacking move noted above), the naturalising move in PoS has taken another turn, epitomised in the Society for Philosophy of Science in Practice (SPSP, founded in 2007) following the idea that scientists obviously acquire knowledge from doing science, but asking: 'given they don't follow philosophical rules – how do they do so?' The ambition for such philosophers is to acquire a stranger-insider knowledge of a specific science by looking deeply into practices within particular scientific activities (as other commentators, e.g. SSK, were already doing earlier). This is, if you like, another kind of standpoint: philosophers as apprentice scientists, going into the scientific field – as field-workers – to observe the science in action, by literal apprenticeships in labs, or field work, or by very careful study of a limited space/place/project through literature and note-books, spawning specialist case studies of different modes of doing science (following Hacking's 1992 list, e.g. experimental science in physics, case studies in sociology, simulations in genetic engineering, and model organisms in evolutionary biology).

However, the SPSP point was/is to remain philosophers, outsiders who get insider experience of how scientists' knowledge-making works, from which philosophical reflections can be drawn. Those reflections may appear stuck to the particular science they are studying, but the point is to draw out the philosophical analysis from their studies for thinking about how that mode or way of doing science works. These reflections are not general judgement 'rules' about the good/bad, right/wrong (though they may be so locally), but aim at a more generic level, philosophical insights about how experiments work, how taxonomic work goes on, etc., and so how scientists come to know the things they think they know. In this view, philosophers are strangers – outsiders who recognise that scientists get to knowledge in different ways from themselves, and their role is to bring a philosophical perspective to understand how those processes and practices (specific field- and context-based scientific rules) enable scientists to grow scientific knowledge in reliable ways. That is, the philosophers learn and reflect upon the scientists' rules to develop their own philosophical understanding, not tell them philosophical rules about how they should have done something. This is the philosopher as an observer in the various fields of science, not by standing to one side, or outside, as many of the standpoint positions offer. The SPSP community is closer to the SSK community, whose observational standpoint was inside their field of interest though the latter's strong theoretical glasses were outsider ones.

The Resident Field-Worker?

Wade is clearly, and has always been, a resident in economics, and so, as I noted at the start, can never really fit with Simmel's notions of being a stranger in economics. For that label to work – to bring that outsider objective perspective from philosophy into economics – Wade would have to be a fully fledged resident in economics, yet somehow not an insider. An alternative, and perhaps the best way, is to picture Wade as a field-worker from economics, going into the philosophical field to really understand how philosophy works, and then making sense of it to bring it into his economics community. In this respect, Wade's practices are close to those of the SPSP philosophers – but in reverse. As economist, he does his field work in philosophy to study how that field goes on and then translates it for his home community of economists.

Wade might even be labelled a 'resident field work', a label from Rob Kohler (2019) who investigates the kind of field work that entails residency next to, or inside, the domain of study. Such work can be characterised as participant observer field work – as exhibited by anthropologists (the key innovator being Malinowski), sociologists (Anderson on living as a hobo, Whyte in Boston gangland), and in natural history wildlife (Goodall). This labelling comes from yet a different way of characterising the 'doing' of science, contrasting field work with lab work, computer work, armchair thinking, and so forth. But Kohler's specific notion of *resident* field work also contrasts with another kind of field work that we do find in economics, one that remains detached from its object of study in the wild. Perhaps the nearest fieldwork examples of both kinds we have in economics are the development economists of the mid-late 20th century. Some travelled extensively in the field in order to understand the peculiarities of particular sites, and engineer recipes for development – such as Wolfgang Stolper in Nigeria who lived there for 2 years or Albert Hirschman who had years of involvement in Latin America. Their resident field experience can be contrasted with the more detached experience of very short field visits, often only a few days, by members of economic missions from international agencies such as the World Bank or IMF. Reading the reports of those resident field-workers, one has the sense of how their strong engagement with the local community, the community in which they are temporarily resident, requires the kind of commitment to understanding that makes it possible for them to explain, articulate, and enlighten their own economics community back home. This is indeed the role that Wade has played, not short-term visits but rather the deep engagement that only comes from doing resident field work in philosophy,

Wade's experience from his residency as a field-worker in philosophy has enabled him – as we see in *RWR* – to explain and get us readers to understand the exact relevance of the PoS of several generations to economists. But there is something else in his observations that I find really special in Wade's commentaries on the philosophers of science he treats, exhibited in his pithy insights that conclude his accounts of very difficult philosophical materials. My favourite is his summary of the position held by Ayres and Dewey: "Science doesn't touch God, but it does touch home." (*RWR* p 235). No other writer in the philosophy of economics can produce these one-liners – the benefit of his own personal, mid-western, standpoint perhaps?

Notes

1. Our labels are indicative of this narrow mindset; historians of physics do not call themselves 'historians of physical thought' and philosophers of physics do not call themselves 'physical methodologists'. In the wide range of sciences, perhaps only the biologists have succeeded in creating conferences at which philosophers and historians of biology and biologists congregate together into an integrated community.
2. This account quotes and paraphrases from Wolff's '(1950)' translation of Simmel (1908).
3. The earlier story saw the 'industrial revolution' created out of Northern European roots based on the 'scientific revolution' but has had to be rewritten in the last 20 years to take account of more advanced Asian prowess in technology in the period before the industrial revolution.

References

Ashmore, Malcolm (1989) *The Reflexive Thesis: Wrighting Sociology of Knowledge*, Chicago, University of Chicago Press.

Crombie, Alistair C. (1988) "Designed in the Mind: Western Visions of Science, Nature and Humankind", *History of Science*, 26, 1–12.

Forrester, John (1996) "If *p*, Then What? Thinking in Cases", *History of the Human Sciences*, 9(3), 1–25.

Hacking, Ian (1983) *Representing and Intervening*, Cambridge, UK, Cambridge University Press.

Hacking, Ian (1992) "'Style' for Historians and Philosophers", *Studies in the History and Philosophy of Science*, 23(1), 1–20.

Kohler, Robert E. (2019) *Inside Science: Stories from the Field in Human and Animal Science*, Chicago, University of Chicago Press.

Nelson, Richard R. and Sidney G. Winter (1982) *An Evolutionary Theory of Economic Change*, Cambridge, Belknap Press/Harvard University Press.

O'Brien, Patrick (2013) "Historical Foundations for a Global Perspective on the Emergence of a Western European Regime for the Discovery, Development, and Diffusion of Useful and Reliable Knowledge", *Journal of Global History*, 8(1), 1–24. doi:10.1017/S1740022813000028

Simmel, Georg (1908)[1950] "The Stranger," in *The Sociology of Georg Simmel*, Translated by Kurt H. Wolff, New York, NY, The Free Press, 402–208.

Sutton, John (1990) "Explaining Everything, Explaining Nothing?", *European Economic Review*, 34, 505–512.

2 Reflections without Rules

Reflections about Rules after Twenty Years

Marcel Boumans

Can We Do Without Rules?

Exactly twenty years ago, *Reflections without Rules* was published. This "survey of recent developments in the field of economic methodology [and] contemporary science theory as it relates to economics and economic methodology" (Hands 2001, pp. 1–2) has been written in a time when the general view was that there were no longer "barbarians at the gates": history had come to an end. Rules, needed to be followed to be or to become a legitimate empirical science, were considered to be otiose, no longer needed in economics and in economic methodology. The title of Wade's book seems to reflect that ethos.[1]

Twenty years later we are wiser and sadder: the barbarians were able to enter the gates and even to destroy the towers in the same year when Hands's *Reflections* was published. A few years later, in 2007, the world entered a period of Great Recession, the most severe since the 1930s. And while I am writing this chapter, we are suffering from a severe COVID-19 pandemic, in scale only comparable with the 1918 influenza pandemic. This chapter discusses the impact of these events on what "reflections without rules" mean for us today, and in what sense Hands's *Reflections* is still relevant for us today.[2]

The events of the past two decades actually do not allow us *not* to reflect on the rules of economics as well as those of economic methodology. Economists were – rightly, in my view – taken to be accountable for the economic disaster that started in 2007. In July 2010, the US Congress held a hearing entitled "Building a Science of Economics for the Real World" with the purpose "to examine the promise and limits of modern macroeconomic theory in light of the current economic crisis."

> [T]he insights of economics, a field that aspires to be a science and for which the National Science Foundation (NSF) is the major funding resource in the Federal Government, shape far more than what takes place on Wall Street. Economic analysis is used to inform virtually every aspect of domestic policy. If the generally accepted economic models

DOI: 10.4324/9781003266051-4

inclined the Nation's policy makers to dismiss the notion that a crisis was possible, and then led them toward measures that may have been less than optimal in addressing it, it seems appropriate to ask why the economics profession cannot provide better policy guidance. Further, in an effort to improve the quality of economic science, should the Federal Government consider supporting new avenues of research through the NSF?

(Congress 2010, p. 3)

Robert Solow, among some other economists, was invited to testify as an expert witness. In his opening statement, he emphasized the particularity of the event: "It must be unusual for this Committee, or any Congressional Committee, to hold a hearing that is directed primarily at an analytical question. [...] It may be unusual for the Committee to focus on so abstract a question, but it is certainly natural and urgent" (p. 14).

David Colander, who was also invited as expert witness, explained in his statement "how the economics profession can do better:" he urged for a "structural change" that would "increase the number of researchers explicitly trained in interpreting and relating models to the real world" (p. 44). The skills involved in interpreting how models apply to the world

would require a knowledge of institutions, methodology, previous literature, and a sensibility about how the system works – a sensibility that would likely have been gained from discussions with real-world practitioners, or better yet, from having actually worked in the area. The skills involved in interpreting models are skills that currently are not taught in graduate economics programs, but they are the skills that underlie judgment and common sense.

(Congress 2010, p. 44)

This 2010 hearing was preceded by a congressional hearing a year before on a similar but more restricted topic, "The Risks of Financial Modeling: VaR and the Economic Meltdown," for which Colander also provided a testimony. Attached to this 2009 testimony, he added a report from the 2008 Dahlem, German Workshop whose unambiguous title was: "The Financial Crisis and the Systematic Failure of Academic Economics." The report was a year later published in *Critical Review*. This report called for an ethical code:

Economists, as with all scientists, have an ethical responsibility to communicate the limitations of their models and the potential misuse of their research. Currently, there is no ethical code for professional economic scientists. There should be one.

(Colander et al. 2009, p. 252)

To be more precise:

> Economic policy models should be theoretically and empirically sound. Economists should avoid giving policy recommendations on the basis of models with a weak empirical grounding and should, to the extent possible, make clear to the public how strongly – or weakly – the data support their models and the conclusions drawn from them.
>
> (Colander et al. 2009, p. 261)

In other words, the events between the publication of *Reflections without Rules* and now urge us to reconsider the role, or even the necessity, of rules in economics. While at the end of the twentieth century, Hands could optimistically de-emphasize the relevance of rules-based methodology, twenty years later we no longer can afford this position.

The Practice Turn

One of the goals of *Reflections* is to "enthusiastically discuss, the new methodology," the "sea change within the broadly defined field of economic methodology" (Hands 2003, p. 549). Hands identifies three "turns" that determine this sea change: the "naturalistic turn," the "sociological turn," and the "economic turn." The naturalistic turn is "a turn away from *a priori* philosophy and toward a philosophical vision that is informed by contemporary scientific practice. According to this view, the theory of knowledge should employ the same scientific tools we use to investigate any other aspect of nature; epistemology so informed is naturalized epistemology" (Hands 2001, p. 129). For the sociological turn, sociological theory is an important resource to be used in science theory, and the economic turn employs economics for that purpose.

The naturalistic turn towards a philosophical vision that is informed by scientific practice not only emerged in economics and economic methodology but also in history, philosophy, and social studies of science where it is called the "practice turn." In 2014, Léna Soler, Sjoert Zwart, Michael Lynch, and Vincent Israel-Jost collected contributions that reflected on this turn in these various fields. In their introduction to the resulting volume, they made a few observations that can also be applied to Hands's *Reflections*.

> Rather than being unified as a positive program, the practice turn is more united by statements about what must avoided, and by a view of the sorts of inquiry that are devalued. [...] The most recurrent critical themes are directed against (often a caricature of) the logical or empirical positivist approach against the classic philosophy of science, such as those of Popper, or even Lakatos. These studies are often called [...] "the received view."
>
> (Soler, Zwart, Lynch and Israel-Jost 2014, p. 11)

In similar vein, the rules which, according to Hands, economic methodology could be better without are the rules of the approach that goes under the following names: Received View, the Legend, and traditional philosophy, names which cover both positivism as well as the philosophies of Popper and Lakatos. Although the title of Hands's *Reflections* seems to suggest *any* rules, the book itself was targeting at a very specific set of rules, namely the rules of the Legend.

But the contributions shared also some "positive" positions, which were summarized by the following list of moves:

- from a priori and "too" idealized to empirically based and empirically adequate accounts of science;
- from normative to descriptive perspectives on science;
- from present-centred reconstructions of past science to historically adequate reconstitutions of past science "from inside";
- from decontextualized, intellectual, explicit, individual, and "purely cognitive" to contextualized, material, tacit, collective, and psycho-social characterizations of science;
- from scientific products to scientific processes;
- from science as contemplation of the world to science as transformation of the world.

The meaning of positive here is thus not only non-negative but also non-normative, empirically based, and descriptively adequate.

Although the editors noted that this mainly descriptive turn made many contributors realize that a "purely descriptive" ideal had damaging effects, and that some kind of normativity had to be reintroduced, they did not clarify what kind of normativity that has to be. One of the contributors, Andrea Woody, however, showed the kind of normativity that could possibly be reintroduced.

Woody claims that the turn to practice is a "retreat from a certain sort of abstraction." The "retreats" she distinguishes are as follows:

- Conception to representation
- A priori to empirical
- Ideal agent to human practitioner
- Knowing subject to social epistemology

This four-dimensional "retreat from abstraction" faces, according to Woody, two distinct and substantial challenges. One of these challenges is actually the kind of position we have to take towards normativity:

> When we build philosophy on strong intuitions and a priori reasoning, in effect, the normativity of the analysis is built in from the get-go. But when we turn to practice and take it seriously, there is a possibility that

we will all become social scientists of a more thoroughly descriptive stripe, that is, more akin to certain anthropologists and sociologists, only without the proper training and skill set. What is required, instead, is a framework for analysing practice that allows us to make assessments regarding the effectiveness or appropriateness of particular practices or actions situated within those practices.

(Woody 2014, p. 125)

In other words, Woody's proposal of a retreat from abstraction suggested the need to reintroduce normativity by situating knowledge claims locally, that is to say by assessing them in terms of the epistemological and methodological norms of the practices in which they arise.

Open Science and its Enemies

Although Soler et al. (2014) and Woody (2014) describe the practice turn as a move from universal normativity to situated normativity, they do not discuss the reason for this retreat from universalism. Hands also does not discuss the need for turning away from universalism in his *Reflections*, but he did so implicitly in his (2004) contribution to *The Elgar Companion to Economic and Philosophy* on constructivism. According to Hands, philosophers have traditionally approached the subject of scientific knowledge from the "what is?" perspective. This kind of question begs for an essentialist answer, "an answer in terms of the underlying essential nature of the subject matter in question" (p. 198). However, the question "what determines scientific knowledge?" elicits a more naturalistic response. This change of questioning also has consequences for normativity: it shifts the responsibility for what counts as scientific onto the relevant scientific agents. "For the traditional approach, the domain of inquiry is circumscribed by the (philosophical) inquirer; in the constructivist framework the domain of inquiry is circumscribed by the subjects themselves (the scientists)" (p. 198).

The reason for the need of a retreat from universalistic normativism is because it is based on essentialism. Elsewhere (Boumans 2021) I have argued that this kind normativism has even impeded a complete turn to practice because of its essentialist nature. Universalism creates a tension between the studies of particular practices, which are local both in space and time, and the search for general norms of good science that not only yield these particular practices but are also considered to be essential for any kind of research practice.

Universalism presents itself by insisting that the concepts to be used for the analysis of research practices, such as "model" and "explanation," need to be defined in a clear, concise, and unambiguous way. By these definitions, the concepts are transcended from the real world to an abstract world of ideas, where they exist purified from any idiosyncrasy or particularity.

It should be noted, that the philosopher of science who most explicitly took a clear position against the essentialist nature of universalism is Karl

Popper. In his article, 'Poverty of Historicism' (1944) and his book *The Open Society and its Enemies* (2002, first published in 1945), he characterized "methodological essentialism" as the view "that it is the task of pure knowledge or 'science' to discover and to describe the true nature of things, i.e. their hidden reality or essence" (p. 33). Essences are aspects of the world that do not change in time or in place – they are universal in this respect. According to Popper, essentialism not only believes in the existence of universals, but it also stresses their importance. "Singular objects, it points out, show many accidental features, features which are of no interest to science. [...] Science must strip away the accidental and penetrate to the essence of things. But the essence of anything is always something universal" (pp. 94–95).

According to methodological essentialism, there are three ways of knowing: "we can know [a phenomenon's] unchanging reality or essence; and that we can know the definition of the essence; and that we can know its name" (2002, p. 34). Typical essentialist questions are what Hands calls "what is" questions, like "what is matter?", "what is force?" or 'what is justice?' It is believed, according to Popper, that a penetrating answer to such questions reveals the essential meaning of these terms and thereby the true nature of the essences denoted by them.

In opposition to this essentialism, Popper proposed what he called "methodological nominalism": "methodological nominalism aims at describing how a thing behaves in various circumstances, and especially, whether there are any regularities in its behaviour" (2002, p. 34). And therefore, the questions will also be different, they will more of the kind of "how" questions. As a consequence, Popper saw a different role for language, namely language as an "instrument of scientific description": words are considered as "subsidiary tools for this task, and not as names of essences" (p. 34). Popper saw the task of science to describe the behaviour of phenomena and suggested that "this is to be done by freely introducing new terms wherever necessary, and by re-defining old terms wherever convenient, to the utter neglect of their original meaning, words being merely regarded as useful instruments of description" (1944, p. 95).

Essentialism presupposes a well-ordered and harmonious world, which allows for a neat categorization, and where definitions can have the epistemological role of peepholes to this hidden world. Essentialism aims at purity, which, according to Mary Douglas (2002), is the aim of a rigorous ordering in categories. But science is too messy for such a categorization, not as well-ordered and harmonious as it is often presented. "The final paradox of the search for purity is that it is an attempt to force experience into logical categories of non-contradiction. But experience is not amenable and those who make the attempt find themselves led into contradiction" (p. 200).

One of the few philosophers who took these insights as starting point of her own approach is Mary Morgan, literally in her (2012) *The World in the Model* whose very first sentence says that "science is messy." To do justice to this messiness of science, Morgan does not aim at a "fortified philosophy," but instead at a "naturalized philosophy of science for economics": "The messy details are important – not just because, as we know, bald narratives lack credibility, but rather because the devil is often in the details, and thus larger, and important, matters cannot be understood and explained without them" (p. vx).

As a result, Morgan's approach is nominalistic. Typical of her approach is a carefully chosen vocabulary. The study of a certain research practice is highly sensitive to not only the choice of concepts used for that purpose but also to the way these concepts are used. They can restrict or even simplify the analysis too much, particularly when they themselves are restricted by a definition.

The main tool of philosophy is language, but it is a problematic tool. Clarification can come from clear concepts, often meant in the sense of being clearly defined. However, when it comes to this kind of analysis, definitions can limit the study of a practice unnecessarily. One reason is that practitioners often use concepts in a much looser way than philosophers have defined them, and even if they accepted the philosopher's definitions, these more strictly defined concepts do not easily translate to another practice. This is the reason, I believe, you will not find any commitment to a definition in Morgan's work, not even for the subject she became most well-known for: models. Instead, Morgan discusses the ways in which models function in science and the qualities that make them useful in science. This attitude determines also the kind of questions that are considered to be relevant. In Morgan's work, "how" questions are dominant, and "what" questions are non-existent. Even though concepts should not be closed down by a definition and should instead remain open-ended, the analysis of each practice requires its own working vocabulary to gain the desired insights. Many, if not all, of Morgan's projects involve the development of a specific vocabulary appropriate for that project. This vocabulary should function as a useful instrument of investigation.

Going Local

The naturalistic approach implies locality, in the sense of that research should be understood and analysed as being situated in a particular practice. This was also emphasized in Hands's (2003) reflections on the review of *Reflections* by Jochen Runde (2003). We need to step down from the pristine world of universals and get our hands dirty in the local details (as the heterodox economists, represented here by Runde, were claiming). For the study of epistemic agents and institutions, we should not use a narrow set of universal normative rules, because "there is room for normative evaluation of local moves in the game of scientific economics without endorsing the simple universal rules of traditional methodology" (Hands, 2003, p. 550).

As acknowledged by Woody and Hands, to reinstall normativity but now locally situated, we need a framework for making assessments regarding particular practices or actions situated within those practices. But what kind of framework is most appropriate and useful? One suggestion, implicitly suggested by Woody, is that one employs the framework that is part of one's specific expertise and skill set. Because the training and skill set of most of the people engaged with economic methodology are economists, a consequence of the practice turn might be that economic methodology has to be economics of scientific knowledge.[3] I understood *Reflections* not wishing to go that direction per se, because Hands raises the issue of reflexivity: "In what sense can economists use a conception of scientific knowledge based on ideas from economics to evaluate the scientific standing of economics or a particular economic theory?" (Hands 2001, p. 390). As Hands (p. 391) notes: if one wants to evaluate something then one needs a standard of evaluation that is based on something other than the thing being evaluated.

Hands, however, presents an interesting economic twist to the problem of local normativity, actually an Austrian twist. To avoid having "central planning authority" rules, "one is deducing 'this rule emerged' from 'no one intended it to happen'" (Hands 2001, p. 392). There are a few reasons why we should be in favour of emerging rules. First, this Austrian notion of natural rules seems to generate less tension with naturalism than rules imposed by some kind of authority. And second, such an authority has never existed, or as I put it myself: science has no intelligent design. "Whatever rules that scientists have chosen to play by, those rules have emerged from within the context of scientific play. Science was not started by an epistemological philosopher-king" (*Ibid.*).

This Austrian twist, however, implies often a certain kind of justification of the emerging rules, what is called naturalistic legitimation: what emerges naturally, thus without intervention or control, is good. When applied to science, the legitimacy of science having a privileged position with respect to other bodies of knowledge is the result of its undeniable successes in the areas of medicine and technology. Thanks to developments – or progress – in these disciplines over the last two centuries, death rates have fallen dramatically and the standard of living has increased across much of the modern world. These successes have created the widely shared belief that science is intrinsically good: science improves the quality of our lives and also increases the survival chances of the human race. Science legitimizes itself by its own natural achievements.

It is therefore no surprise that this kind of legitimacy of a system or process is questioned whenever a system or process is associated with a crisis, and if it produces a disaster instead of success. In science, its naturalistic legitimation was for the first time most severely disputed when the atomic bomb was set off above Hiroshima and shortly after a second bomb above Nagasaki. This event and the effects of the deadly radiation for many years to follow showed an opposite, horrifying face of science: science was capable of damaging the quality of life and even threatening the survival of the human race.

For that reason, John von Neumann, who was involved with the Manhattan Project, warned that science "has outgrown the age of independence from society" and should be regulated by society. In his testimony before the Special Senate Committee on Atomic Energy in 1946, he stated that:

> It is for the first time that science has produced results which require an immediate intervention of organized society, of the government. Of course science has produced many results before which were of great importance to society, directly or indirectly. And there have been before scientific processes which required some minor policing measures of the government. But it is for the first time that a vast area of research, right in the central part of the physical sciences, impinges on a broad front on the vital zone of society, and clearly requires rapid and general regulation It is now that physical science has become "important" in that painful and dangerous sense which causes the state to intervene. Considering the vastness of the ultimate objectives of science, it has been clear for a long time to thoughtful persons that this moment must come, sooner or later. We now know that it has come.
>
> (von Neumann 1963, p. 499)

In addition to these dramatic developments, the rise of "big science" after World War II, requiring large amounts of funding, made society aware of the necessity of a legitimation of science on alternative grounds, and of the need to think about eventual desired directions along which science could develop. More recent discussions on genetic engineering and stem cell research show that these issues of legitimation continue and remain part of science, including economics as discussed at the beginning of this chapter, reflected by the questions raised at the 2010 Congress hearing in response to the financial crisis.

Critique

What are the rules that make science less harmful? On the one hand, they should not be determined by the particular practice that needs to be assessed, but, on the other hand, they should not be essentialist. The proposal I would like to suggest is the alignment of Kantian immanent critique.

The original motivation of the logical positivists, and of philosophers like Imre Lakatos and Mark Blaug of the Popperian tradition, was to protect society from harmful science, which they called pseudo-science. For them, the harm was caused by non-humanistic ideologies that were presented as scientific theories. It was therefore necessary to formulate demarcation rules to draw a line between science and pseudo-science. As is now well known and acknowledged, whatever lines are been drawn, they do not do what they are supposed to do: to make a division between objective knowledge and ideology. Nor do they prevent science from developing weapons of mass destruction. The positivist and Popperian demarcation does not protect us from harmful science.

The discussions induced by the practice turn have implied a better way to reduce the harmfulness of science, namely demarcation, not as a division between science and pseudo-science, but as a delineation of the scope and domain of a certain body of knowledge. We should stop presenting our economic models as they are representing truth and tell society how much uncertainty is involved in our policy advices – Colander's ethical code. Surely, our models are validated, but we should tell what this validation means: its relation to truth and what aspect of the model is validated and what not. This code is of course not strong enough to protect us from destructive science, but it is nevertheless a first necessary step to a less harmful science.

One of the reason that economics is still not a harmless science is that most of the economic textbooks still present their materials as if it meets the rules of the Received View. The current textbooks show a remarkable contrast with the original template of these kinds of textbooks, Paul Samuelson's *Economics*. In the introductory chapter, Samuelson (1980, p. 12) enumerates the following "basic problems of methodology": "subjective elements of introspection and value judgment; semantic issues of ambiguous and emotional meanings; probability laws of large numbers, both of normal-error and fat-tailed skewed type; fallacies or reasoning and fallacies of inference." Equally important, besides making these problems explicit, is that there is no claim in his textbook that these problems can be solved. "So let us be forewarned" (p. 19).

Concluding Remarks

Hands's *Reflections without Rules* appeared at a time when the intense debates about the rules of proper science had come to an end. This ending was not a closure; it did not mean that any consensus was reached, except the commonly shared view that the rules of the Received View were passé. It was mainly a "turn" or a "move away." Like in the dominant economic view of the 1990s, undisturbed emerging systems were considered to be good, so the only ethical rule was no rule.

I must admit that it is not clear whether Hands's *Reflections* draws the same conclusions, though it touches on this – what I call – Austrian view, and title seems also to reflect this view. But the relevant question is whether this view still bears relevance after a decade of major crises. According to the authors of the Dahlem report not anymore, and I do agree. We need an ethical code in particular when economic knowledge can do harm. But the nature of these rules are different than those of the positivists: (1) know what you know and (2) be honest about it.

Philosophy and history of science and science studies therefore still have an important role to play, these are the fields that can help to map out what we know, what the often implicit rules are of how we gain that knowledge, and in what sense we can trust it. These can never be universal rules but have to be situated locally and historically and sociologically contextualized.

Acknowledgements

I am grateful to John Davis for his helpful comments on a previous version of the paper.

Notes

1. In the book, Hands is clearer about what kind of rules he is referring to: the rules of the Received View, that is the methodological rules of the logical positivists and Popperians. Although "simple rules-based economic methodology has quietly and unceremoniously passed from the scene" (p. 393), the space opened by this disappearance was not replaced by any other universal rules-based methodology. Hands does not regret this empty space, or even question it.
2. It is of interest to compare this reflection on *Reflections* after twenty years with Hands (2019) and Davis (2020). The latter two were written as reflections on twenty years of economic methodology after stepping down as editors of the *Journal of Economic Methodology* which they were for fifteen years.
3. Likewise, Davis (2020) suggests that one of the two possible scenarios for the future development of economic methodology is 'meta-economics,' the field that studies economics.

References

Boumans, Marcel (2021). Retreat from normativism. *Journal of Economic Methodology* 28 (1), 60–66.

Colander, David, Michael Goldberg, Armin Haas, Katarina Juselius, Alan Kirman, Thomas Lux, and Brigitte Sloth (2009). The financial crisis and the systemic failure of the economics profession. *Critical Review* 21 (2–3), 249–267.

Davis, John D. (2020). Change and continuity in economic methodology and philosophy of economics. *Revue de Philosophie Économique* 21 (2), 187–210.

Hands, D. Wade (2001). *Reflections without Rules. Economic Methodology and Contemporary Science Theory*. Cambridge: Cambridge University Press.

Hands, D. Wade (2003). Reflecting on three reviews of *Reflection without Rules*. *Journal of Economic Methodology* 10 (4), 548–556.

Hands, D. Wade (2004). Constructivism: the social construction of scientific knowledge. In J. B. Davis, A. Marciano, & J. Runde (eds), *The Elgar Companion to Economics and Philosophy*. Cheltenham, UK, and Northampton, MA: Edward Elgar.

Hands, D. Wade (2019). Economic methodology in the twenty-first century (so far): Some *post-reflection* reflections. *Revue de Philosophie Économique* 20 (2), 221–252.

Morgan, Mary S. (2012). *The World in the Model. How Economists Work and Think*. Cambridge: Cambridge University Press.

Popper, Karl (1944). The poverty of historicism, I. Economica. *New Series*, 11 (42), 86–103.

Popper, Karl (2002). *The Open Society and its Enemies*. London and New York: Routledge.

Runde, Jochen (2003). Is reflecting without rules enough? *Journal of Economic Methodology* 10 (4), 535–541.

Samuelson, Paul (1980). *Economics*, 11th edition. New York: McGraw-Hill.

Soler, Léna, Sjoert Zwart, Michael Lynch, and Vincent Israel-Jost (eds) (2014). *Science After the Practice Turn in the Philosophy, History, and Social Studies of Science*. New York and London: Routledge.

von Neumann, John (1963). Statement of John von Neumann before the Special Senate Committee on Atomic Energy. In A.H. Taub (ed), *John von Neumann, Collected Works, Volume VI* (pp. 499–502). Oxford: Pergamon Press.

Woody, Andrea I. (2014). Chemistry's periodic law. Rethinking representation and explanation after the turn to practice. In L. Soler, S. Zwart, M. Lynch, & V. Israel-Jost (eds), *Science After the Practice Turn in the Philosophy, History, and Social Studies of Science* (pp. 123–150). New York and London: Routledge.

3 Social Aspects of Economics Modelling

Disciplinary Norms and Performativity

Caterina Marchionni

Introduction

About twenty years ago while an MPhil student at the *Erasmus Institute for Philosophy and Economics,* I had the immense privilege of taking a course taught by Wade Hands, during which we examined the most recent developments occurring in philosophy of science at the time. The course syllabus was largely based on Wade Hands' impressive book *Reflections without Rules* (2001a) which was then about to be published. Hands (2001a,b) taught us how the breakdown of the *Received View* – the mainstream of philosophy of science roughly before Kuhn – opened up the space for new approaches to both the philosophy of science and the philosophy of economics. Several features of this historical and intellectual trajectory are noteworthy, but here I am particularly interested in the recognition that "science is fundamentally a collective endeavour engaged in by scientific communities and that consideration of its sociality matters to understanding scientific knowledge." (Hands 2001b: 54). In particular, with the breakdown of the Received View, it became increasingly clear that science is not the purview of the lone individual nor is it carried out in complete autonomy from the surrounding society and its values. More importantly, neither condition is necessary to uphold its epistemic performance.

The recognition that the social and the epistemic are inextricably intertwined in ways that make it impossible to understand the former without the latter can be traced back to the sociology of science and to science studies more broadly. But whereas at least early on sociologists of science tended to emphasise the debunking implications of this recognition, recent philosophy of science has set out to show that the influence of the social on science is not always an obstacle to its epistemic project. This is the path taken by social epistemology, especially that branch concerned with studying and designing the social institutions of science. Hands (2001a) also emphasised how economic methodology in the early 2000s had largely abandoned an "off the shelf" view of economic methodology, that is, the tendency among early methodologists to apply what general philosophical theories say about methods to economics and check whether how well they fit. If they did not, then

DOI: 10.4324/9781003266051-5

the problem was with economics. According to Hands (2001a), philosophers of economics had started to pay increasing attention to the specificities of economics as a science, including the social dimensions of its knowledge production activities; a trend, which I believe, continues to this day.

In this spirit, this chapter reviews some selected issues in social epistemology (broadly understood) in the context of economics' modelling practices.[1] Just like any other science, the identity of economics is shaped and maintained by the adherence to a set of shared commitments and norms about which methods to use, what counts as a good explanation, and what features a good model should have. Economics also has significant policy relevance and societal influence – more than any other social science in fact. Its knowledge-producing activities greatly affect policy making and society at large. Whatever distortions the norms of economics bring in on its own models are consequential beyond the science itself. I will focus on two interrelated themes. The first is the role that norms about explanation play in shaping the *kind of models* economists build and deem valuable. The second concerns the effects that the *content* of economic models has on society, specifically through the phenomenon of performativity. The main message is not only that understanding the epistemic performance of economics requires us to examine its social structure, but also that evaluating economics' epistemic project requires us to consider its broader societal consequences.

In economics, a good explanation is one that shows how the phenomenon to be explained is the result of individual-level behaviours, a preference that derives from its commitment to *methodological individualism*. The latter holds that "social phenomena must be explained in terms of individuals, their physical and psychic states, actions, interactions, social situation and physical environment" (Uhden 2001, 354). A good explanation also shows that phenomena, which were previously thought to be different, can be explained in terms of the same, preferably small, set of causal factors or mechanisms. The latter is interpretable as the endorsement of the ideal of *explanatory unification*, "the urge 'to explain much by little'" (Mäki 2001: 488). These norms play a special role in defining the identity of economics because they tend to play a bigger role in determining the kind of models that are built compared to the exigencies of the subject matter. Markets, for example, certainly fall within the subject matter of economics. Yet, there are different ways of modelling markets, and what makes a certain model of a market an *economic* model is the application of certain modelling tools to it. We will see more examples of this later in this chapter.

Second, economics has the power of shaping the phenomena it tries to represent. Performativity can also occur in other human sciences, but it is more likely to occur in economics because of its perceived superior epistemic authority. The point is not that there is something particularly mysterious about economics performativity. Economics, its models, in certain contexts, in some of our societies, enjoy a solid epistemic authority both among the public and in policy making. Insofar as the agents represented in the models react to the models themselves, then such models have causal effects on the objects they aim to represent.

Does this mean that economic models do not represent at all? I do not believe so. The models of economics can still accurately represent aspects of real-world phenomena, even though the modelling choices made along the way are as much the result of empirical considerations as of (more or less explicit) beliefs about what counts as a good explanation. Similarly, the distinction between economic models contributing to *causally* changing certain features of social phenomena vis-à-vis the popular yet mysterious idea that they constitute them ensures that we can hold on to a realist interpretation of economic modelling. Acknowledging the influence of the social on the epistemic, and of the epistemic on the social, does not necessarily commit one to antirealism – as philosophers of science and social epistemologists have made abundantly clear.

The rest of the chapter is organised as follows. The second section introduces the concept of disciplinary norms. It argues for their role in two scientific episodes in the recent history of economics: geographical economics and the economic theory of networks. The third section explains what is and what is not problematic about the commitment to this particular set of explanatory norms on the part of economics. The fourth section then turns to examine performativity. Rather than a social constructionist thesis, I consider it as a thesis about the effects of economics as a social institution on other institutions: it is because economics and economists have epistemic authority in certain contexts and because that epistemic authority is transmitted and amplified through a certain social organisation that economic models trigger performative effects, effects that in turn can produce modifications on the social phenomena themselves. It is this "performative" aspect that might give us pause for concern: given the higher performative potential of economics and its apparent superior power, then we should worry about the possibility that our societies will end up resembling the models of economics with their own unique set of blind spots. The fifth section concludes the paper.

Economic modelling shaped by norms about explanation

The debate over what defines the scope of the science of economics has a long history. Traditionally, the domain of economics is defined by the range of phenomena (production, consumption, distribution, and exchange) that it studies. Alternatively, or in conjunction, the domain of economics is identified by the kinds of causes it appeals to. According to Jon Stuart Mill, economics is concerned with phenomena that occur as a result of people's "pursuit of wealth." The more recent Robbinsian definition expands the range of phenomena belonging to the domain of economics further to include any aspect of human behaviour that can be studied as "a relationship between ends and scarce means which have alternative uses." On this latter account, the domain of economics can encompass anything from market behaviour to marriage, implying "no limitations on the subject-matter of Economic Science" (Robbins 1932, 16). That means that the identity of economics came to lie elsewhere, namely in its theoretical (rational choice theory and game theory) and empirical apparatus (econometric techniques, experimental techniques, etc.). This approach is most vividly exemplified in Gary Becker's work, which applies the economics method well beyond the traditional boundaries of the field (Becker 1976).

Whereas the emphasis of economics on a set of methods rather than a domain of phenomena might be relatively uncommon, all disciplines and fields are defined by, and develop around, a set of norms and values shared by members of the scientific community. A particularly important role is played by norms about explanation: what to explain and how to best explain it. In economics, where scientific modelling is a prevailing tool of knowledge production, such norms influence what should count as a good economic model. They also influence the way in which new concepts and techniques are adopted and imported into economics, how they are modified and applied so that they can be recognised as economic ones. It is contested whether economics is nowadays still characterised by a strong mainstream that adheres to a shared set of methodological norms (see Davis 2006). Even so, as especially the case of networks that I discuss below makes clear, when new tools or concepts are incorporated into the mainstream of economics, they are moulded according to its norms.

Norms about explanation contribute to define a discipline's identity. They develop and adjust to meet the demands set by the kinds of phenomena a discipline is concerned with. They develop alongside prevailing modelling methodologies. Yet, neither of them fully accounts for such norms. Disciplinary norms take a life of their own (Woody 2003, 2015). As fields develop, such norms come to indicate how phenomena should be modelled, partly independently of considerations having to do with attributes and characteristics of the phenomena under investigation. Mäki and Marchionni (2011a) described disciplinary conventions as "enabling and constraining principles that shape scientific inquiry characteristic of a discipline." We took them to suggest what should and should not be done by determining which virtues of inquiry should be sought for. I prefer to refer to them as *social norms*. As conventions, they are the result of social processes; economists are socialised into them through training and social interactions. But the term *norm* also highlights their normative status within the discipline: they tell economists what it is expected of their models and explanations.

It is important to note that the adherence to norms about explanation is a pervasive feature of science. It is not just some special characteristics of economics. What makes economics different is the particular set of norms to which it adheres. As anticipated above, a good explanation in economics (i) shows how the phenomenon to be explained result from the decisions and interactions of rational agents and (ii) unifies several phenomena under a small number of similar mechanisms.

To highlight the role that norms about explanation play on the modelling practices of economics, I discuss two examples I am familiar with from previous work: geographical economics (see e.g., Marchionni 2004, Mäki and Marchionni 2011a,b) and the economic theory of networks (Marchionni 2013). In both cases, interdisciplinary clashes afforded the opportunity to "observe" the way in which such commitments contributed to shaping their modelling practices. In particular, geographical economics encountered fierce resistance among economic geographers, who also study the interplay of geography and economic activity. Economists' approach to spatial phenomena such as agglomeration was rather different from that of geographers, however; even the very concept of geography was thought to be at odds with how geographers conceived of it: in the models of economics it lacked "real communities in real historical, social and cultural settings with real people, going about the 'ordinary business of life'" (Martin 1999, 77). For economists, however, an unrealistic depiction of geography was worth the price: it enabled them to show how agglomeration phenomena could be traced back to the same small set of economic mechanisms. In the case of the economics of networks, economics developed its own distinctive approach not only compared to both the old and new sociological work on networks, but also compared to the highly popular work of physicists who claimed to have unearthed universal laws underlying network phenomena in both the natural and social domains. Economists stressed that their models, which combined graph theory and game theory, succeeded to obtain network phenomena from individual choices and to do so from a small set of basic mechanisms. For models of network formation, however, this meant that the models were able to derive networks with relatively simple architectures (Goyal 2007).

Geographical economics and the recovery of space

Geographical economics is an approach to spatial agglomeration founded in the early 1990s by Paul Krugman, who was later awarded a Nobel Prize in economics in 2008 "for his analysis of trade patterns and location of economic activity."[2] Geographical economics entered a domain of phenomena that was already well populated: the same kind of phenomena fell within the purview of urban economics, regional economics, and economic geography. Partly as a result, the early proponents and founders of the field found themselves in need of stating in quite explicit terms what their approach was supposed to add to existing ones. For a methodologist, this constituted a precious occasion to observe the social dynamics of science: What kind of justifications was proposed? How were they received in neighbouring fields, both within and outside economics? From this, it was possible to extract information about what the scientists from different disciplines thought as particularly important.

The early geographical economic models derived either agglomeration or dispersion of economic activity as the result of the relative balance of centripetal and centrifugal forces. The comparative strength of each force depended on the value of a few parameters such as increasing returns and transportation costs. But what geographical economics were particularly proud of is that these forces were traced back to the rational choices of consumers, firms, and workers (see e.g., Fujita, Krugman and Venables 1999; Fujita and Thisse 2000). According to geographical economists, this had not been done before in economics or neighbouring fields. That the geographical economics models were able to explicitly derive agglomeration this way and that they did so within a general equilibrium framework was regarded as one of its main theoretical accomplishments. According to the standard narrative of some of its early proponents, geographical economics was celebrated for its capacity to provide the much-needed *micro foundations* to theories of agglomeration.

The second celebrated contribution of geographical economics was the *unification of both phenomena and theories*. According to its proponents, the great advantage of the geographical economic framework was that it succeeded in bringing together and explaining under the same framework diverse stylised facts about agglomeration at different spatial scales such as the emergence of international core–periphery patterns, the existence of cities and the persistence of industrial clusters. Doing so also meant the integration of previously separate sub-fields in economics. As the Nobel Prize Committee put it, Krugman "integrated the previously disparate research fields into a new, international trade and economic geography."[3] The unification of phenomena and fields was made possible by the development of a flexible but rather unrealistic modelling framework that heavily relied on what Paul Krugman himself referred to as "modelling tricks." That unification was achieved at the expense of realisticness was not regarded as a problem, however. It was the price to pay to be able to build models capable of explaining agglomeration in the way economists regarded as appropriate. Whether the "modelling tricks" of geographical economics are so unrealistic to make it too hard to determine whether their results are simply artefacts of those tricks is an open question, one that I will not try to settle here.

Whereas geographical economics was highly celebrated in economics, leading up to the awarding of the Nobel Prize in economics to Krugman, it was harshly criticised by scientists working in neighbouring fields, notably in economic geography, a subfield of human geography. Not only were the models of geographical economics considered deficient, but the allegedly dismissive attitude of economists towards the work done in economic geography also indisposed many commentators (see e.g., Mäki and Marchionni 2011b). In addition, the alleged superiority of economics was partly reflected in the *World Development Report 2009* which emphasised the importance of the spatial dimension of economic development but drew almost exclusively on geographical economics literature. This is a feature of the culture of economics, and its surroundings, to which we will come back later on, as it is relevant to identifying the undesirable (epistemic and social) consequences of a strict adherence to a certain set of explanatory norms.

Network theory and the recovery of social relations

The development of geographical economics is not an isolated case. In a very different area of economics, the economic theory of networks, we can observe the same influence of disciplinary norms about explanation on the way phenomena are modelled. The economic theory of networks combines graph theory applied to the study of networks and the tools of game theory. In its basic outline, the theory assumes that forming links is not only costly but also valuable and that agents decide whether and with whom to form links by weighing their costs and benefits. The strategic element of such network models results from the fact that an agent's utility function depends on the activities undertaken by the agents with whom she is linked. There are several features of this episode that are worthy of investigation, but the one I am interested in here is how this way of approaching networks in economics is very much determined by the adherence to the same disciplinary norms we have identified above: namely, the importance of having micro foundations and of unifying previously separate phenomena in terms of relatively small number of basic mechanisms. The way I interpret these requirements is in terms of norms about what counts as a good explanation in economics.

As in the previous case, the development of the theory of networks took place in a domain that was populated by other fields. Approximately at the same time as the first economic models of network formation appeared, physicists had started to apply graph theory to several kinds of networked phenomena, including social phenomena. Sociology also had a long history of studying networks, mainly through the method of social network analysis. At about the same time, however, analytical sociologists began to build simulation models that also provided individual-level explanations of the emergence of social networks. According to economists, the distinctiveness of the economics approach to networks was its capacity to remedy certain shortcomings in the interdisciplinary literature devoted to modelling network formation: the absence of micro foundations and the lack of generality. They argued that the generative models of both sociology and physics were less explanatory than those of economists. The physics models are silent about why nodes form links in the way they do, whereas the models of sociologists are unsatisfactory because they appeal to different kinds of processes to account for different network explananda (cf. Marchionni 2013).

The economics approach, it is said, can remedy these shortcomings, and it does so in a distinctive way. First, the economic models provide mechanistic underpinnings. In particular, such mechanisms are at the micro level, where "micro" refers to the level of individuals, households and firms. For example, economist Sanjeev Goyal (2007) claims that the differences between economics' approach and physicists' approach to networks "can be traced to a substantive methodological premise in economics: social and economic phenomena must be explained in terms of the choices made by rational agents" (Ibid.: 7; my emphasis). In a similar spirit, Matthew O. Jackson (2007) writes that the models of economics address "[...] the how, but not the why. Insights from the economic perspective complement Watts and Strogatz' approach and instead of offering a process that will exhibit such features, offer an explanation of why people would tend to form networks with such features" (Jackson 2007: 32). For example, economists' models of network formation typically assume that agents form links, which involve some cost for the agents, to gain access to the benefits available to the agents with whom they form links. The mechanism of network formation thus describes the inter-action between actions of the agents (which links to form and with whom) and the associated payoffs; it is this interaction that gives rise to (equilibrium) networks that display different kinds of structures.

Analogously to the case of geographical economics, economists modelling networks have also emphasised the virtues of unified explanations. What they see as the main deficiency of the simulation models of sociologists is that their behavioural assumptions are formulated so as to fit a particular expla-nanda. There is no attempt to show that various network phenomena can all be traced back to the same kind of individual-level mechanisms. Unlike the previous case, however, the appearance of the economics of networks did not arouse strong reactions in other fields. Speculatively, there might be two reasons. First, the economics theory of networks did not have much traction outside the scientific domain, not compared to network science in general. Second, if there was any interdisciplinary power imbalance, this was mostly in favour of the models of the physicists, who not only are perceived to be the most epistemically authoritative but have also managed to entice the public's imagination as testified by the popularity of works such as Barabási (2002). Its direct influence on policy has also not been particularly significant, though the influence of network science in general has been. It is thus rather difficult at this point to single out the specific contribution of economics (though for an attempt to do so, see Elliott, Goyal, and Teytelboym (2019) and the other articles in the same special issue).

Disciplinary norms and blind spots

Norms about explanation affect the kind of models economists build and value as well as the kinds of interdisciplinary interactions they engage in. Such norms are to some extent justified by the specificities of a field's subject matter, but as a field develops, these norms typically tend to take a life of their own. Their application is therefore not justified every time anew by appeal to the characteristics of the phenomena to which they are applied. It is the domain of economics that changes concomitantly to where the norms find suitable applications. This is the other side of the coin of the phenom-enon mentioned above whereby the domain of phenomena that fall within the purview of economics coincides with the domain of phenomena where its style of modelling and explanation is successfully applied. Finding "novel applications" is as much a matter of reconceiving phenomena as much as re-purposing old tools or moulding new ones to render them fit for purpose. The economic theory of network is a wonderful example in this respect. The discovery of a tractable way of studying network phenomena in a game-theoretical framework was no small feat.

That fields are committed to certain ways of modelling is not a problem per se, however. In fact, knowledge production is a social activity, and the function of disciplinary norms is to contribute to maintain the cohesiveness of the field, its identity (see Woody 2003, 2015). The existence of such norms is perfectly compatible with capturing real and important aspects of the phenomena to which the norms are applied. This is crucial to keep in mind. At the same time, the commitment to such norms sometimes over and above the exigencies of the subject matter implies that some features of the phenomena studied in the field are systematically disregarded. A rigid adherence to such norms, that is, can lead to significant blind spots. This is more than a mere possibility. Explanations have different virtues, and such virtues often trade off with one another. If a scientific field systematically favours explanations that fare well on some dimensions of explanatory power, then other dimensions tend to be systematically neglected.

For example, unification typically occurs by omitting specific information about the phenomena unified (Morrison, 2007). Reducing the range of features included in a model enables its application to a wider range of phenomena on the one hand (a gain in breadth or generality) but results in a loss of information about aspects of specific phenomena on the other (a loss in detail or completeness). This is what happens in both the cases discussed above. To be applicable to a large variety of kinds of agglomeration phenomena at different spatial scales, geographical economics ignores features that are specific to each of the phenomena or their kinds (Mäki and Marchionni 2011b). Similarly, the abstract mechanisms captured in the economists' model of networks might not only reveal important aspects of networked phenomena but also leave out a lot of information specific to different kinds of empirical phenomena. Matthew O. Jackson (2007: 22), for example, writes that abstracting from the full details of a setting yields explanations of "why certain regularities appear in social and economic networks."

Fields will differ not only on what they take to be a good explanation but also on what are legitimate ways of solving the trade-off between different explanatory desiderata. Let us consider the dispute between economic geography (a subfield of human geography) and geographical economics. The subject matter of economic geography substantially overlaps with that of geographical economics, but the field is more interdisciplinary and eclectic. While economics has incorporated space by way of abstracting away from the details specific to certain places and geographical scales in favour of a unified approach, economic geographers have complained that the trade-off should be solved in favour of specificity rather than generality. They believe this will enable them to explain a larger range of aspects of phenomena of agglomeration, including what happens in particular places and hence what renders particular instances of agglomeration different from others (Martin 1999). Now this approach can also lead to blind spots: insofar as agglomeration phenomena do have common features, we will not be able to detect those features without focusing on what kind of mechanisms can explain those commonalities.

If a field does not have an absolute monopoly on a set of phenomena, the presence of blind spots need not cripple our epistemic projects. We can think that rather than at the level of different kinds of models within a field, it is the diversity of fields that can help us achieve a more comprehensive understanding of social phenomena. Things get more complicated though at the macro-level of interdisciplinary interactions and of interactions between science and the surrounding society. Different fields of inquiry are perceived to have different epistemic authority both within science and outside it. This implies that a field's blind spots are likely to matter more, the more societal and policy influence on policy makers a field has. The situation becomes even more problematic if a field's perceived epistemic authority is such that its models can shape the very phenomena they represent, in ways that are not transparent to either the modellers or the users. If performative models all share the same kind of blind spots, then we might be worried that we are unintentionally shaping our behaviour and institutions to reflect those blind spots.

The social effects of economic modelling

The idea that economics is performative also derives from the sociology of knowledge. Wade Hands (2013: 305) defines the basic idea of *performativity* as follows:

> [E]conomics performs – shapes, conditions, formats, etc. – the economy, rather than simply describing it. Economic theory conditions behaviour and institutions in ways that have significant effects on the economy itself; in other words, the economy is constructed, at least in part, by economic theorising.

In other words, the models of economics not only capture (for better or worse) people's behaviour and institutions but also change them. I use performativity to broadly refer to situations whereby an economic model, and more generally an explanatory and modelling style, affects behaviour and institutions by means of its diffusion and uptake among relevant actors. Hence, my concern is not with broad philosophical theses according to which economic performs the economy, or in Callon's words, that "economics, in the broad sense of the term, performs, shapes and formats the economy, rather than observes how it functions" (Callon 1998, 2). For a scientific item such as a theory or model to shape social reality, it needs to be taken up and acted upon. Not all of economics will have this power (see Brisset 2016), nor is this a phenomenon that exclusively occurs in economics. Performativity, I think, is better thought of in terms of local empirical hypotheses about interactive causal mechanisms between science and the world. Even if I do not claim that performativity only occurs in economics, I do believe that it is more likely to be found in economics than in other social sciences.[4] The reason is simple: economics' epistemic authority and political influence are generally much stronger, which contributes to sustain an image of economics as superior to other social sciences (Fourcade et al. 2015).

If, as we have seen above, the social structure of a discipline affects its epistemic products by creating blind spots that are hard to detect from inside that structure, and if such epistemic products reshape the phenomena they are supposed to 'merely' represent, then the discipline's social dynamics has wider social implications that should be object of concern. As MacKenzie (2006: 275) puts it: "performativity prompts the most important question of all: what sort of a world do we want to see performed?" This should be no news for the students of science. What it does is to further strengthen the case for understanding economic modelling as both an epistemic and a social activity with both epistemic and social consequences, some of which, as we will see below, should be object of ethical scrutiny.

I believe performativity is a real possibility, albeit one that should not be overstated. First of all, even though performativity is sometimes thought of as a thesis about economics *constituting* its object of study, we do not need the extraordinary metaphysical concept of constitution to understand performativity, at least not for my purposes. We can do just as well with the more mundane concept of causation, or interactive causal mechanism: this or that model has caused changes to its target (Mäki 2013). Second, for a model to have performative effects, a set of "felicitous" conditions must be in place (MacKenzie 2006). As I mentioned above, not every model will have the kinds of effects we are interested in here. Such conditions range from attributes of the model, which makes it more usable or its results more likely to be believed, or more easily acted upon, to features of the agents that use, believe, or act in line with the model. It is because economic models more often encounter such felicitous conditions, in virtue of the place of economics in our societies, which makes economics a special case in the social science.

If we agree that performativity can and does occur, what does this imply for economic modelling? For one, performativity has epistemic consequences: it makes rigorous testing of economic models harder. In such cases, we might want to find ways of avoiding performativity or minimising its effects, for example, by finding ways of endogenising agents' reactions into our economic models. But, if as we have seen above, performativity also has societal consequences, some of which might be undesirable, then we need to evaluate the desirability of those consequences and take appropriate action on the basis of such evaluations (see also Roscoe 2016). Should economists refrain from modelling certain phenomena in certain ways if we are worried that they might mould people's behaviour in ways that we find undesirable? Or are there other ways to avoid undesirable performative effects? For example, suppose that it is indeed the case that studying economics makes us more self-interested because genuinely altruistic behaviour is hard to represent in economic models (e.g., Frank et al. 1993, and for a more recent discussion, see Ferraro et al. 2005). Suppose in addition that we, as a society, wish to minimise rather than promote self-interested behaviour, what should be done? For another example, feminist scientists have argued that some of the values the economic approach endorses display an androcentric bias (Nelson 1995). Again, if true (and I have no reason to doubt it is), and if such models contribute to reshaping the world in line with the model, then economists' models can end up reinforcing current gender disparities. We might hold that the undesirability of the consequences warrants a ban on teaching certain kinds of economics models or that in fact the costs of such a ban far outweigh the benefits. But first we need to decide if the epistemic project of realistically representing how people behave in the wild should always, or almost always, prevail. I will not try to address these issues in this chapter but only offer two related observations.

First, questions about the responsibilities of economists regarding the performative effects of their models and how to balance the epistemic and the moral should be of concern philosophers of economics (Roscoe 2016). The current philosophical literature on values in science has argued that scientists have a general moral responsibility towards the societal effects of their scientific actions (Douglas 2003). This responsibility does not replace the responsibility of other agents, such as science communicators or then even of those whose actions are directly affected by the models. Yet, it does imply that economists need to think hard about what the unintended performative effects of their models might be and how to mitigate them when such unintended effects are undesirable. This is not a substantially different issue from the complaint that the policy recommendations of economics should not be trusted because they rely on a partial framework.[5] Nor is it different, I believe, from the question of whether scientists have responsibilities for the societal effects of their scientific claims as discussed in Douglas (2003)'s and related literature. What makes performativity a special case is that its effects are more difficult to spot compared to the case in which a model or scientific result is explicitly relied upon to formulate and justify policy options.

The second observation concerns the implications of the view that economists are responsible for the performative effects of their models. It is important to clarify that the point is not to blame or praise individual economists for specific effects of their models (whether they be positive or negative), but rather to think hard on how to design the institutions of economics so that the effects of performativity are recognised and possibly mitigated. The social structure of economics, broadly understood to encompass its relations to other disciplines as well as with the society at large, is where we are more likely to find the most effective ways of mitigating possible undesirable effects of performativity without however stifling economics' epistemic project, or its usefulness for policy. These range from re-balancing current power asymmetries among disciplines to improving the design of the science-policy interface in ways that take the ethical dimension of performativity into account. Therefore, it is not obvious that the best or the only way to address whatever problematic implications performativity has on our societies is to try and fix the norms about explanation that define economics – even when we believe that the undesirable effects of performativity are due to their blind spots. Doing so might itself have unintended consequences that are deleterious for economics' epistemic project. As we have seen above, norms about explanation play an essential role in defining a field's identity – there is no field of inquiry interested in explanation that does not adhere to one or another set of norms. In addition, it is unclear that there would be a set of norms that would yield the most complete or best explanation of social phenomena.

Concluding remarks

In his reflections on the development of the field of economic methodology, Wade Hands (2001b) identified developments that would define the field in the years to come. One such development was the interest in models, encapsulated in his thesis no. 5: "Abstraction, Idealisation and Modelling are important issues in economic methodology and the use of and/or appropriateness of such concepts also (like realism) has little to do with how these terms have been defined and debated within the philosophy of physical science" (Hands 2001b: 53). Another was the attention in economic methodology to the social dimensions of scientific knowledge production, one of the points advanced in thesis no. 8, the recognition, that is, that the "economics profession, like all organizations of scientific practitioners, is a social organization and much (for some, all) of what is produced by this institution is a result of its sociality" (Hands 2001b: 54–55).

Time has proven Wade Hands right. In this chapter, I have explored some points of contact between these two theses, an area of philosophical inquiry we could call the *social epistemology of economic modelling practices*. It goes beyond the initial focus on the role that abstraction and idealisation play in economic modelling to tackle the way in which the social organisation of economics, both within it and in relation to other fields and to society, not only hinders the epistemic project but also sustains it. I offered an account of how norms about explanation affect the way economists model phenomena. I suggested that the systematic preference for certain kinds of explanation tend to obscure some aspects of the phenomena and hence create blind spots. I argued that this need not be a problem. Adherence to shared norms is what keeps fields together and allows for knowledge production.

This does not mean that this aspect of science has no problematic features. Insofar as epistemic authority and policy influence are not evenly distributed among the sciences, or allocated based on actual epistemic performance, then the blind spots of a science can have undesirable societal consequences. I discussed one way in which they can do so, namely, performativity. Under a certain range of conditions, economic models also shape the phenomena they describe, making them more like the models. This means that the disciplinary norms economists subscribe to also have effects beyond the science itself. Examining economics in its peculiarity and attending to its social aspects, both internally and externally, seems to require an approach that blurs the boundary between the epistemic and the social, between the epistemic and the ethical. I believe this is the direction that the philosophy of economics will take, one that Wade Hands' interest in the intersection between the sociology of science and economic methodology has contributed to opening.

Notes

1. There is more to say about the social dynamics of economics as a science, including how norms about eponymic credit are assigned (Hands 2006).
2. https://www.nobelprize.org/prizes/economic-sciences/2008/krugman/facts/.
3. https://www.nobelprize.org/prizes/economic-sciences/2008/krugman/facts/.
4. For example, Healy (2015) discusses the performativity of social network analysis and de Basshuysen et al. (2021) that of epidemiological models.
5. For example, Rigg et al. (2009) complained that the exclusive reliance on the geographical economics literature in the World Development Report 2009, with its blind spots due to, as they put it, "the way that certain forms of evidence and approach are privileged over others," resulted in inadequate policy recommendations.

References

Barabási, A.L. (2002). *Linked: The New Science of Networks*. Cambridge: Perseus Publishing.

Becker, G. (1976). *The Economic Approach to Human Behavior*. Chicago, IL: University of Chicago Press.

Brisset, N. (2016). Economics is not always performative: some limits for performativity. *Journal of Economic Methodology, 23*(2), 160–184.

Callon, M. (1998). The embeddedness of economic markets in economics. In M. Callon (Ed.), *The Laws of the Markets*. Oxford: Blackwell, 1–57.

Davis, J. B. (2006). The turn in economics: neoclassical dominance to mainstream pluralism?. *Journal of Institutional Economics, 2*(1), 1–20.

Douglas, H. E. (2003). The moral responsibilities of scientists (tensions between autonomy and responsibility). *American Philosophical Quarterly, 40*(1), 59–68.

Elliott M. L, Goyal S., & Teytelboym A. (2019). Networks and economic policy. *Oxford Review of Economic Policy, 35*(4), 565–585.

Ferraro, F., Pfeffer, J., & Sutton, R. I. (2005). Economics language and assumptions: how theories can become self-fulfilling. *Academy of Management Review, 30*(1), 8–24.

Frank, R.H., Gilovich, T.R., & Dennis, T. (1993). Does studying economics inhibit cooperation? *The Journal of Economic Perspectives, 7*(2), 159–171.

Fourcade, M., Ollion, E., & Algan, Y. (2015). The superiority of economists. *Journal of Economic Perspectives, 29*(1), 89–114.

Fujita, M., & Thisse, J-F. (2000). *Economics of Agglomeration. Cities, Industrial Location, and Regional Growth*. Cambridge: Cambridge University Press.

Fujita, M., Krugman, P., & Venables A. (1999). *The Spatial Economy. Cities, Regions and International Trade*. Cambridge, MA: MIT Press.

Goyal, S. (2007). *Connections: An Introduction to the Economics of Networks*. Princeton, NJ: Princeton University Press.

Hands, D. W. (2001a). *Reflections without Rules*. Cambridge: Cambridge University Press.

Hands, D. W. (2001b). Economic methodology is dead-long live economic methodology: thirteen theses on the new economic methodology. *Journal of Economic Methodology*, 8(1), 49–63.

Hands, D. W. (2006). Priority fights in economic science: paradox and resolution. *Perspectives on Science*, 14(2), 215–231.

Hands, D. W. (2013). Introduction to symposium on 'reflexivity and economics: George Soros's theory of reflexivity and the methodology of economic science'. *Journal of Economic Methodology*, 20(4), 303–308.

Healy, K. (2015). The performativity of networks. *European Journal of Sociology/Archives Européennes de Sociologie*, 56(2), 175–205.

Jackson, M.O. (2007). The study of social networks in economics. In J. Rauch (Ed.), *The Missing Links: Formation and Decay of Economic Networks* (pp. 19–43). New York: The Russell Sage Foundation.

MacKenzie, D. (2006). *An Engine, Not A Camera: How Financial Models Shape Markets*. Cambridge, MA: MIT Press.

Mäki, U. (2001). Explanatory unification: double and doubtful. *Philosophy of the Social Sciences*, 31(4), 488–506.

Mäki, U. (2013). Performativity: saving Austin from MacKenzie. In *EPSA11 Perspectives and Foundational Problems in Philosophy of Science* (pp. 443–453). Springer, Cham.

Mäki, U., & Marchionni, C. (2011a). Economics as usual: geographical economics shaped by disciplinary conventions. In *The Elgar Companion to Recent Economic Methodology*. Cheltenham (UK): Edward Elgar Publishing.

Mäki, U., & Marchionni, C. (2011b). Is geographical economics imperializing economic geography?. *Journal of Economic Geography*, 11(4), 645–665.

Marchionni, C. (2004). Geographical economics versus economic geography: towards a clarification of the dispute. *Environment and Planning A*, 36(10), 1737–1753.

Marchionni, C. (2013). Playing with networks: how economists explain. *European Journal for Philosophy of Science*, 3(3), 331–352.

Martin, R. (1999). The new 'geographical turn' in economics: some critical reflections. *Cambridge Journal of Economics*, 23, 65–91.

Morrison, M. (2007). *Unifying Scientific Theories: Physical Concepts and Mathematical Structures*. Cambridge: Cambridge University Press.

Nelson, J. A. (1995). Feminism and economics. *Journal of Economic Perspectives*, 9(2), 131–148.

Rigg, J., Bebbington, A., Gough, K. V., Bryceson, D. F., Agergaard, J., Fold, N., & Tacoli, C. (2009). The World Development Report 2009'reshapes economic geography': geographical reflections. *Transactions of the Institute of British Geographers*, 34(2), 128–136.

Robbins, L. C. (1932) *An Essay on the Nature and Significance of Economic Science*. London: MacMillan.

Roscoe, P. J. (2016). Performativity matters: economic description as a moral problem. In I. Boldyrev & E. Svetlova (Eds.), *Enacting Dismal Science: New Perspectives on the*

Performativity of Economics. Perspectives from Social Economics, Palgrave MacMillan, pp. 131–150. https://doi.org/10.1057/978-1-137-48876-3_6.

Uhden, L. (2001). *Methodological Individualism: Background, History, and Meaning*. New York, NY: Routledge.

van Basshuysen, P., White, L., Khosrowi, D., & Frisch, M. (2021). Three ways in which pandemic models may perform a pandemic. *Erasmus Journal for Philosophy and Economics*, *14*(1), 110–127.

Woody, A. I. (2003). On explanatory practice and disciplinary identity. *Annals of the New York Academy of Sciences*, *988*(1), 22–29.

Woody, A. I. (2015). Re-orienting discussions of scientific explanation: a functional perspective. *Studies in History and Philosophy of Science Part A*, *52*, 79–87.

Part II

The methodological dimensions and implications of Paul Samuelson's economics

4 Unification and Pluralism in Economics

Sheila Dow

Introduction

Wade Hands (2020) adds to his many important contributions to the philosophy and methodology of economics in an intriguing exploration of the concept of pluralism in relation to Paul Samuelson. He does so by identifying *both* unification and pluralism in Samuelson's classic work, *Foundations of Economics*. Samuelson's deliberate strategy was to promote unification at the derivational level in the form of mathematical structure while allowing pluralism at the explanatory level of theory. This explanatory plurality consists of the comparative statics of his microeconomics, based on constrained optimisation, and the dynamics of his macroeconomics. While Hands points out that this is a narrow form of pluralism, yet he sets out to argue that Samuelson was pluralist 'in spirit'. The purpose here is to take Hands' thought-provoking analysis as a starting point for exploring further unification and pluralism in Samuelson's work, and in economics more generally.

There are multiple discourses on unification and pluralism, complicating any interpretation and discussion of a particular analysis. Unification refers to promoting unity, while pluralism refers to promoting plurality. But then unity and plurality can apply to a range of levels, i.e. within a range of different domains. Furthermore, there may or may not be scope for interrelations between unity and/or plurality at the different levels (Dow 1997a, 2001). These levels are respectively:

1 ethics;
2 ontology, the real subject matter of enquiry;
3 epistemology, or the scope, and procedure, for building knowledge about that subject matter;
4 methodology, or the range of methods of theorising and the basis for theory appraisal;
5 theory, or explanation.

There is further the matter of context in the form of philosophy of science, from which emerges the justification for particular forms of and domains for

DOI: 10.4324/9781003266051-7

unification and pluralism. We begin therefore by exploring the nature and significance of Samuelson's philosophy of science, and then broaden the discussion to consider different approaches to unification and pluralism. Hands completes his paper with some reflections on the departure of mainstream economics from Samuelson's framework. In the fourth section, we build on these reflections to offer an account of pluralism in mainstream economics.

Samuelson's philosophy of science

Fortunately for our purposes, Samuelson reflected on his own philosophy of science, giving us an insight into his own thinking, including notably in his debate with Friedman (Samuelson 1963) and also in a later reflective essay (Samuelson 1983). Of course, there is scope for disparity between professed methodology and practice, an important component of the Samuelson-Friedman debate. Furthermore, as with all important thinkers, Samuelson's views evolved over his career. But we can still learn about Samuelson's influences, his motivation and his mode of thought. In the process, we examine whether Samuelson's pluralism extended beyond the domain of explanation.

Hands (2020) shows that Samuelson was heavily influenced by mathematical physics and especially by thermodynamics, 'the archetype of a successful scientific theory' (Samuelson 1983: 8–9).[1] It is therefore not surprising that Samuelson should take the physical sciences as his model for economics. In so doing, he was following a tradition of aiming to make economics more scientific in the sense of being more like the physical sciences. Indeed Samuelson's substantial influence facilitated the agenda of moulding economics in the image of the physical sciences as it evolved in the twentieth century (Mirowski 1989). He did note the epistemological difference between economics and the physical sciences arising from our direct experience of economic subject matter: 'I abhor the sins of scientism' (Samuelson 1983: 8). But he carried over the unification goal, common in the physical sciences, in terms of developing a general formal mathematical framework. 'Central to Samuelson's book was the idea that there were common mathematical structures underlying different problems, both within economics and across disciplines' (Backhouse 2015: 347).

Samuelson (1983: 8) traced his philosophy of science to the father of logical positivism, Ernst Mach:

> Unpopular these days are the views of Ernst Mach and crude logical positivists, who deem good theories to be merely economical descriptions of the complex facts that tolerably well replicate those already observed or still-to-be-observed facts. Not for philosophical reasons but purely out of long experience in doing economics that other people will like and that I myself will like, I find myself in the minority who take the Machian view.

Machlup (1964) challenged this identification of explanation with description (see further Wong, 1973; Hands 2001, p. 63). In his reply to Machlup, Samuelson (1964) acknowledged that there were outstanding issues over the subjectivity involved in identifying facts, making reference to Kuhnian paradigms. He saw these issues as applying more to the social sciences than the physical sciences. Like Kuhn (1962), Samuelson saw the social sciences as immature, still evolving, allowing for contemporaneous paradigmatic differences. But these he classified as 'warts' on the surface of the 'face' (Samuelson 1983: 10); the latter was the proper focus of social science. Samuelson further reduced the significance of different perspectives on reality by referring to their source in psychological factors, rather than more fundamental epistemological factors. Indeed, awareness of this type of plurality did not shake his emphasis on the primacy of facts over deductive reasoning. 'I am primarily a theorist. But my first and last allegiance is to the facts' (Samuelson 1983: 7).

Recognising the scope for plurality but only within limits is characteristic of Samuelson's philosophy of science; he could be said to subscribe to a form of inexactness.[2] Thus, he regarded theory failings as marginal deviations from true descriptions/explanations: inaccuracies which could in principle be corrected (Samuelson 1964: 736–7). Later, Samuelson (1983: 9–10) repeated his recognition of epistemological plurality, this time with respect to econometric analysis: 'I do recognize that truth has many facets. Precision in deterministic facts or in their probability laws can at best be only partial and approximate'.

At the ontological level, there are indications that Samuelson identified plurality in the subject matter beyond the micro–macro distinction. He justified different lines of enquiry (explanatory pluralism) thus: 'I am an eclectic economist ... only because experience has shown that Mother Nature is eclectic' (Samuelson 1983: 9). But he had earlier asserted that '[n]ature seems to show an inexplicable simplicity' and inferred that theoretical simplicity was therefore an appropriate appraisal criterion (Samuelson 1964: 739). So it seems that, for Samuelson, ontological eclecticism, like epistemological pluralism, is present but limited, holding no implications for methodology.

Finally, Samuelson (1983: 6) also reveals some plurality with respect to ethics. He noted that his motivation to pursue economics, unlike other economists, was not an ethical motivation, yet his pursuit was guided by ethics: 'Although positivistic analysis of what the actual world is like commands and constrains my every move as an economist, there is never far from my consciousness a concern for the ethics of the outcome'. Nevertheless he argued that rational argument combined with facts could resolve ethical differences, noting 'the sad fact that our hearts do often contaminate our minds and eyes'. His example of ethical differences referred to views as to the appropriate relative roles for markets and for the state, something which was amenable to mainstream economic analysis. Other examples like the role of ethics in individual and collective behaviour would have posed more fundamental challenges. But, given the apparent assumption that ethical differences can be expressed within the formal framework, we find again that Samuelson does not allow pluralism to threaten the integrity of the methodological framework.

In addition to his positivist focus on evidence, Samuelson was a realist in the sense that he was motivated to analyse real economic problems. In particular, he developed dynamic analysis in an attempt to address the important macroeconomic issues raised by Keynes. But unlike Keynes, he saw mathematics as the best medium for presenting facts. Indeed for Samuelson, mathematical expression and derivation were necessary for economics to be regarded as a science, encompassing both description and explanation. His motivation was to develop a mathematical framework which would synthesise and define economics. It was the resulting overall mathematical structure and Samuelson's neoclassical synthesis that unified post-war economics. Samuelson's allegiance arguably was just as much to his methodological framework as to the facts.

What we have seen is that Samuelson identified a degree of plurality in most domains: ethics, nature, knowledge and explanation. Yet the plurality is conditioned by his positivist methodology: '*what ultimately shapes the verdicts of the scientist juries is an empirical reality out there*' (Samuelson 1983: 10, emphasis in original). The way in which Samuelson treated different paradigmatic accounts as distortions (sources of inexactness) is paralleled in his theoretical propensity to contemplate only disequilibria which would naturally self-correct. This parallel is best understood at the level of his mode of thought whereby he saw differences in reality, perception and theory as deviations from truth. His corresponding theoretical focus on general equilibrium was well suited to the task of generating and testing explanations and providing technical adjudication on those ethical issues which could be expressed in terms of the framework. Unity in mainstream economics was thereby to be achieved, and pluralism tamed, by unity at the methodological level.

Unification and pluralism: different domains and justifications

Samuelson carried over into economics the powerful drive towards unification in the physical sciences. There is a large philosophical literature on unification in science, some of which Hands sets out in relation to Samuelson, exploring different views on the relations among ontological unity, derivational unity and explanatory unity. For Mäki, explanatory unity requires ontic unity (whereby what appear to be different phenomena are shown to be of the same kind), as well as, 'ideally', derivational unity (Mäki 2009, p. 87; see also Mäki 2001). Morrison's (2000) alternative unificationist approach allows for plurality of explanation, providing a philosophical reference point for Samuelson's approach.[3]

These views hold in common a scientific requirement for methodological unification by means of mathematical expression and empirical testing. But there is a circularity in that a deductivist mathematical framework *requires* that the subject matter is such that the resulting explanations can be derived mathematically and tested against facts as a full representation of that reality. The epistemological justification for unification presumes a particular type of ontology whose identification depends on a particular type of epistemology. This circularity poses a particular problem for the justification for unification since methodology is not neutral with respect to ontology and epistemology.

All epistemologies rely on an ontology, whether explicit or implicit, and Lawson (1997) teases out the ontology implicit in an economic methodology focused on deductivist mathematical modelling. It is a closed-system ontology of the kind that not only allows but also justifies derivational unification by means of deductivist mathematical frameworks (see further Chick and Dow 2005). Furthermore, Lawson focuses on the limitations of identifying ontology only with the empirical level rather than also the underlying structures, powers, mechanisms and tendencies. These are potentialities which may be countervailing and yet not always active, and thus not identifiable from observed events. By identifying reality for the purposes of economic analysis purely in empirical terms, Samuelson thus limited the scope of ontology. Again there is a circularity among the methodological, epistemological and ontological levels. Furthermore, the epistemological step is absent from justifying the ontological assumption that the subject matter is suited to a common general mathematical framework even when 'Mother Nature is eclectic'.

The very notion of unification as a necessary feature of science thus requires justification. It is not a universal goal of science, far less a universal demarcation principle. Indeed, the persistence of paradigmatic differences within the physical sciences shows that unification has not been achieved. There is a long tradition of alternative approaches to the philosophy of science that support pluralism, or different forms of unification, in all domains, including methodology and ethics. These pluralist approaches to science derive from alternative types of ontological account, in particular, those which are holistic in emphasising interactions and processes which are evolutionary in a non-deterministic fashion, rather than emphasising equilibrium outcomes.[4] Such accounts defy the possibility of ontological unification in the sense outlined above, not least because the subject matter itself is understood as a plurality and also because it cannot be fully captured by empirical data (Dow 1997a, Davis 2021). Furthermore, ethical stances are built into the process from the ground up, motivating and delineating lines of enquiry. If it is not taken as given that the subject matter is a unified closed system for which a unified closed-system epistemology is suitable then positivist methodologies lack justification.

For a system to be closed, a number of conditions need to be satisfied; failure to satisfy any one of those conditions renders the system open (Chick and Dow 2005). There is therefore a range of possibilities for open-system ontology, justifying a range of open-system epistemologies, i.e. methodological pluralism. Just as with a closed-system ontology, an open-system ontology is a matter of belief, albeit justified by reason and evidence. But reason and belief in turn are conditioned by the character of the ontology and its corresponding epistemology and thus the preferred methodology. The particular source(s) of openness of an ontology thus ground(s) a methodological approach, or school of thought.

Ontology can then be said to unify a particular epistemological approach, not in the sense of ontic unity but by founding different approaches on different ontologies. Each may or may not promote pluralism of theory and/or method. But this type of unification is more usefully thought of as *philosophical consistency*. Indeed, the term 'unification' is not normally used within the pluralism discourse. The preferred term is 'monism', which is used as a way of categorising the exclusivist focus of mainstream methodology on mathematical modelling. Far from regarding monism as a goal, as unification is in mainstream economics, it is regarded as an inferior alternative to pluralism for building knowledge with respect to an open-system ontology.

Given the recognition that theory and empirical evidence cannot be demonstrated to provide a true explanation with respect to an open-system ontology, even as an approximation, it is common (although not necessary) for a pluralist epistemology to justify a pluralist methodology. While the official discourse of mainstream economics instead requires a unified methodology in the form of mathematical formalism, McCloskey (1983) demonstrates that multiple methods are in practice employed in unofficial mainstream discourse. Yet, even if only sociologically rather than logically, a demarcation criterion of mathematical formalism in official discourse is critical if implemented as part of the power structure of the discipline (see, e.g., Lee 2009; Akerlof 2020).

The issue is much more complex than mathematics/no-mathematics. First, mathematics itself evolves with changing understandings of consistency and rigour (Weintraub 2002; Dow 2003). In particular, it is critical whether the consistency and rigour refer to internal deductive logical structures or to application to reality. In any case, as with the closed-system/multiple-open-systems categorisation, there is a multiple categorisation ranging from an exclusive reliance on deductivist mathematics to no-mathematics, with all sorts of possibilities in between.[5] There is a wide variety of mathematical traditions, of which deductivism is only one, just as there are many forms of logic other than classical logic.[6] Furthermore, pluralist methodologies may well include formal mathematical methods alongside other methods of argument (Chick 1998). Any formal model is a closed system, but if this closure is provisional, to be modified in relation to other forms of argument, mathematical models can form *part* of a pluralist methodology, consistent with an open-system ontology and epistemology.

To pursue, as Samuelson did, an exclusivist mathematical strategy is to assume that the subject matter is adequately described and explained by his formal mathematical system. But there is a considerable literature on the limitations of mathematical frameworks which purport to offer representations of the economy. These limitations have particular force when these models are put forward as approximating complete representations such that model results have direct policy implications.[7] A policy recommendation can then be understood to follow directly from the model as a technical result to which political values are added. Colander (1992) does make the case for a pluralist methodology for policy application. But he assumes that the closed-system methodology for deriving the core theoretical results which are to be applied is retained as being the most scientific; only at a later stage are considerations of history, institutional arrangements, ethics etc. to be brought into consideration.[8]

It is common to encounter Samuelson's view that mathematics is 'just' a language, which facilitates more precise, rigorous analysis than verbal argument, although the meaning of rigour with respect to mathematics itself has evolved over time (Weintraub 1998; see also Davis, 1999). But, given the limitations of this language in representing an evolving open-system reality, the method itself limits the subject matter. It does so in a way that prescribes both ontology and epistemology. The circularity between ontology and epistemology therefore extends also to methodology: the chosen methods determine the scope of the subject matter and its analysis. Mathematical formalism is not neutral (Chick and Dow 2001). Samuelson's formal mathematical interpretation of Keynes's *General Theory* provides a good case study for considering this non-neutrality.

Samuelson on Keynes: a case study of mathematisation

Keynes employed an open-system methodology which included mathematics. He used limited formal mathematical models as an 'organised and orderly way of thinking out particular problems' at a preliminary stage of any analysis (Keynes 1936, p. 297). He deliberately held back from combining his analysis into a comprehensive formal mathematical system, but he was pragmatic in exploring simplified mathematical relations, such as the consumption function, in a partial analysis.[9] This methodology was consistent with his open-system philosophy (see, e.g., O'Donnell 1990, 1997; Chick 1998; Chick and Dow 2001). Keynes presented his theory as general in its derivation from an open-system epistemology characterised by uncertainty; neoclassical theory was a special case which required certainty or certainty-equivalence, a condition only rarely satisfied.

Keynes was explicit that what had been abstracted from (as a simplification) needed to be brought back to the fore before any policy conclusions could be justified.

> It is a great fault of symbolic pseudo-mathematical methods of formalising a system of economic analysis, ... that they expressly assume strict independence between the factors involved and lose all their cogency

and authority if this hypothesis is disallowed; whereas, in ordinary discourse, we can keep at the 'back of our heads' the necessary reserves and qualifications and the adjustments which we will have to make later on, in a way in which we cannot keep complicated partial differentials 'at the back' of several pages of algebra, which assume they all vanish.

(Keynes 1936, pp. 297–8).

Samuelson is noted for championing a version of Keynesian macroeconomics within his neoclassical synthesis. The dynamic analysis which sits alongside optimisation-based microeconomic analysis in the *Foundations* was an attempt to address the evident possibility of the labour market not clearing. But this approach succeeded in portraying Keynesian macroeconomics as a special case of a Walrasian system whereby price and wage rigidities could prevent speedy reversion to full-employment general equilibrium. Samuelson's philosophy of science meant that his enquiry was driven by real-world observation. But he regarded it as necessary for scientific rigour in operationalising his analysis that it be encompassed within his deductive mathematical framework.

The fact that Keynes made only limited use of formal mathematical expression encouraged Samuelson (1946: 188) to doubt Keynes's mathematical abilities. Furthermore, '[a]s for expectations, the *General Theory* is brilliant in calling attention to their importance and in suggesting many of the central features of uncertainty and speculation. It paves the way for a theory of expectations, but it hardly provides one' (ibid.: 192).[10] By a 'theory of expectations', Samuelson presumably meant a mathematical theory which would fit into his optimisation model, which was precluded by Keynes's (1921) theory of probability. Samuelson was seeing Keynes through the lens of his own methodological unification.

For Keynes, fundamental uncertainty, as the general outcome of an open-system ontology, underpins not only economic institutions and behaviour but also the theorising of economists. The early focus of post-Keynesianism was on challenging the mainstream representation of Keynes's economics as a special case of Walrasian economics, rather than the reverse, with Davidson (2006, 2015) making this case explicitly with respect to Samuelson's interpretation. It is telling that Hicks (1980–81), the key figure in developing the form of IS-LM framework, which took hold in Samuelson's neoclassical synthesis, grew to doubt the robustness of that framework in that it disregarded expectations and the consequences for equilibrium analysis of the potential for their disappointment.

The different interpretations of Keynes were recognised by Coddington's (1976) classification in terms of 'hydraulic Keynesianism' which he associates with Samuelson and 'fundamentalist Keynesianism' which he associates with Joan Robinson and George Shackle. In fact, Samuelson and Robinson engaged in a lengthy correspondence. But Gram (2019) shows how their early shared interest in expectations and uncertainty was not sustained as their methodological judgements increasingly diverged. Coddington (1982) even described some fundamentalist Keynesians as verging on 'nihilism': without being able to quantify probabilities, a mathematical framework could not generate definitive results. He was applying the demarcation criterion of Samuelson's derivational unification to dismiss any theorising outside that framework.

Pluralism in modern mainstream economics

The third form of Keynesianism identified by Coddington was the 'reconstituted reductionists', referring to the work of Clower and Leijonhufvud to relate market failure at the macroeconomic level to behaviour at the microeconomic level. This line of enquiry was taken over by mainstream macroeconomics in the form of the microfoundations agenda, undermining Samuelson's project by promoting theoretical unification. Samuelson had deliberately developed an alternative route to explanation at that level since optimisation could not be applied at the macro level without the introduction of the representative agent. But the power of the unificationist microfoundations logic meant that Dynamic Stochastic General Equilibrium (DSGE) models came to dominate mainstream macroeconomics. They provided the benchmark on which to build a response to the crisis, perpetuating what Haldane and Turrell (2018) describe as a monoculture within macroeconomics (see also Kuorikoski and Lehtinen, 2018).

But the failure of DSGE models to account for the financial crisis has spawned debate over the future of mainstream macroeconomics, as in the Oxford-based Rebuilding Macroeconomic Theory Project (Vines and Wills 2018, 2020).[11] One route they consider was to develop DSGE models further in order to explain financial crises, i.e. to promote explanatory unification in a continuing departure from Samuelson. This requires moving beyond the representative-agent framework and addressing the substantial challenge of building in money and a financial sector (see Rogers, 2018, on the nature and extent of the challenge). An alternative would be to accept that macroeconomics will proceed as an applied field independent of microfoundations, in the spirit of Samuelson. But the conclusion is that, while structural econometric models (SEMs) can usefully be developed at the macroeconomic level alongside DSGE models, the design of a more satisfactory core DSGE model is still the ultimate goal (Vines and Wills 2020). The proposed strategy is to proceed by means of small satellite models, established empirically to represent parts of the economy (such as the financial sector) excluded by DSGE modelling. These are to amplify the core DSGE model to encompass the wider institutional and behavioural considerations which have dominated post-financial-crisis discourse. But the ultimate goal of a synthetic DSGE model shows that the hold over mainstream economics of the ideal of both derivational and explanatory unification has been remarkably tenacious.

There is still scope for Samuelsonian explanatory plurality in that formal models can perform diverse roles suited to different purposes, particularly with respect to theory, testing and application (Morgan and Morrison, 1999). Indeed, the tensions which had arisen from the strictures of the DSGE framework created the space for the development of alternative explanatory strategies outside the optimising framework and in some cases outside Samuelson's general mathematical framework. Hands argues that theoretical pluralism was thus restored by means of some methodological plurality in diverse fields such as game theory and behavioural economics; there is no longer a common formal basis for unification in mainstream economics.

How far can any such plurality survive absorption in the enhanced-DSGE project? Kuorikoski and Lehtinen (2018: 255) argue that the kinds of modifications being called for are incompatible with the framework:

> many of the most central assumptions, such as intertemporal optimization, never change in DSGE models: even if the modifications concern the behavioural assumptions, the core optimization model is never abandoned. In other words, altering this assumption to make it more realistic is only possible if the whole DSGE framework is abandoned.

At the same time, the grip of derivational unification is evident in those fields such as behavioural economics which are looked to for explanatory pluralism. For example, Camerer and his colleagues introduce their substantial behavioural economics reader as follows:

> At the core of behavioral economics is the conviction that increasing the realism of the psychology underlying economic analysis will improve the field of economics *on its own terms*—generating theoretical insights, making better predictions of field phenomena, and suggesting better policy. This conviction does not imply a wholesale rejection of the neoclassical approach to economics based on utility maximization, equilibrium, and efficiency. The neoclassical approach is useful because it provides economists with a theoretical framework that can be applied to almost any form of economic (and even noneconomic) behavior, and it makes refutable predictions.
>
> (Camerer, Loewenstein and Rabin 2004,
> p. 1, emphasis in the original)

Similarly Hong and Stein (2007, p. 126) spell out the pressure for behavioural finance to fit into the standard mainstream approach if it is 'ever to approach the stature of classical asset pricing'.

Most significantly for our discussion of Samuelson, macroeconomists who espouse external consistency still aspire to derivational unification, i.e. internal consistency, as the ideal. Even those who are the most forceful critics of DSGE modelling and who thus promote explanatory pluralism aspire to explanatory unification:

> We can think of an SEM as incorporating theory in a rough and ready way, but it is clearly better to incorporate it more rigorously. Internal

consistency is a goal worth trying to achieve. That alone provides a rationale for the microfoundations project.

(Wren-Lewis 2018: 67)

Samuelson's approach privileged consistency with the data over internal theoretical consistency and there is an increasing concern with policy application of theory which adds weight to the need for external consistency. As Backhouse and Cherrier (2017) show, there has been a general shift of attention and prestige in economics away from theory to application. This need not hold implications for exclusivist mathematical methodology. While Weintraub (1998) espouses 'rigour' as the unifying principle for science, he advocates attention to rigour in the *application* of mathematics as an alternative to rigour in the form of pure mathematics.

Yet theory of necessity continues to play a central role in application, either explicitly or implicitly in the way in which evidence is understood. The latter was recognised up to a point by Samuelson when he noted the constructed nature of 'facts'. Even if theory is only to be applied in a 'rough and ready' way, what is the proper basis for such modifications to pure theory? Does this accord with Samuelson's mode of thought whereby pluralities and modifications are only marginal? Furthermore, is derivational unification to be retained as the basis for theory formulation? Or should the focus on application be allowed to generate an alternative approach to theorising, and if so, on what grounds?

If the derivational and explanatory unification of DSGE modelling is to be discarded, we seem to be back to the drawing board. Ontology and epistemology need to be specified if the philosophy underpinning a new methodological approach is to be coherent (Dow 1997b). Consistency, both internal within a modelling framework and external with respect to a particular form of evidence, does not address the requirements of other forms of consistency. In particular, philosophical consistency can provide the necessary grounding for methodology.

The fragmentation within mainstream economics, both in terms of content and in terms of methodology, represents a move away from traditional prescriptive methodology. Associated with this has been a shift in the field of methodology itself to a more descriptive role, addressing that plurality (Hands 2001). Davis (2007) identifies that plurality particularly with the importation of methodologies, as well as content, from other disciplines. But without a philosophical framework, there is a danger that mainstream economic methodology is vulnerable to the charge that 'anything goes'. This is a charge more commonly levelled at non-mainstream methodology, but the latter is coherent in its ontological and epistemological groundings, even if the methodology is not consistent with the mainstream approach. Different approaches within non-mainstream thought start from a particular ontology which sets the parameters for an appropriate epistemology and methodology.[12]

Methodological pluralism, with different methodological approaches stem-ming from different ontologies, may use alternatives to classical logic which are more consistent with the relevant ontology (King 2012; see also Dow 2016). The methodology may or may not include use of formal mathematics, and econometric expression of evidence, depending on its groundings. But there is a common characteristic of some specified forms of open-system methodology for the investigation of an open-system ontology. This justifies a pluralist approach whereby no one model and no one form of empirical testing can constitute a sufficient argument for policy-making. Anything does not go.

Conclusion

In contemplating Samuelson's combination of derivational unification with his explanatory pluralism, the question arose as to the justification for unifi-cation in the first place. It was concluded that the justification is circular, with unification requiring the type of ontology, epistemology and methodology which justifies it. Promoting unification is a scientific convention in the sense that there are alternative bases for science which cannot be *categorically demon-strated* to be either better or worse in relation to some notion of truth. While we found various aspects of plurality in Samuelson, he did not allow this to challenge his derivational unificationism. The plurality he identified at the ontological and epistemological levels was a sort of approximation to truth, a feature of what we might call his mode of thought.

We explored an alternative in the form of pluralism based on an open-system approach. The plurality in ontology and epistemology here is substan-tive rather than deviations from some central truth. Such an approach is based on philosophical consistency in place of unification. Any particular ontology determines the possibilities for knowledge, including its type and scope. In turn, this pluralist epistemology justifies the choice of methodology. This type of approach characterises the different schools of thought which operate outside the economics mainstream.

So what are we to make of developments within the mainstream which seek to use a different methodological framework from Samuelson's uni-fying approach? Tensions remain and we have seen how difficult it is for mainstream macroeconomics to break away from the DSGE framework as a unificationist ideal. Even while the emphasis is on empirical application, the goal of unification remains, as does the role of deductive mathematics and empirical realism.

But if methodological unification is to be abandoned, on what basis is theorising to proceed? The onus is on economists to be able to justify their methodological approach in terms of ontology and epistemology – whether a Samuelsonian approach or some alternative. Including accounts of such philosophical groundings fits well with the dominant (critical) descriptive practice of the 'new methodology'.

Notes

1. A full account of this influence is provided by Backhouse (2015).
2. See Hausman (1992: ch. 8) for a full discussion of inexactness.
3. The third approach considered is that of Kitcher's (1989), who sees derivational unification as ensuring explanatory unification without reference to ontology.
4. See Chick (1995) for an account of such an approach in chemistry, discussed in relation to economics.
5. It is important to distinguish between mathematisation and formalism; arguably all theory requires some form of formal (logical) argument, even if expressed only verbally.
6. See Feynman (1965) on Babylonian mathematics, for example (see further Dow 2003).
7. See Lawson's (2009) critique of Colander et al.'s (2009) search for a new model to replace the old in the wake of the financial crisis.
8. Ethical judgements are in fact built into all theory, whether acknowledged or not.
9. Keynes also accepted the usefulness of econometric analysis. But in his debate with Tinbergen, such analysis was only justified if it could be demonstrated that the structure underpinning a particular relationship was stable (Garrone and Marchionatti 2009).
10. These views of Keynes's *General Theory* are echoed by Lucas (1980).
11. This is not to be confused with the UK's ESRC-financed Rebuilding Macroeconomics project based at NIESR (https://www.rebuildingmacroeconomics. ac.uk/). This project was a response to the call from the ESRC for the development of non-mainstream macroeconomic research. The project is pluralist in all domains.
12. In practice, if only for logistical reasons, there is only a limited number of communities coalescing around any one approach (Dow 2004).

References

Akerlof, G A (2020) 'Sins of Omission and the Practice of Economics', *Journal of Economic Literature*, 58 (2): 405–18.
Backhouse, R E (2015) 'Revisiting Samuelson's *Foundations of Economic Analysis*', *Journal of Economic Literature*, 53 (2): 326–50.
Backhouse, R E and B Cherrier (2017) 'The Age of the Applied Economist: The Transformation of Economics Since the 1970s', *History of Political Economy*, 49 (Supplement): 1–33.
Camerer, C F, G Loewenstein and M Rabin (2004) *Advances in Behavioral Economics*. Princeton, NJ: Princeton University Press.
Chick, V (1995) 'Order out of chaos in economics? Some lessons from the philosophy of science', in S Dow and J Hillard (eds), *Keynes, Knowledge and Uncertainty*. Aldershot: Edward Elgar, pp. 25–42.
Chick, V (1998) 'On Knowing One's Place: the Role of Formalism in Economics', *Economic Journal*, 108 (451): 1859–69.
Chick, V and S Dow (2001) 'Formalism, Logic and Reality: A Keynesian Analysis', *Cambridge Journal of Economics*, 25 (6): 705–22.
Chick, V and S Dow (2005) 'The Meaning of Open Systems', *Journal of Economic Methodology*, 12 (3): 363–81.
Coddington, A (1976) 'Keynesian Economics: The Search for First Principles', *Journal of Economic Literature*, 14 (4): 1258–73.

Coddington, A (1982) 'Deficient Foresight: A Troublesome Theme in Keynesian Economics', *American Economic Review*, 72 (3): 480–7.

Colander, D (1992) 'The Lost Art of Economics', *Journal of Economic Perspectives* 6 (3): 191–8.

Colander, D, M Goldberg, A Hass, K Juselius, A Kirman, T Lux, and B Sloth (2009) 'The Financial Crisis and the Systemic Failure of the Economics Profession', *Critical Review*, 21 (2–3): 249–67.

Davidson, P (2006) 'Samuelson and the Keynes/post Keynesian revolution', in M Szenberg, L Ramrattan, and A A Gottesman (eds), *Samuelsonian Economics and the 21st Century*. Oxford, Oxford University Press, ch. 18.

Davidson, P (2015) 'What was the Primary Factor Encouraging Mainstream Economists to Marginalize Post Keynesian Theory?', *Journal of Post Keynesian Economics*, 37 (3): 369–83.

Davis, J B (1999) 'Common Sense: A Middle Way Between Formalism and Post-Structuralism?', *Cambridge Journal of Economics*, 23 (4): 503–15.

Davis, J B (2007) 'The Turn in Economics and the Turn in Economic Methodology', *Journal of Economic Methodology*, 14 (3): 275–90.

Davis, J B (2021) 'Sheila Dow's Open Systems Methodology', presentation to INEM session at ASSA meetings, https://www.aeaweb.org/conference/2021/zoom/download?q=03d628f1-43fd-4b55-aceb-78b5f97607e7

Dow, S (1997a) 'Methodological pluralism and pluralism of method', in A Salanti and E Screpanti (eds), *Pluralism in Economics: Theory, History and Methodology*. Cheltenham: Edward Elgar, pp. 89–99.

Dow, S (1997b) 'Mainstream Economic Methodology', *Cambridge Journal of Economics*, 21: 73–93.

Dow, S (2001) 'Modernism and postmodernism: a dialectical analysis', in S Cullenberg, J Amariglio and D F Ruccio (eds), *Postmodernism, Economics and Knowledge*. London: Routledge, p. 61–76.

Dow, S (2003) 'Understanding the Relationship between Mathematics and Economics', *Journal of Post Keynesian Economics*, 25 (4): 545–8.

Dow, S (2004) 'Structured Pluralism', *Journal of Economic Methodology*, 11 (3): 275–90.

Dow, S (2016) 'Consistency in pluralism and the role of microfoundations', in J Courvisanos, J Doughney and A Millmow (eds), *Reclaiming Pluralism in Economics*. London: Routledge, pp. 32–46.

Feynman, R P (1965) *The Character of Physical Law*. Cambridge, MA: MIT Press.

Garrone, G and R Marchionatti (2009) 'Keynes on economic method. A reassessment on his debate with Tinbergen and other econometricians, 1938-1943', in R Arena, S Dow and M Klaes (eds), *Open Economics: Economics in Relation to Other Disciplines*. London: Routledge, pp. 148–72.

Gram, H (2019) 'Keynesian uncertainty: the great divide between Joan Robinson and Paul Samuelson in their correspondence and public exchanges', in R Anderson, W A Barnett, and R A Cord (eds), *Paul Samuelson: Master of Modern Economics*. London: Palgrave Macmillan, pp. 375–419.

Haldane, A G and A E Turrell (2018) 'An Interdisciplinary Model for Macroeconomics', *Oxford Review of Economic Policy*, 34 (1–2): 219–51.

Hands, D W (2001) *Reflection without Rules: Economic Methodology and Contemporary Science Theory*. Cambridge: Cambridge University Press.

Hands, D W (2019) 'Re-examining Samuelson's operationalist methodology', in R Anderson, W A Barnett, and R A Cord (eds), *Paul Samuelson: Master of Modern Economics*. London: Palgrave Macmillan, pp. 39–67.

Hands, D W (2020) *The Many Faces of Unification and Pluralism in Economics: The Case of Paul Samuelson's Foundations of Economic Analysis*. Tacoma, WA: University of Puget Sound mimeo.

Hausman, D M (1992) *The Inexact and Separate Science of Economics*. Cambridge: Cambridge University Press.

Hicks, J R (1980–81) 'IS-LM: an explanation', *Journal of Post Keynesian Economics*, 3 (2): 139–54.

Hong, H and J C Stein (2007) 'Disagreement and the stock market', *Journal of Economic Perspectives*, 21 (2): 109–28.

Keynes, J M (1921) *A Treatise on Probability*. London: Macmillan.

Keynes, J M (1936) *The General Theory of Employment, Interest and Money*. London: Macmillan.

King, J E (2012) *The Microfoundations Delusion: Metaphor and Dogma in the History of Macroeconomics*. Cheltenham: Edward Elgar.

Kitcher, P (1989) 'Explanatory unification and the causal structure of the world', in P Kitcher and W C Salmon (eds), *Scientific Explanation: Minnesota Studies in the Philosophy of Science*, vol. XIII, Minneapolis, MN: University of Minnesota Press, pp. 410–505.

Kuhn, T S (1962) *The Structure of Scientific Revolutions*. Chicago, IL: University of Chicago Press; second, enlarged edition, 1970.

Kuorikoski, J and A Lehtinen (2018) 'Model Selection in Macroeconomics: DSGE and Ad Hocness', *Journal of Economic Methodology*, 25 (3): 252–64.

Lawson, T (1997) *Economics and Reality*. London: Routledge.

Lawson, T (2009) 'The current economic crisis: its nature and the course of academic economics'. *Cambridge Journal of Economics*, 33: 759–77.

Lee, F (2009) *A History of Heterodox Economics: Challenging the Mainstream in the Twentieth Century*. London: Routledge.

Lucas, R E Jr (1980) 'Methods and Problems in Business Cycle Theory', *Journal of Money, Credit, and Banking*, 12 (4): 696–715.

Machlup, F (1964) 'Professor Samuelson on Theory and Realism', *American Economic Review*, 54 (Sept.): 733–6.

Mäki, U (2001) 'Explanatory Unification: Double and Doubtful', *Philosophy of the Social Sciences*, 31: 488–506.

Mäki, U (2009) 'Realistic Realism About Unrealistic Models', in H Kincaid and D Ross (eds), *The Oxford Handbook of Philosophy of Economics*. Oxford: Oxford University Press, pp. 68–98.

McCloskey, D N (1983) 'The Rhetoric of Economics', *Journal of Economic Literature*, 21: 434–61.

Mirowski, P (1989) *More Heat than Light: Economics as Social Physics, Physics as Nature's Economics*. Cambridge and New York: Cambridge University Press.

Morgan, M S and M Morrison (1999) 'Models as mediating instruments', in M S Morgan and M Morrison (eds), *Models as Mediators: Perspectives on Natural and Social Science*. Cambridge: Cambridge University Press, pp. 10–37.

Morrison, M (2000) *Unifying Scientific Theories: Physical Concepts and Mathematical Structures*. Cambridge: Cambridge University Press.

O'Donnell, R (1990) 'Keynes on Mathematics: Philosophical Foundations and Economic Applications', *Cambridge Journal of Economics*, 14: 29–47.

O'Donnell, R (1997) 'Keynes and formalism', in G C Harcourt and P Riach (eds), *The Second Edition of The General Theory*, vol. 2. London: Routledge, pp. 131–65.

Rogers, C (2018) 'The New Macroeconomics Has No Clothes', *Review of Keynesian Economics*, 6 (1): 22–33.

Samuelson, P A (1946) 'Lord Keynes and the General Theory', *Econometrica*, 14: 187–200.

Samuelson, P A (1947) *Foundations of Economic Analysis*. Cambridge: Harvard University Press.

Samuelson, P A (1963) 'Problems of Methodology: Discussion', *American Economic Review Papers and Proceedings*, 52 (May): 231–6.

Samuelson, P A (1964) 'Theory and Realism: A Reply', *American Economic Review*, 54 (Sept.): 736–9.

Samuelson, P A (1983) 'My Life Philosophy', *The American Economist*, 27 (2): 5–12.

Vines, D and S Wills (2018) 'The Rebuilding Macroeconomic Theory Project: An Analytical Assessment', *Oxford Review of Economic Policy*, 34 (1–2): 1–42.

Vines, D and S Wills (2020) 'The Rebuilding Macroeconomic Theory Project Part II: Multiple Equilibria, Toy Models, and Policy Models in a New Macroeconomic Paradigm', *Oxford Review of Economic Policy*, 36 (3): 427–97.

Weintraub, E R (1998) 'Axiomatisches Mißverständnis', *Economic Journal*, 108 (Nov.): 1837–47.

Weintraub, E R (2002) *How Economics Became a Mathematical Science*. Durham and London: Duke University Press.

Wong, S (1973) 'The "F-Twist" and the Methodology of Paul Samuelson', *American Economic Review*, 63 (3): 312–25.

Wren-Lewis, S (2018) 'Ending the Microfoundations Hegemony', *Oxford Review of Economic Policy*, 34 (1–2): 55–69.

5 In Search of Santa Claus

Samuelson, Stigler, and Coase Theorem Worlds

Steven G. Medema

Prelude

Dear Editor—
I am 8 years old. Some of my little friends say there is no Santa Claus. Papa says, "If you see it in *The Sun*, it's so." Please tell me the truth, is there a Santa Claus?

Virginia O'Hanlon

Virginia, your little friends are wrong. They have been affected by the skepticism of a skeptical age. They do not believe except they see. They think that nothing can be which is not comprehensible by their little minds. All minds, Virginia, whether they be men's or children's, are little. In this great universe of ours, man is a mere insect, an ant, in his intellect as compared with the boundless world about him, as measured by the intelligence capable of grasping the whole of truth and knowledge.

Yes, Virginia, there is a Santa Claus. He exists as certainly as love and generosity and devotion exist, and you know that they abound and give to your life its highest beauty and joy. Alas! how dreary would be the world if there were no Santa Claus! It would be as dreary as if there were no Virginias. There would be no childlike faith then, no poetry, no romance to make tolerable this existence. We should have no enjoyment, except in sense and sight. The eternal light with which childhood fills the world would be extinguished.

Not believe in Santa Claus! You might as well not believe in fairies. You might get your papa to hire men to watch in all the chimneys on Christmas eve to catch Santa Claus, but even if you did not see Santa Claus coming down, what would that prove? Nobody sees Santa Claus, but that is no sign that there is no Santa Claus. The most real things in the world are those that neither children nor men can see. Did you ever see fairies dancing on the lawn? Of course not, but that's no proof that they are not there. Nobody can conceive or imagine all the wonders there are unseen and unseeable in the world.

You tear apart the baby's rattle and see what makes the noise inside, but there is a veil covering the unseen world which not the strongest man, nor even the united strength of all the strongest men that ever lived could tear apart. Only faith, poetry, love, romance, can push aside that curtain and

DOI: 10.4324/9781003266051-8

view and picture the supernal beauty and glory beyond. Is it all real? Ah, Virginia, in all this world there is nothing else real and abiding.

No Santa Claus! Thank God! he lives and lives forever. A thousand years from now, Virginia, nay 10 times 10,000 years from now, he will continue to make glad the heart of childhood.

Francis B. Church
Editor of the New York *Sun* 1897

Introduction

Paul Samuelson loved a good rhetorical flourish almost as much as he loved a good theorem. His writings are replete with both, and they were seldom devoid of meaning. One of the flourishes that Samuelson adopted in his later years involved applying labels such as "Santa Claus economics" and "Santa Claus situations" to, as Wade Hands put it, "mathematical models with extremely strong and empirically unrealistic assumptions" (2016, 425). As Hands went on to emphasize in his wonderful essay on Samuelson's use of this language to describe homothetic general equilibrium models, "Santa Claus economics" was not wholly, for Samuelson, a term of derision. Some Santa Claus models he found useful, others not. But there was one economic result that, in Samuelson's view, could not be captured even in a Santa Claus world: the Coase theorem.[1]

In 1959 and 1960, Ronald Coase made Virginia, and Chicago, believe that there indeed is a Santa Claus. The gift was efficiency in the face of uncompensated spillovers—externalities—situations that, for more than a century, had caused economists to believe that the market system would fail to produce an optimum (Medema 2009). Serious existence questions had been raised by, e.g., J.S. Mill and Henry Sidgwick in the nineteenth century, but some persisted in their belief, pointing out that Adam Smith had told them so back in 1776. But then came Pigou (1920), with his contention that these divergences between private and social interests could only be resolved via direct state action. And he argued this to great effect. Arrow (1951) was forced to assume away externalities to prove efficiency in the marketplace, and subsequent work by Meade (1952) and Bator (1958) only reinforced Pigou's finding. That there is no Santa Claus in these situations was taken as gospel even in Chicago (Stigler 1946), which makes crystal clear the extent of the problem. Any claims for Santa's existence must satisfy certain marginal conditions, and there seemed to be no hope for that. At least not until Coase arrived at the North Pole.

Coase's discovery came almost by accident. His analysis of the political economy of broadcasting was aimed at showing the inefficiencies of the existing regulatory structure, including the U.S. Federal Communications Commission's policy of allocating broadcast frequencies via administrative fiat. His sense that the market would be a more efficient mechanism for allocating frequencies, though, ran into the externality problem—the concern that, left to their own devices, broadcasters would overpopulate the best slices of the frequency spectrum, causing interference problems. Regulation had, for decades, seemed to offer the only way around this problem, but Coase (1959) argued that the market mechanism could do the trick if the government would only assign private property rights in those frequencies and permit their exchange. In fact, he said, it would not even matter to which party the rights were assigned. If the rights were not located where they were most highly valued, market exchange would move them there, assuming that the costs of movement did not get in the way.

Though Virginia had little difficulty accepting this argument, the same could not be said of Chicago.[2] As Stigler (1988) has told us, however, Coase managed to convert the Chicagoans to his way of thinking during a magical evening in Aaron Director's living room. This led Coase, at Director's urging, to write up a more expansive version of his argument in "The Problem of Social Cost" (1960), and the theory of externalities was forever changed. As Coase noted in summarizing his argument,

> It is necessary to know whether the damaging business is liable or not for damage caused since without the establishment of this initial delimitation of rights there can be no market transactions to transfer and recombine them. But the ultimate result (which maximizes the value of production) is independent of the legal position if the pricing system is assumed to work without cost.
>
> (8)

George Stigler, who was only too eager to believe in Santa Claus once presented with an argument he deemed credible, soon labeled this result the "Coase theorem," and the rest is history.

Coase certainly did not see himself as laying out an important new proposition in economic theory—to say nothing of a "theorem"—when writing up his negotiation analysis and the result that flowed from it. One indicator of this is his failure (if it can be called that) to state clearly and precisely the details of the assumptions upon which his analysis rested. This task fell to others, just as had the working out of the unstated assumptions underlying Marshall's analysis in the *Principles* (1890), the search for which occupied a generation of Cambridge economists during the first third of the twentieth century. Another is the absence of any "proof" in Coase's article that would satisfy the strictures of modern economic thinking. Instead, Coase worked out his result through a series of illustrations and called it good. It may be that none of this would have mattered were it not for the growing societal concern with pollution and natural resource use, an issue that caused more and more economists to turn their attention to problems of externality. Coase's result was caught up in this turn and even began to gain traction in certain quarters. Still, there were many who refused to believe, having absorbed the lesson that market forces simply could not deal efficiently with external effects.

And so a debate ensued, one that reflected and to no small extent was driven by both externality-related policy concerns and the ambiguities in Coase's argument. The debate played out on several fronts and across the pages of the profession's leading journals. One of the more striking features of this debate is the wide variety of models and theoretical frameworks used to discuss, evaluate, or otherwise analyze Coase's result—an artifact of the aforementioned ambiguity in Coase's reasoning. Some framed Coase's result in a bargaining context and others in a competitive markets (both partial and general equilibrium) context. And players on both sides lined up with their demonstrations that the Coase theorem did or did not hold water. The parties involved in these debates, though, were often talking past each other, debating very different environments and models, and on different terms. Stabilization was elusive. Those who, like Virginia, very much wanted to believe could certainly find reason to do so. For others, however, the theorem smacked more of the shopping mall Santa who reeks of alcohol and cigarettes.[3]

Grinch[4]

To say that Paul Samuelson was not a fan of the Coase theorem would be something of an understatement. Though he mentioned Coase's result only a handful of times in his writings, the discussion was uniformly critical. It first caught Samuelson's eye already in the early 1960s—well ahead of most economists, it seems—and his reaction was anything but sympathetic. The occasion for his initial commentary was an essay titled "Modern Economic Realities and Individualism," which found Samuelson taking issue with the excesses of the latter in light of the interdependencies associated with the former. One of those excesses was the abuse of Adam Smith's concept of the invisible hand which, according to the individualist's credo, tells us that "anything which results from voluntary agreement is in some sense, *ipso facto*, optimal," obviating the need for government interference in the marketplace (1963, 130). Samuelson considered Coase's (1960) analysis of negotiated solutions to externalities emblematic of this misplaced optimism:

> The view that R. Coase has shown that externalities—like smoke nuisances—are not a logical blow to the Invisible Hand and do not call for coercive interference with *laissez-faire* is not mine. I do not know that it is Coase's. But if it had not been expressed by someone, I would not be mentioning it here. Unconstrained self-interest will in such cases lead to the insoluble bilateral monopoly problem with all of its indeterminacies and non-optimalities.
>
> (Samuelson 1963, 132n)

In laying down this charge, Samuelson became the first to suggest, at least in print, that the emperor had no clothes—that the smoothly operating exploitation of gains from exchange contemplated by Coase made for bad economics and so led to seriously wrongheaded conclusions.[5] But given that the article appeared in *The Texas Quarterly*, a periodical "designed for the general literate reader," and which strove "to seek a balance among the sciences, social sciences, humanities, and fine arts," it should not surprise that it had no influence on the course of events.[6]

Four years later, however, Samuelson pressed the same point in his discussion of "The Monopolistic Competition Revolution" (1967), an essay in honor of Edward Chamberlin and dedicated to elaborating "some of the *theoretical* reasons why perfect competition provides an empirically inadequate model of the real world" (21). One of those reasons had to do with the insufficiency of such models for describing exchange outcomes in the presence of bilateral monopoly:

> the rational self-interest of each of two free wills does not necessitate that there will emerge, even in the most idealized game-theoretic situation, a Pareto-optimal solution that maximizes the sum of the two opponents' profits, *in advance of and without regard to how that maximized profit is to be divided up among them*. Except by fiat of the economic analyst or by his tautologically redefining what constitutes "nonrational" behavior, we cannot rule out a non-Pareto-optimal outcome. We can rule it out only by Humpty-Dumptyism.[7]
>
> (35)

Once again, Samuelson felt compelled to draw attention to the Coase theorem to illustrate his point:

> Some readers have interpreted R. H. Coase ... as having shown how *laissez-faire* pricing can solve the problem of "externalities" and "public goods" harmoniously. The above analysis shows that a problem of pricing two or more inputs that can be used in common is not solved by reducing it to a determinate maximized total whose allocation among the parts is an indeterminate problem in multilateral monopoly. It should come as news to no economist or game theorist that duopoly, oligopoly, bilateral and multilateral monopoly are indeterminate in their solution.
>
> (36n.18)

Of course, a glance at the list of attendees at Director's little soirée informs us that game theorists were in short supply that evening.

Given this attitude, it is no surprise that Samuelson did not elect to include a discussion of the Coase theorem in his best-selling textbook, *Economics*, until the 1985 edition. Coincidentally or not, this was when William Nordhaus joined him as a co-author, and well after it had become commonplace for textbook authors to take up Coase's result within their pages. Time, though, clearly had not affected Samuelson's attitude. Having established the externality problem and the potential for governmental corrective action, Samuelson and Nordhaus informed their readers that "A startling analysis by Ronald Coase suggested that voluntary negotiations among the affected parties [to an externality] would in some circumstances lead to an efficient outcome" (1985, 718). Such an outcome "might" occur, they said, "when there are well-defined property rights and the costs of negotiation are *low*" (718, emphasis added).[8] But Samuelson and Nordhaus strongly resisted the argument that efficient bargains *will* occur, basing their opinion on the same game-theoretic considerations that Samuelson had spoken of in the 1960s. In fact, their discussion of these concerns, elaborated in a footnote, is nearly as long as the in-text presentation of the theorem. But the lesson was clear and, lest the readers be inclined to give Coase's result actual credence, theoretical or otherwise, Samuelson and Nordhaus made sure to point out that "there is no theorem from game theory proving that an *invisible hand* will lead a pair or more of bargainers to the Pareto efficient level of pollution" (1985, 719n.6).

Apart from the textbook mentions, Samuelson left Coase's result alone for a quarter-century but then took it up twice in the first half of the 1990s. A 1993 essay on altruism and Darwinian selection finds Samuelson railing against the idea that the individual pursuit of self-interest, channeled through a Darwinian survival of the fittest process, generates outcomes congruent with the social interest. A goodly amount of self-interested behavior is "socially harmful", he said, and "this lack of congruence is not a freak of rare paradox." Indeed, it is congruence itself that is the rare bird, as reflected in the finding that "constant returns to scale *sans* externality *cum* perfect competition singularly entails Pareto optimality of prices" (1993, 145). That which survives, then, is not necessarily, or even likely, to be optimal:

> Darwin's evolution is indeed mere sound and fury, signifying nothing normative, rather than denoting a process of meaningful Spencerian triumph. Natural selection is not an empty tautology about survival of those who survive. It is a lawful process subject to shrewd predictions and testable refutations. But in general it does not act to maximize any scalar magnitude.
>
> (145)

Social Darwinism, Samuelson argued, was nothing more than "a perverted borrowing from what can be validly established for biology" and its imitation makes for very poor economics:

> When I contemplate strong claims by a Richard Posner that law has evolved historically à la Pareto, or arguments that a Coase Theorem ensures that deadweight loss is at its feasible minimum, I fear that von Neumann and Morgenstern are spinning in their graves and Charles Darwin is wondering why he left his barnacles, pigeons, and earthworms.
>
> (145)

For Samuelson, then, the Coase theorem seems to have been little more than "a perverted borrowing from what can be validly established for" economics. Then again, a nodding acquaintance with Samuelson's various commentaries on Chicago suggests that, in his opinion, there was a good deal of such perversion going on in Hyde Park.

It was not until 1995, in a symposium on the Coase theorem published in *Japan and the World Economy*, that Samuelson finally went to some lengths in spelling out the source of his uneasiness with Coase's result. The issue, at one level, was its departure from the real world. But Samuelson had developed and proved all manner of theorems that entailed departures from the real world. With the Coase theorem, the issue was clearly something deeper.

Samuelson certainly understood what was at stake if the Coase theorem was correct. Yes, the theorem proclaimed the efficient resolution of externalities—a challenging enough proposition in itself—but its import went well beyond this: "Follow the bare-bones logic," Samuelson said, "and *nothing institutional matters* in economics" (1995, 2, emphasis added). Indeed, this could well be the most important insight to emerge from Coase's result. But Samuelson was mystified that anyone could, even in theory, buy into the logic that gets one there. Reminding his readers of the evening when Coase converted the skeptical crowd of Chicagoans to his way of thinking, Samuelson asked, "Did 21 savants buy this palaver?" (2)

The "dubious major premise of Coase argumentation," from where Samuelson stood, was its wholesale glossing over of the enormous potential for strategic behavior within the negotiation process (3). And once one grants this possibility, outcomes are indeterminate and, "generally speaking," not Pareto optimal. Nor was Samuelson willing to buy claims that vague hand-waving related to the shadowy and elusive assumption of zero transaction costs negated these issues. "[T]hat one can usefully capture the content of the game-theoretic interactions between ranchers and farmers or parent and child under the rubric of 'transaction costs'" was, for Samuelson, nonsensi-cal. "Is there some coherent proof that, without transaction costs, real-life rivals must find their way to Pareto-Optimal frontiers?" (4) Certainly not for Samuelson, who made clear that economists had already been told what is needed to guarantee efficiency:

> Only in certain *Santa Claus situations*—constant returns to scale, infinite divisibility, free entry, dispersed ownership of each grade of factor, shared knowledge, complete markets—only then will Smithian self-interest be compelled to achieve Pareto-Optimality"
>
> (6, emphasis added)

It will not escape the reader that Santa, so conceived, bears a striking resem-blance to Samuelson's brother-in-law.[9]

What emerges, then, is this: The problems with the Coase theorem, as Samuelson understood it, went well beyond detachment from the real world.

His position was that there *is no* Coase theorem, no Santa Claus world that, teamed with economic logic, can get us around the problems associated with strategic behavior. To suggest otherwise, for Samuelson, was simply a bridge too far.

Enter Rudolph: Guiding Santa's Sleigh[10]

George Stigler did believe in Santa Claus, at least post-1960. Of course, Stigler also announced to the participants in a bicentenary conference on Smith's *Wealth of Nations* (1976) that ol' Adam was "alive and well and living in Chicago" (Meek 1977, 3). It is important to remember, though, that Stigler was once in the same camp as Samuelson, the editions of his price theory textbook prior to 1966 laying out a fairly standard Pigouvian story about externalities. But, like St. Paul on the road to Damascus, Stigler was converted and quickly became a zealous champion of the cause. Or, lest we confuse our Christmas stories, emerged as our Rudolph, with his illuminating nose, pulling Santa's sleigh.[11]

It has been suggested that Stigler did *not* fully buy into Coase's argument on that fateful evening at Director's home. But whatever his initial reaction, there can be no question that Stigler came to embrace Coase's result in the years that followed. In fact, he seems to have been mesmerized by it. It was Stigler, after all, who gave Coase's result the name by which it has come to be known—the "Coase theorem"—in the 1966 edition of his price theory textbook (1966, 113). Two years later, he gave the theorem prominent play in a lecture at the University of Michigan Law School,[12] and over the next quarter-century, he published a half-dozen papers that drew on the theorem. Beyond this, his 1988 *Memoirs* devotes the better part of a chapter to this topic—comparing Coase with Archimedes along the way—and his archives are littered with drafts of ideas, often fragments, related to the theorem that he set down on paper but never fully developed.[13]

What Coase had demonstrated, in Stigler's view, was that "under perfect competition private and social costs will be equal," a finding that, he noted for his student readers, is "more remarkable ... to us older economists who have believed the opposite for a generation, than it will appear to the young reader who was never wrong here" (1966, 113). But yet, Stigler continued, though the Coase theorem "seems astonishing ... it should not be." In fact, he considered it nothing more than an illustration of some basic economic analysis long and widely accepted in the field and thus a result upon which all economists should agree. After all, he pointed out, "Laws often prove to be unimportant" when their effects are subjected to economic analysis, as illustrated by the invariant economic incidence of a sales tax (113)."[14] For Stigler, then, the Coase theorem was a revolutionary result that should not have been revolutionary. That it seemed so was only because the profession had been in the clutches of some bad economics.

Stigler was well aware that Coase's result relied on the fiction of zero transaction costs, and he understood the implications of this assumption better than most. "The world of zero transaction costs," he said, "turns out to be as strange as the physical world would be with zero friction." In such a world, Stigler continued, "Monopolies would be compensated to act like competitors, and insurance companies and banks would not exist" (1972, 12). His 1988 commentary on the theorem fleshes this out even further:

> Still, zero transaction costs are a bold theoretical construct. It implies, for example, that in buying an automobile one knows the prices all dealers charge (with no cost to anyone in time or money), that one is completely certain what all warranties for replacement of defective parts or provision of services mean and has complete confidence that they will be fulfilled (without controversy), and so on. Zero transaction costs mean that the economic world has no friction or ambiguity.
>
> (Stigler 1988, 75)

Yet, despite this severe detachment from reality, Stigler ascribed tremendous import to Coase's finding. Why? Stigler does not tell us explicitly, but the reason seems clear when one examines the corpus of his writings: He saw in Coase's result an extension of the first fundamental theorem of welfare economics, which demonstrates that perfectly competitive markets generate efficient outcomes (Arrow 1951). The first fundamental theorem, of course, assumed away externalities on the grounds that they are a barrier to efficiency. Yet, the Coase theorem suggests that externalities are no barrier at all.

The "theorem" label, then, was more than simply a manifestation of Stigler's literary cleverness—though it certainly was that, in part. The correspondence between Coase's result and the first fundamental theorem explains both Stigler's terse wording, as against Coase's more lengthy exposition of his result, and Stigler's grounding of it in the assumption of perfect competition—not to mention his desire to codify the result as a "theorem." This also helps us to understand why, though Stigler's 1966 presentation of Coase's result makes much of both the efficiency and allocative invariance principles, his "Coase theorem" does not—being content with the simple assertion that efficiency is assured. In Stigler's hands, the "Coase theorem" is a result about the efficiency properties of competitive markets rather than, as it was typically interpreted at the time, a contribution to the theory of externalities *per se.*[15]

For Stigler, unlike for Samuelson, there *is* a Santa Claus world that will guarantee efficiency in the presence of externalities. Yet, having come this far, one might reasonably ask, "Does any of this matter?" After all, we are talking about Santa Claus worlds, with seemingly no bearing on the world in which we live and within which externality policy is made. As it happens, though, it *does* matter, and for reasons both theoretical and practical.

Whoville vs. Mt. Crumpit[16]

The juxtaposition of Stigler's view of the Coase theorem with that of Samuelson leaves us in a rather interesting position. For Stigler, the "Coase theorem" is a bargaining result that teaches us about the efficiency properties of competitive markets. Samuelson, on the other hand, rejected the Coase theorem precisely because an efficient outcome is assured only under the "Santa Claus" conditions of perfect competition, and the Coase theorem's bargaining process is far-removed from this realm. How, then, do we reconcile, or at least explain, these divergent claims? And, in particular, how could Stigler simply assume that any necessary negotiations were likely to come off without a hitch—that bilateral monopoly problems and the like would not generate the inefficiencies which Samuelson considered inevitable? If Samuelson was correct in his assertion that the Coase theorem lies beyond even the reach of Santa Claus economics, Stigler was serving up nonsense on stilts.

Let's begin with Stigler's assessment of the discipline imposed on market participants by perfect competition. Those who fail to minimize costs do not survive, meaning that it is in the interests of those involved in externality situations to reach an agreement that exploits the gains from exchange. Indeed, the survival of at least one of them depends on it. This insight lies at the heart of Stigler's attraction to Coase's analysis. In a brief article published in the *Yale Law Journal* shortly before his death, Stigler opened his discussion by saying, "Ronald Coase taught us, what of course we should have already known, that when it is to the benefit of people to reach an agreement, they will seek to reach it" (1989, 631). This, then, was the fundamental insight to be taken from Coase. Though his target was undoubtedly the legion of theorem critics, Stigler's elaboration on this point almost seems to have been pointed directly at Samuelson:

> Does the proposition require proof? One would think not. It is similar to a proposition in international trade: The prices of internationally traded goods in two national markets will differ by no more than the cost of movement of the goods between the markets. Suppose that I started to test the proposition and found that a pair of prices differed by more than the costs of movement. I would immediately abandon the test and embark on lucrative arbitrage transactions. Similarly, if I found that Coase's famous grain farmer and cattle rancher were making foolish decisions with respect to the damage to grain from wandering cattle, I would buy the enterprises and reap a capital gain from efficient reorganization.
> (631)

This is all well and good, but not everyone is George Stigler. Though his argument does seem to guarantee end-state efficiency, it neatly sidesteps the actual negotiation processes that are so integral to Coase's result and were of so much concerns to Samuelson.

But this is not the end of the story. To understand how Stigler got from *A* to *B*, we need to examine his treatment of the "perfect knowledge" requirement of perfect competition and how this—and deviations from it—relate to the negotiation processes contemplated by Coase. Note what Stigler says here:

> If there is not perfect knowledge, there will be an array of prices at which transactions will take place, and almost all real markets display such an array. There will often be scope for higgling, and to this extent a situation termed bilateral monopoly arises.
>
> (1966, 88)

So far, he seems to be playing right into Samuelson's hands. But then Stigler goes on to note that,

> if the scope for higgling is small, the departure from competition is small.
>
> (88)

Stigler allowed that the perfect knowledge assumption is almost always violated in the real world. The question is whether this entails any significant consequences. This, though, is where his assumption of perfect competition takes on an additional role. If the parties to the externality, whether Coase's rancher and farmer or the polluting factory and the laundry of externality illustration lore, sell their products in perfectly competitive markets, well-known market clearing prices serve as the key ingredients to the negotiation process, providing much of the information most relevant to negotiation. The scope for higgling is thus greatly reduced, meaning that "the departure from competition" will be "small." In short, we can rely on the Coase theorem to generate efficient results in a world approximating that of perfect competition.

Even if one is willing to accept Stigler's logic here, however, we are still left with a result that applies only to that Santa Claus situation. This would seem to be rather poor grounds on which to anchor a theorem to which Stigler ascribed potentially wide-ranging relevance. For Stigler, however, the model of perfect competition was anything but a purely abstract, theoretical construct, as he made clear to the readers of his textbook:

> If the reader bristles at the acceptance of assumptions such as perfect knowledge and complete product homogeneity, he is both wrong and right. He is wrong in denying the helpfulness of the use of pure, clean concepts in theoretical analysis: they confer clarity and efficiency *without depriving the analysis of empirical relevance.* He is right if he believes these extreme assumptions are not *necessary* to the existence of competition: it is sufficient, for example, if each trader in a market knows a fair number of buyers and sellers, if all traders together have a comprehensive

knowledge so only one price rules. The reason for not stating the weakest assumptions (necessary conditions) for competition is that they are difficult to formulate, and in fact not known precisely.

(1966, 89)

This suggests that, for Stigler, the model of perfect competition is neither a purely theoretical exercise nor a literal depiction of reality. Instead, it is a tool for analysis, one that combines "clarity and efficiency" with "empirical relevance," the latter because it gives rise to empirically testable propositions.

In Stigler's mind, at least, real-world markets tend to approximate the strictures of perfect competition sufficiently closely, in many circumstances, to make it a useful interpretive and prescriptive tool.[17] His attitude on this score is neatly captured in his discussion of Edward Chamberlin's monopolistic competition approach, which Stigler famously dismissed in a lecture given at the London School of Economics in the late 1940s:

> Chamberlin's vision was clearly a legitimate way of looking at economic life. One may even argue that it was more congruent with untutored observation, and in this sense more 'realistic.' But these are points, not of unimportance, but of complete irrelevance, despite the part they played in securing popularity for his theory.
>
> (1949, 14)

Instead, he continued, the "paramount" question is whether "a theory incorporating this viewpoint contain[s] more accurate or more comprehensive implications than the neoclassical theory" (14). For Stigler, the answer to this question was a resounding, "No"—that despite its claims of greater "realism," the theory of monopolistic competition added little, if anything, to the standard competitive model as an explanatory or predictive construct. His 1966 defense of the competitive model, quoted above, is simply a restatement of the same point from a different angle.

Stigler's message, then, was this: The typical market is characterized by conditions that can be regarded as reasonable approximations of the competitive environment. The Coase theorem's efficiency and invariance claims hold under competitive conditions. Therefore, the Coase theorem tells us that externalities will be efficiently internalized in many real-world situations. So conceived, it combines "clarity and efficiency" with "empirical relevance," just as does the competitive model. And so Stigler called for empirical studies of the magnitude of transaction costs, doubtless in the hope that their findings would support his views of the theorem's practical utility (1989, 631).

Samuelson's view of the relative merits of the competitive and monopolistic competition frameworks could hardly have been more different, and the distinction sheds a good deal of light on their respective attitudes toward the Coase theorem. Samuelson had Stigler squarely in his sights when disparaging those who proclaimed the theoretical and empirical virtues of the competitive model and made no bones about his dim view of Stigler's position:

> If the real world displays the variety of behavior that the Chamberlin-Robinson models permit—and I believe the Chicago writers are simply wrong in denying that these important empirical deviations exist—then reality will falsify many of the important qualitative and quantitative predictions of the competitive model. Hence, by the pragmatic test of prediction adequacy, the perfect-competition model fails to be an adequate approximation. When Friedman claims (*Essays*, pp. 36–37) that a tax will have the type of incidence on the cigarette industry that it would on a competitive industry, he is at most showing that some predictions of the latter theory are adequate. To the degree that other predictions are falsified—consumer price approximately equal to marginal cost, advertising cost equal to zero—the competitive model fails the pragmatic predictive test.
>
> (1967, 21)

This inadequacy, Samuelson argued "forces us to work with some version of monopolistic or imperfect competition" (21). It was not sufficient—indeed, wholly wrongheaded—to take refuge in Santa Claus models when a superior alternative was close at hand:

> Chicago economists can continue to shout until they are blue in the face that there is no elegant alternative to the theory of perfect competition. If not, the proper moral is, "So much the worse for elegance" rather than, "Economists of the world, unite in proclaiming that the Emperor has almost no clothes, and in pretending that the model of perfect competition does a good enough job in fitting the real world."
>
> (21–22)

To stand with Chicago on this score, he continued, meant "taking the coward's way" out by avoiding the important and challenging questions that the economy puts squarely in front of us and "fobbing off in their place nice answers to less interesting easy questions" (22).

Our protagonists' respective attitudes toward perfect and monopolistic competition, then, tell us a good deal about their views of the Coase theorem. It is safe to say that each applied the same set of methodological precepts to the Coase theorem as he did to his analysis of competitive markets. Just as we can assume that the competitive model is a useful (incredibly misleading) description of the operation of vast swaths of the marketplace, we can assume that the Coase theorem aptly describes (bears no correspondence to) many situations of externality. Stigler almost certainly would have agreed with Samuelson's (1963, 132n) contention that the "insoluble bilateral monopoly problem with all its indeterminacies and non-optimalities" essentially forecloses the consummation of efficient bargains; the difference is in the domain that each ascribed to those insoluble problems. For Stigler, the prevalence of competitive markets largely negated such worries, allowing for his seemingly boundless optimism that agents would be able to higgle their way to efficient solutions in a wide variety of circumstances.

The Wonders that Are Unseen and Unseeable in the World[18]

It is not difficult to understand why Stigler wanted very much to believe in Santa Claus. Though many, and perhaps most, economists view the first fundamental theorem as a purely theoretical exercise (albeit a very important one), it was more than just this for Stigler. Given the practical utility he found in the competitive model, it reinforced a presumption of "efficient until proven otherwise" for a wide range of market outcomes. In this sense, the Coase theorem is consistent with Stigler's (1961) pioneering analysis of information problems in economics. There, he showed that, once the costs of acquiring information are taken into account, "some important aspects of social organization take on new meaning" (1961, 213), with activities (such as advertizing) often presumed inefficient now seen in a different, more efficient light. One could argue that Stigler's Coase theorem in some sense did for externality problems what his 1961 article did for information problems, showing them to be less detrimental to efficiency than commonly believed and, in the limit, of little concern.

The more difficult issue is getting at why Samuelson failed to believe. One can certainly sympathize with his concerns about realism; yet this only takes us so far, as Samuelson was all too eager to use unrealistic models in his own work. From models of international trade to his (co-)development of the efficient markets hypothesis, Samuelson showed himself time and again willing to theorize about frictionless worlds.[19] We can also grant his concerns about the vagueness surrounding the concept of transaction costs, but this does not preclude the serious theoretical probing of life in their absence—a world without frictions and where agents possess full and complete information. More to the point, under this and other restrictive assumptions, the efficiency and invariance claims made by Coase *are* valid:

> Theorem: *If agents are rational and the costs of transacting are zero, resources will be allocated efficiently independent of how rights over those resources are initially distributed. Moreover, if utility functions are uniformly affine and the registration of subjective values is not wealth-constrained, this efficient allocation of resources is independent of the initial rights structure.*[20]

A world of zero transaction costs, as defined here, is characterized by fully specified property rights, transferable utility, and costless information. The last of these requires that all information relevant to the transacting process and its effects can be acquired costlessly by all individuals affected by the transaction. And given that information is costless, everyone possesses all relevant information, including knowing everything about everyone else.[21] In this "transactions costs-free fairyland," as Alan Randall (1975, 741n.44) called it, the strategic behavior that so concerned Samuelson is impossible, or at least without effect. Is this unrealistic? Of course, but surely no more (or less) so than homothetic utility. A Santa Claus world indeed, but it *is* a Santa Claus world.

If we were to bring charges against Samuelson here, they would be for insufficient theoretical imagination. But that is a hard one to make stick, given the extent of Samuelson's endowment with that gift. It may be, though, that Hands' analysis of Samuelson provides us with an explanation here, just as it does for Samuelson's dim view of homothetic utility:

> In the homothetic Santa Claus case, the competitive equilibrium is the unique social welfare maximum (associated with the utility function of the representative agent) and this is a much stronger defense of the free market than Samuelson believed pure economic theory could, or should, provide. As he noted in the final paragraph of his Nobel lecture (quoting Herbert Davenport): "There is no reason why theoretical economics should be a monopoly of the reactionaries ...."
>
> (2016, 431–32)

The Coase theorem undeniably provides a much stronger defense of the free market than do homothetic general equilibrium models, overcoming *all* of the classic objections to market failure—monopoly, externalities, and public goods. The seeming inevitability of the last had been hammered home by Samuelson (1954; 1955) only a few years before Coase published his classic article, and utilizing arguments similar to those he later leveled against the Coase theorem. When it came to these classic market failure situations, it seems that Samuelson could not even allow himself to search for a North Pole, as if to admit the existence of a Santa Claus world here was to admit too much. Then again, Samuelson was anything but alone in this, perhaps because, like so many others, he feared the consequences that might follow if economists and policy makers began to believe too fervently.

Yes, Virginia, There Is a Santa Claus

"Anecdotes do not a science make," as Samuelson pointed out in his 1995 discussion of the Coase theorem (Samuelson 1995, 4). The currency of stories about farmers and ranchers, physicians and confectioners, or polluting factories and laundresses is of little more value than the sight of a rotund, bearded fellow in a red suit at the local Macy's in December, though each has the ability to deceive the innocent. But the reality that the farmer and the rancher may not be able to agree on the division of surplus and that the guy in the red suit goes home to Queens rather than the North Pole is no evidence against Santa Claus.[22]

Does it matter whether one believes in Santa Claus? Indeed it does, as the history of economics shows us time and again. Trim away the beards and remove the red suits, and you find Smiths, Says, Langes, Arrows, and even Keyneses. Each taught us, or allowed us, to see things in ways that we previously did not. And so too for the Coase theorem. Though for Samuelson this seems to have been little more than a reason to avert one's eyes, the lessons learned from the literature of the last six decades suggest otherwise (Medema 2020). The Coase theorem at once alerted economists and others to the possibilities of markets and market-like mechanisms and to the forces that preclude their smooth functioning, or their functioning at all. Whether, when all of the effects are totaled up, Santa left economics a shiny new toy, a lump of coal, or some combination of these when he landed in Aaron Director's living room is a matter of taste. What is unmistakable, however, is that economics would be very different if, instead, Santa had set down his sleigh 1000 miles away, in Cambridge.

> "Alas! how dreary would be the world if there were no Santa Claus! It would be as dreary as if there were no Virginias."

Or no Chicagos.

Acknowledgements

I would like to thank Bruce Caldwell and John Davis for instructive comments on earlier versions of this paper. The financial support provided by the National Endowment for the Humanities, the Institute for New Economic Thinking, and the Earhart Foundation is gratefully acknowledged, as is the excellent assistance offered by the staff of the Hanna Holborn Gray Special Collections Research Center at the University of Chicago's Regenstein Library.

Notes

1. Hands, by the way, does not mention Samuelson's discussions of the Coase theorem in his article.
2. On Virginia, see Buchanan (1962, 341n.1). In conversations with this author some forty years later, Buchanan evidenced an almost "ho-hum" attitude toward what Coase had done in 1960.
3. Medema (2020) provides a discussion of these debates, as well as a wealth of references to related primary- and secondary-source literature. Other discussions, from somewhat different perspectives, can be found in Bertrand (2019) and Zelder (1998).
4. For the uninitiated, see Seuss (1957).
5. That is, Samuelson recognized that strategic behavior possibilities imply a variety of potential equilibria, not all of which are efficient. This is all well and good.

Whether it goes to the Coase theorem proper, however, is another story. See section V, below, as well as Medema (2020).

6. https://tshaonline.org/handbook/online/articles/nnt01, accessed May 20, 2020. Among its many illustrious contributing authors before it ceased publication in 1978 were Frank Lloyd Wright, Aaron Copland, Robert Penn Warren, Allen Tate, John Wain, J. W. H. Auden, and Lyndon B. Johnson. Samuelson's paper was presented at a December 1962 symposium on individualism in twentieth-century America, organized for the American Studies Association of Texas. I thank Roger Backhouse for bringing this symposium information to my attention.

7. The relevant reference here is Lewis Carroll's *Through the Looking Glass*: "'When I use a word,' Humpty Dumpty said in a rather scornful tone, 'it means just what I choose it to mean—neither more nor less.'" See, e.g., https://www.gutenberg.org/files/12/12-h/12-h.htm.

8. Why Samuelson specified "low" transaction costs rather than, following Coase (1960, 2–8), zero transaction costs is a mystery, though this version of Coase's result was not (and still is not) uncommon in the literature. One possibility is that Samuelson wanted to make the theorem 'operational,' which would then more obviously allow him to register his concerns about bilateral monopoly.

9. That brother-in-law, of course, is Kenneth Arrow.

10. The readers upon whom this reference is lost are encouraged to familiarize themselves with the classic television special, references to which can be found on the web.

11. Stigler's treatment of the Coase theorem is also discussed at length in Bertrand (2018), Marciano (2018), and Medema (2011).

12. Memorandum from Richard Posner to George Stigler, 4 Jan 1971, George J Stigler Papers, Box 11.

13. See Stigler (1988, ch. 5).

14. For the non-economist reader, the lesson here is that the effects of a sales tax on a good's price and on the quantity of the good bought and sold will be the same whether the tax is imposed on buyers or on sellers.

15. In recent years, the Coase theorem has become loosed from its original externalities context and is often seen as a general proposition about the efficiency of exchange and/or as a general invariance result. The latter is reflected in the propensity to view Ricardian equivalence, the Modigliani-Miller theorem, and other such invariance results as "special cases" of the Coase theorem. See, e.g., Allen (1999, 904–5) and Medema (2020, 1089–90).

16. Again, for the uninitiated, Whoville is a town full of believers in Santa Claus, and Christmas. Mt. Crumpit, which overlooks Whoville, is the home of the Grinch. See Seuss (1957). Any resemblance to certain 'freshwater' and 'saltwater' cities is purely coincidental.

17. A useful background discussion to this topic is found in Hammond and Hammond (2006). Of course, Milton Friedman's (1953) essay, "The Methodology of Positive Economics," also bears on all of this.

18. See "Prelude," above.

19. That is, one cannot simply write off Samuelson's position as seeing transaction costs as endemic to the bargaining process. Transaction costs are also endemic to the market process—an 'institutional' feature of the world—but Samuelson was repeatedly willing to overlook them in that venue.

20. Proof: For efficiency, see, e.g., Robson (2012) and Mas-Colell et al. (1995, 356–9). For invariance, see Bergstrom (2017). For a more fulsome defense of this version of the theorem, see Medema (2020).

21. This is a roundabout way of saying that incomplete information and asymmetric information are manifestations of transaction costs.

22. And while anecdotes may not "make" a science, they can certainly affect the path of its development, whether unintentionally or via their place in a narrative strategy. On the role of narrative in economics, see the forthcoming special issue of *History of Political Economy* dealing with this subject, edited by Mary Morgan and Tom Stapleford.

References

Allen, Douglas W. 1999. "Transaction Costs." In *Encyclopedia of Law and Economics*, edited by Gerrit De Geest, and Goudewijn Bouckaert, 893–926. Aldershot: Edward Elgar.

Arrow, Kenneth J. 1951. "An Extension of the Basic Theorems of Classical Welfare Economics." In *Proceedings of the Second Berkeley Symposium on Mathematical Statistics and Probability*, 507–32. Berkeley and Los Angeles, CA: University of California Press.

Bator, Francis M. 1958. "The Anatomy of Market Failure." *Quarterly Journal of Economics* 71 (3): 351–79.

Bergstrom, Ted. 2017. "When Was Coase Right?" *Working Paper*, University of California, Santa Barbara.

Bertrand, Elodie. 2018. "George Stigler: The First Apostle of the Coase Theorem." In *Understanding the Enigmatic George Stigler: Extending Price Theory in Economics and Beyond*, edited by Craig Freedman, 445–75. London: Palgrave Macmillan.

Bertrand, Elodie. 2019. "Much Ado About Nothing? The Controversy Over the Validity of the Coase Theorem." *European Journal of the History of Economic Thought* 26 (3): 502–36.

Buchanan, James M. 1962. "The Relevance of Pareto Optimality." *Journal of Conflict Resolution* 6 (4): 341–54.

Coase, Ronald H. 1959. "The Federal Communications Commission." *Journal of Law and Economics* 2 (1): 1–40.

Coase, Ronald H. 1960. "The Problem of Social Cost." *Journal of Law and Economics* 3 (October): 1–44.

Friedman, Milton. 1953. "The Methodology of Positive Economics." In *Essays in Positive Economics*, 3–43. Chicago, IL: University of Chicago Press.

Hammond, Daniel J., and Claire H. Hammond. 2006. *Making Chicago Price Theory: Friedman-Stigler Correspondence 1945-1957*. London: Routledge.

Hands, D. Wade. 2016. "The Individual and the Market: Paul Samuelson on (Homothetic) Santa Claus Economics." *European Journal of the History of Economic Thought* 23 (3): 425–52.

Marciano, Alain. 2018. "Why Is "Stigler's Coase Theorem" Stiglerian? A Methodological Explanation." *Research in the History of Economic Thought and Methodology* 36A: 127–55.

Marshall, Alfred. 1890. *Principles of Economics*. London: Macmillan.

Mas-Colell, Andreu, Michael Dennis Whinston, and Jerry R. Green. 1995. *Microeconomic Theory*. New York, NY: Oxford University Press.

Meade, James E. 1952. "External Economies and Diseconomies in a Competitive Situation." *Economic Journal* 62 (245): 54–67.

Medema, Steven G. 2009. *The Hesitant Hand: Taming Self-Interest in the History of Economic Ideas*. Princeton, NJ: Princeton University Press.

Medema, Steven G. 2011. "A Case of Mistaken Identity: George Stigler, 'The Problem of Social Cost,' and the Coase Theorem." *European Journal of Law and Economics* 31 (1): 11–38.

Medema, Steven G. 2020. "The Coase Theorem at Sixty." *Journal of Economic Literature* 58 (4): 1045–128.

Meek, Ronald L. 1977. *Smith, Marx and After: Ten Essays in the Development of Economic Thought.* London: Chapman and Hall.

Pigou, A.C. 1920. *The Economics of Welfare.* London: Macmillan.

Randall, Alan. 1975. "Property Rights and Social Microeconomics." *Natural Resources Journal* 15 (4): 729–47.

Robson, Alex. 2012. *Law and Markets.* Houndmills, Basingstoke: Palgrave Macmillan.

Samuelson, Paul A. 1954. "The Pure Theory of Public Expenditure." *Review of Economics and Statistics* 36 (4): 387–9.

Samuelson, Paul A. 1955. "Diagrammatic Exposition of a Theory of Public Expenditure." *Review of Economics and Statistics* 37 (4): 350–56.

Samuelson, Paul A. 1963. "Modern Economic Realities and Individualism." *Texas Quarterly* 6 (Summer): 128–39.

Samuelson, Paul A. 1967. "The Monopolistic Competition Revolution." In *The Collected Scientific Papers of Paul A. Samuelson*, vol. 3, edited by Robert C. Merton, 18–51. Cambridge, MA: MIT Press, 1972.

Samuelson, Paul A. 1993. "Altruism as a Problem Involving Group versus Individual Selection in Economics and Biology." *American Economic Review* 83 (2): 143–8.

Samuelson, Paul A. 1995. "Some Uneasiness with the Coase Theorem." *Japan and the World Economy* 7 (1): 1–7.

Samuelson, Paul A., and William D. Nordhaus. 1985. *Economics.* New York, NY: McGraw-Hill.

Seuss, Dr. 1957. *How the Grinch Stole Christmas!* New York, NY: Random House.

Smith, Adam. 1976. *An Inquiry Into the Nature and Causes of the Wealth of Nations.* Oxford: Oxford University Press.

Stigler, George J. 1946. *The Theory of Price.* New York, NY: Macmillan.

Stigler, George J. 1949. "Monopolistic Competition in Retrospect." In *Five Lectures on Economic Problems*, 12–24. London: London School of Economics and Political Science.

Stigler, George J. 1961. "The Economics of Information." *Journal of Political Economy* 69 (3): 213–25.

Stigler, George J. 1966. *The Theory of Price*, 3rd edn. New York, NY: Macmillan.

Stigler, George J. 1972. "The Law and Economics of Public Policy: A Plea to the Scholars." *Journal of Legal Studies* 1 (1): 1–12.

Stigler, George J. 1988. *Memoirs of an Unregulated Economist.* New York, NY: Basic Books.

Stigler, George J. 1989. "Two Notes on the Coase Theorem." *Yale Law Journal* 99 (3): 631–3.

Zelder, Martin. 1998. "The Cost of Accosting Coase: A Reconciliatory Survey of Proofs and Disproofs of the Coase Theorem." In *Coasean Economics Law and Economics and the New Institutional Economics*, edited by Steven G. Medema, 65–94. Boston, MA: Kluwer.

6 Neo-Samuelsonian Methodology, Normative Economics, and the Quantitative Intentional Stance

Don Ross

Introduction

Hands (2013) was the first prominent commentator on economic methodology to explicitly signal notice of a new entrant among the competing philosophies of core economic methods, which he called 'contemporary revealed preference theory' (CRPT). CRPT, on Hands's reconstruction, differs from 'original' Samuelson-Houthakker revealed preference theory (RPT) in three main respects:

i   it applies over finite, measured, choice sets, rather than infinite, necessarily hypothetical ones; technically, it implements Afriat's (1967) Generalised Axiom of Revealed Preference (GARP) instead of Samuelson's Weak Axiom of Revealed Preference (WARP) or Houthakker's Strong Axiom of Revealed Preference (SARP);

ii in interpreting utility functions (and preferences) as summaries of observed instances of an agent's choice behaviour, it denies that utility functions (or preferences) causally explain choices or other aspects of behaviour;

iii in allowing that economic agency arises at scales other than that of whole individual people, it extends the reach of RPT to apply to any entities that are behaviourally sensitive to incentives; thus it extends the domain of microeconomic analysis to include non-human organisms, coordinated coalitions of organisms, and perhaps internal functional modules within nervous systems.

As Hands makes clear in his careful presentation, CRPT is not a 'paradigm shift' *against* earlier interpretations of RPT, but the product of technological evolution from them. Samuelson interpreted RPT compatibly with (ii). Numerous economists following Afriat's innovation applied (i). Followers of Gary Becker, though often only loosely committed to RPT, set precedents for (iii). What distinguishes CRPT, on Hands's story, is its fusion of (i)–(iii) so as to attempt to assemble a relatively full-bodied philosophy of economics.

DOI: 10.4324/9781003266051-9

Hands introduces CRPT by reference to three sources: Bernheim and Rangel (2008), Binmore (2009a, 2009b), and Gul and Pesendorfer (2008). Later he adds reference to Ross (2000, 2005, 2008, 2011) as being 'the most philosophically sophisticated defense of CRPT' (Hands 2013, pp. 1104–1105). In work published subsequent to Hands's paper, particularly Ross (2014), I rounded off corners and added brushwork to this structure, and also motivated a more descriptive name for it: 'neo-Samuelsonian philosophy of economics' (NSPE). This is the version of CRPT that will be in play in what follows. Consequently, except when quoting or closely paraphrasing Hands, I will drop references to 'CRPT', a label that is bound to become increasingly awkward as the years accumulate upgrades and refinements to the view.

NSPE adds, as Hands notes, two main supporting elements to his characterisation of CRPT.

First, and most importantly, it interprets preferences and beliefs – the propositional attitudes (PAs), as Fodor (1978) nicely called them – in accordance with the now-dominant view in the philosophy of mind known as 'externalism' (Burge 1986; Dennett 1987; McClamrock 1995; Bogdan 1997, 2000, 2009, 2010, 2013; Clark 1997). Externalism comes in weak and strong forms. In the weak form due to Putnam (1975) and now endorsed by almost all philosophers, it recognises that truth conditions on beliefs depend on semantic facts of which the bearers of the beliefs in question might not be aware. As expounded in Ross (2005), what is relevant to NSPE is the more general cognitive externalism according to which PAs do not designate theoretically constructed internal representational structures in brains, but descriptions of observed and forecast patterns in intentional behaviour, including verbal behaviour. People understand and predict one another's behaviour by adopting what Dennett (1987) calls *the intentional stance* towards one another: ascribing mutually coherent sets of beliefs and preferences that make sense of behaviour as aiming at goals that are conditional on perceptions about how the world is.

Intentional stance taking is a skill that children are required to learn to participate in human society. This includes learning to take the intentional stance towards their *own* behaviour. This self-referential construction of networks of PAs creates distinctive individual personhood that allows for recruitment into shared projects with others. The view that PAs are constructed in shared ascription rather than discovered as expressions of representations in individual brains is sometimes mistakenly thought to assign PAs the status of mythical objects. However, as Dennett has stressed, being 'virtual' objects of social negotiation is a way of being real, not a way of being fictional. Money is similarly virtual, but its reality is self-evidently robust. Dennett (1991a) proposed a general account, using resources from computational and information theory, for distinguishing 'real patterns', including virtual ones, from descriptions of patterns that are used merely for convenient shorthand. Ross (2000) and Ladyman and Ross (2007) (LR) repaired some technical deficiencies in Dennett's account, and LR's has become the standard theory of real patterns cited for applications and criticism in the philosophy of science.

As Ross (2014) explains, this view of PAs amounts to bringing cognitive science into alignment with Afriat-style RPT, the opposite direction of reconciliation to that favoured by behavioural economists in the broad camp of Thaler (1992) and Camerer et al. (2005). It also makes Hands's feature (iii) of CRPT natural: it follows from externalism that an agent need not have a nervous system to have (real) beliefs and preferences, so institutions can be fully-fledged, and not merely metaphorical, economic agents.

Second, NSPE takes a relaxed attitude to conformity of revealed preferences with axioms of either GARP or expected utility theory (EUT). If RPT is to be applied to actual rather than normatively idealised PAs, it must allow for the fact that the latter are *noisy* patterns (Dennett 1991a). Axioms provide crucial baseline specifications to be adjusted in the face of empirical choice data, but the target form of economic theory is structural and statistical; see Bourgeois-Gironde (2020) for examples of such instrumental use of axioms, and Wilcox (2008, 2021) for deeper challenges to consistent application that call for conceptual refinements. For example, as Wilcox argues, relative risk aversion must be understood as relative probabilistic risk aversion, which is crucially *not* equivalent to deterministic risk aversion with error. The sources of noise in pattern identification and specification, given externalism about PAs, arise partly from stochastic psychological mechanisms, but may equally be generated by fluctuating social dynamics, to which the very meanings of PAs are sensitive. PAs are not, in general, *inferred from* observed behaviour through processes cognitive scientists call 'mindreading' (Nichols and Stich 2003). Zawidzki (2013) reviews evidence against the hypothesis that such inferences are frequently actual or indeed even typically possible in real-time social interactions.[1] Rather, Zawidzki argues, as fundamentally social constructs PAs successfully describe statistical tendencies in behaviour because they are instruments by which behaviour is *regulated* through processes of *mindshaping*. Ross and Stirling (2021) provide a formal characterisation of mindshaping in game-theoretic terms, which Ross et al. (2021) extend to contexts involving risk.

Adjusting the focus from CRPT as Hands frames it to the more comprehensive NSPE implies removal of Gul and Pesendorfer (2008) (GP) from the corpus of representative literature. Their blunt denial that any results from psychology can be relevant to any economic model specification is implausible dogmatism on its surface, and inconsistent with their own methodological examples (e.g., Gul and Pesendorfer 2001), which incorporate the assumption that people have well defined *private* preferences over succumbing to short-term temptations. Since this assumption is a folk theoretical myth according to some externalist cognitive scientists, it is not innocent of psychology as per GP's official methodology. A similar objection applies to recent work of Bernheim (2016), which relies on the assumption that 'true' preference content can in principle be identified with outputs of (deliberative or latent) internal mental processes. In the economics literature, Infante et al. (2016) and Sugden (2018) have emphasised the absence of support from cognitive science for this assumption. Therefore, in what follows, my core reference texts for methodological views consistent with NSPE will be Smith (2008), Binmore (2009a), and Ross (2014). NSPE as promoted in Binmore (2009a) and Ross (2014) explicitly incorporates preferred strategies for econometric estimations of structural utility functions. These strategies are illustrated, and accompanied by methodological reflections, in Andersen et al. (2008), Harrison and Rutström (2008), Harrison and Ng (2016), and Harrison and Ross (2018).

Hands argues that CRPT avoids generic challenges raised against earlier versions of RPT. He considers Hausman's (1992, 2000, 2008, 2012) and Sen's (1973 and elsewhere) linked family of arguments to the effect that preferences cannot explain behaviour independently of beliefs. These arguments begin with analysis of folk-psychological explanation, and then rely on the assumption that economic consumer theory is a formalisation or regimentation of folk psychology. CRPT/NSPE is untroubled by this kind of objection, because it disavows straightforward interpretation of economic theory in terms of folk psychology. Although externalism about PAs does not eliminate preferences or beliefs from scientific ontology, in denying that these denote internal states or processes it breaks with the aspect of folk psychology on which Hausman's arguments rely. Hausman (1995) contends that unless preferences are understood as causes of choice, economists are forced to fall back on instrumentalist philosophy of their science. NSPE directly answers this objection: the core original motivation of Dennett's Real Patterns ontology that NSPE refines and incorporates is to explain how PAs can be actual, virtual, elements of the cognitive-behavioural nexus without being taken to be internal states or processes.

Hands goes on to argue, however, that the strategy by which CRPT escapes allegations of incapacity to explain behaviour succeeds by surrendering its power to normatively favour some choices over others. Both Hausman's and Sen's criticisms anticipated this problem, Hands says. He discusses two senses in which economists often proffer normative guidance: on which items in a set of policy options would make agents better off, and on which patterns of choice allow agents to be deemed practically rational. Though Hands's discussion involves various strands and sub-arguments, it can be boiled down without too much loss of accuracy as follows. Both welfare and rationality assessments as economists typically perform them inherit their plausibility from the folk-psychological assumption that agents should do what they believe is most likely to best satisfy their preferences (given constraints). Thus in breaking with folk-psychological foundations, CRPT/NSPE abandons the source of normative force, in general, in economic analysis. This implies a reductio against CRPT/NSPE because economists are committed to doing policy science.

In what follows I will argue that Hands's critique reveals an important and very broad fact about the normative reach of economics: that ambitions are often attributed to it that it cannot and should not aspire to achieve. Welfare is not equivalent to human well-being, and even if economists can often successfully identify welfare consequences of policies (as, I will argue, they can and do), agents should only follow their advice *to the extent that* welfare is what the agents in question care about. Fortunately for the relevance of economists' interest in policy, a dominant institutional practice in modern societies is for people to be explicitly hired by principals to implement welfare improvements as agents. As for rationality *in general*, I will argue that this is not an idea with which economists should professionally concern themselves at all. I will grant a sense in which philosophers can usefully worry about rationality in general, but the sense in question does not incorporate rational *choice* as axiomatised in the powerful tradition of Bernoulli, von Neumann, Morgenstern, and Savage.

I referred above to ambitions 'attributed to' economics. Disciplines, of course, only 'have ambitions' metaphorically. Econom*ists* have ambitions literally, which vary from economist to economist. Towards the end of the essay, I will suggest – though leaving the work of demonstration to future occasions – that economists' ambitions with respect to normative authority have tended systematically to be inflated by philosophers' and other critics' interpretations, thus creating balloons ripe for popping. It is precisely one of the attractions of NSPE that it can help economists spot and resist such inflationary pressure.

Hands musters an additional criticism of CRPT/NSPE, questioning its claim to generality as a philosophy of economics. In particular, he raises doubt that a methodology for consumer choice theory should reasonably be extended across other areas of economics. In pressing this criticism, I will argue, Hands fails to fully appreciate the force of his own other arguments. These generated the conclusion that microeconomic choice theory has been taken to commit overreach. The overreach in question is not with respect to modelling choice itself, wherever it is found; rather, it is in extension to some *personal* policy domains, which typically implicate considerations from beyond economists' zone of focus. But *all* of microeconomics concerns choice: incentivised choice is indeed its defining subject matter. The basis for generalising NSPE across all of microeconomics emerges most clearly precisely when sweeping normative aspirations are tempered.

The chapter is structured as follows. In the second section, I argue that economists should not interpret their models of choice as aspects of the philosophical project of conceptualising general rationality. The conclusions of this discussion feed into the third section, which addresses the limits and value of welfare analysis given NSPE. The brief fourth section concerns the scope of NSPE in response to Hands's criticism on that front and the fifth section concludes.

Rationality in general

I will defend the following claims:

i   Rationality, as an everyday normative designation, has multiple potential interpretations that are disambiguated for specific application by
contexts.

ii The idea of rationality (irrationality), as *general* potential characteristics
of people, because it implies transcendence of contexts, is not coherent
except within a carefully developed, venerable, and valuable philosophical tradition that resists presentation in other than discursive and narrative form.

iii What economists model as rationality is a specific, very useful, and technical idea that conforms only to occasional applications of the everyday
notion and has no very direct relationship to the general rationality of
the philosophers.

iv Normative philosophical decision theory is a confused enterprise that
systematically confuses (ii) and (iii) above.

Culturally, 'rationality' is as thick and complex a concept as 'beauty' and
'moral goodness'. As with these other thick concepts, its normal use depends
on clarity of contexts. If I can show that you believe that some proposition
is true only because you wish it were true, then I can call you irrational
with respect to that belief.[2] If I can show that you chose some action only to
increase the probability of some outcome that your action in fact makes less
likely, but you persist despite evidently understanding my demonstration, I
can call you irrational with respect to that combination of ends and means.

If, then, I say that you are 'generally' irrational, perhaps I merely mean that
you are unusually statistically likely to be soundly diagnosed as irrational in
a range of actual and projected specific, contextualised, instances. But this
apparently innocuous extension is problematic.

Objections of Sen's type systematically arise. In the first example above, the
critical force of labelling wishful beliefs as irrational is very limited, because
such beliefs often make people happier or more productive. In the second
example, what sets people up for valid labelling as irrational with respect
to practically self-defeating actions are narrowly instrumental and strongly
partitioned motivations for the actions in question. The large proportion of
human actions that do not have such characteristics, and with which actions
that *do* have these characteristics are usually entangled, give examples of this
kind very limited leverage as grounds for attributing general irrationality.

Confident diagnoses of local irrationality thus depend on the availability
of conditions that make some choice patterns or beliefs relatively isolable
from an agent's wider cognitive and behavioural ecology. This is what we
should expect, given that the intentional stance depends on *assuming* general

coherence of belief and preference. Thus local departures can be identified relative to that frame, but only *as* local. If we think of the intentional stance account of PAs as a form of irrealism about them, then, since this strategy is logically similar to the variety of RPT adopted under NSPE, then we invite Hausman's (1995) charge of instrumentalism against CRPT. But this is where the combination of the realist interpretation of the intentional stance (again, see Ladyman and Ross 2007) and externalism about PAs bites: it is an empirical matter which entities can be constructed as agents, and the crucial contingent requirement is that describing them by reference to *generally* coherent PAs leads to successful prediction and explanation of their behaviour.

Attempting to motivate a diagnosis of general irrationality by piling up instances of local irrationality confronts the problem that there is no general counting protocol for 'instances'. Consider the special kinds of potential local irrationalities with which economists concern themselves. The more finely we distinguish choice options, the more inconsistencies we will identify, because agents are limited in their capacities to notice and respond to informational discriminations. Empirical and analytical work is required, with respect to any given case of inconsistency, to determine whether the case is best modelled as an instance of subject error or unexpectedly wide indifference over prospects. And attributing error requires, in the scientific setting, specifying a *kind* of error: perceptual discrimination (Fechner) error implies different out-of-sample behaviour from errors of representational framing or errors of implementation (trembling hands). To the economist, this problem calls not for exercises in interpretative hermeneutics, as apparent error from the qualitative intentional stance demands of the historian or literary critic, but for theoretically guided experimental design that is well integrated with good econometrics. The economist's tools allow her to operate a *quantitative intentional stance* (Alekseev et al. 2018).

Consider an example as applied to a single consumer. Suppose that, after becoming richer, someone becomes less sensitive to price changes in a regularly purchased item such as toilet paper. Is she rationally avoiding spending her more valuable marginal time on attending to toilet paper options, or does she believe, on the basis of no good evidence, that her habitual brand is superior to an equally accessible alternative, so is worth a premium? Or perhaps she's correlation averse with respect to intertemporal risk, so her maintenance of a brand-centred habit is minimisation of the prospect of a negative utility shock when she takes home an untested substitute. Economists know better than to necessarily believe her when she asserts a belief that 'Huggies are the best', if her report is not controlled by manipulation of salient incentives. We might be able to experimentally demonstrate, to a scientific standard of evidence, that she is more rational, with respect to toilet paper, or perhaps household staples in general, than her unincentivised survey responses suggest. The results of such studies, of representative samples of consumers, are worth real money to toilet paper manufacturers and to supermarket managers deciding how to stock their shelves.

Note that although the specific data-generating process we identify matters for these purposes, it does *not* matter to them whether we stigmatise some but not other processes as 'irrational'. One might nevertheless suppose that *some* responses to price changes that we can hypothetically imagine would imply not only local but more serious and general irrationality. Suppose, in the example above, that the subject revealed that she would still choose Huggies if the price were raised to $1,000 per pack. This might license real doubts about her sanity. It is important that our methodological standard for regarding such a preference as revealed is high: behaviour in the lab that implied such a preference, if the actual experimental stakes were much smaller, would lead us to doubt our experimental design or our theoretical specification.

But doesn't this hypothetical concession suggest that contextualised consumption research can tell us something about general rationality after all? It seems that we think we know that no generally rational person is *completely* insensitive to prices. In fact I think that this is true, but it is a truth that is of no significance for policy purposes because the preference we imagine being revealed would never actually be observed. Truths of the kind at issue here matter to theory and modelling. For a more grounded example, economists learned something important about the relationship between risk and utility when they explained why St Petersburg lotteries aren't marketed outside of economics labs. But our relevant question here is: should we interpret the resulting knowledge about theory and modelling as knowledge about general rationality? A sufficiently risk-loving person might buy a St Petersburg lottery, if there were enough such people to induce their supply. There is no evident basis for pronouncing these hypothetical gamblers 'generally irrational'. But that isn't the point of the St Petersburg thought experiment; its point is to show that a good theory of subjective utility should take account of risk.

Perhaps the following proposition could be defended: it would be a mark of general irrationality for a person to make choices with complete obliviousness to risk (e.g., to choose the lottery with the highest outcome among its prospects no matter what). Again we consider a proposition that has no practical policy significance for economists: no set of real agents economists will ever model includes any risk-oblivious ones, for the same reason they will not include any price-oblivious ones: such agents do not actually exist.[3]

There is an obvious objection to the claim that price-oblivious and risk-oblivious agents don't exist. It might simply be pointed out that some real *people* – my mother in her final years as a dementia victim, for example – are oblivious to risk as a special case of being oblivious to almost everything. I have argued elsewhere, however (Ross 2012), that economists working from the quantitative intentional stance cannot usefully model such people as economic agents. A natural, non-technical way of explaining why not, which is the language that many economists would actually use, is to say 'they are not rational'. True to everyday usage though this is, if an economist says it and intends it strictly, then she is accidentally philosophising, and not doing so well.

According to the Dennettian account of agency that is among the foundations of NSPE, agents just are partially self-regulated systems that respond to changes in incentives. The disappearance of this responsiveness towards the end of my mother's life was thus equivalent to her disappearance from the class of agents. Economic analysis is usefully applicable to agents – to *all* agents. It is not applicable to any non-agents. But then *if* something counts as an agent, the range of technical devices available to economists for recovering real patterns in the agent's choice behaviour have no systematic relationship to the practical motivations that govern folk applications of the rationality concept (or the *useful* philosophical idea of general rationality to which I will turn presently). None of widened indifference bands, nor Fechner error, nor trembling hands are typically associated by economists with irrationality[4]; whereas hypothesised computational or framing errors are.[5] This, I am arguing, is an instance of economists harmfully swallowing some out-of-date philosophy: the ontologies in which 'computational processing error' is constructed as a concept are stretched beyond the restricted bases in which they are used by cognitive scientists.[6] Why is a hand that trembles due to poor nervous system calibration outside cortex not regarded as evidence of irrationality, whereas a hand that trembles due to low tonic dopamine levels in midbrain is taken to impugn rationality? There is a (complicated) explanation for these semantics in the history of science, and in its relationships to folk psychology and metaphysics, but this explanation is not a justification for maintaining a scientifically arbitrary distinction.

My mother's dreadful disease changed her gradually, not suddenly. So why not say that she lost her agency gradually, and mark this by saying that she became progressively less rational? Again, that is a natural enough thing to say for casual purposes. But as a target of economic analysis, what happened to my mother was that she steadily discriminated less and less among outcomes to which she had earlier responded as imperfect substitutes. Her indifference bands became progressively wider. But at each point in her decline, she was highly behaviourally responsive to what she *did* still distinguish with respect to substitutability. She remained an agent until the point, which preceded her death by many months, at which she ceased to implement any preferences at all.[7]

My mother *did* gradually lose a lot of capacities other than agency. For most normative purposes relevant to her carers, and to the range of public policies that governed both this care and the legal rights and obligations that still applied to her (e.g., she still owed taxes), the most important thing she lost was capacity to share general assessments of the significance of her life (or of anything) with others. As she become increasingly unable to discriminate between particular people, and to understand speech, and to identify herself with any past experiences, she ceased to have opinions (in the sense of Dennett 1991c) about how to integrate what was best for her with what others regarded as good, for her and for themselves.

I think that philosophers do something useful in trying to articulate how loss of this kind warrants being regarded as loss of a kind of 'general rationality', in a sense that has deeper intellectual roots than careless folk conceptions, and a far older history than scientific economics. In particular, my mother became decreasingly generally rational in the sense that Aristotle intended, which has been extensively critically refined by philosophers working loosely within a project they inherit from him.

This Aristotelian tradition is by its nature discursive and entangled within a broader nexus of humanistic scholarship. It resists brief summary if anything does, but with that warning duly issued I will condense it to tweet length: it studies the deliberate personal and social management of emotions to create preconditions, dependent on good luck, for long-term personal and interpersonal peace. Some (relatively) recent philosophers who have made major contributions to it, whom I mention to help non-specialists gather what I am talking about, are Bernard Williams (1981, 2006), Martha Nussbaum (1997), Valerie Tiberius (2010), and Allan Gibbard (1990). My aim here is to promote just two points about this tradition: that it is semantically appropriate to regard its practitioners as studying general rationality, and that economists who conceive of themselves as students of rationality are interested in something largely unrelated to it.

Philosophers in the Aristotelian tradition are working witness to what many economists will regard as an audacious belief: that it is possible to make discoveries about non-trivial and non-obvious principles and commitments that characterise wise living for people trying to balance social flourishing with freedom of thought, open-ness to experience *and* particular historical-cultural identifications. There are two aspects of this project that make it audacious by reference to economists' standard assumptions about the sovereignty of strictly subjective value judgement.[8] The first audacious idea is that it is possible to promote *general* propositions intended to be *objectively* true about wise social and personal living, notwithstanding full alertness to the heterogeneity of human personalities and proclivities, without implying any kind of moral tyranny. The second audacious idea is that it is possible for some particular people to be trained experts in such promotion, who may reasonably request deference from non-experts.

These propositions are audacious for a combination of two reasons: first, they seem *prima facie* implausible; second, if they are true then well-trained Aristotelian philosophers assume remarkable responsibility. There is no general analytic argument to be made for the audacious propositions. The only possible proof is in demonstration: read the best exemplars, such as the philosophers I mentioned above. It is possible to be a reasonably well-informed sceptic about the propositions: I think that Karl Popper was one (though not his general intellectual friend Hayek). It is no part of my aim to convince such sceptics. I do, however, seek to persuade economists that *casual* scepticism here is rash.

First, it is mulish to insist that what the Aristotelian philosophers study is not really rationality. The entire point of the project is to gain insights into how a thoughtful person should control and temper her impulses and tendencies to lazy thinking. Hands (2013) points out that CRPT/NSPE takes to its logical conclusion economists' identification of 'rationality' (in their special sense) with choice consistency. The Aristotelian philosophers are also interested in consistency, but only *secondarily*, and to the extent that some manifestations of inconsistency undermine principles of wise judgement about general values. Inconsistency with respect to responses to price changes in toilet paper is not among such manifestations. Inconsistency with respect to the value of trying to prevent biodiversity collapse, or of seeking to thwart the ambitions of cruel people, or to looking for reasons to judge people generously, are among such manifestations. I conceded earlier that a hypothetical person who was oblivious to prices or risks would signal general irrationality. But these strange insensitivities would be indicators that they were too cognitively *and* emotionally peculiar to likely be generally rational; they would not in themselves be the *substance* of the general irrationality they suggested. And I don't think that philosophers should be any more *interested* in these outlandish thought experiments than economists should be.

The basic point is that economists have no proper business, unless they mean to develop a sideline in promoting aggressive reductionism about value, in denying any of the following claims: there are generally better and worse general ways of forming and implementing opinions on important social and moral questions; 'generally better and worse' doesn't grant trumping authority to consistency, or normally refer to any *purely* subjective states of individual opinion holders; and 'rationality' in Aristotle's sense is something that people who are emotionally attracted to peacefulness should want to encourage.

Second, economists invite confusion about their very important project, of trying to comparatively quantify opportunity costs of public and private choices, with vigilance about unintended consequences factored into the estimations, if they adopt rhetoric that seems to reduce Aristotelian general rationality to the necessary conditions for identifying and estimating choice functions as utility functions. Few economists intend such reduction, because few economists are aggressively philosophical. However, it is common for them to defend 'rational' economic man as a normative idealisation. Most see that 'man' is a remnant of old blind spots, but fewer see that 'rational' is too. It is the semantic trace of a bruised conviction, which was particularly widespread in general mid-20th century culture, that all important normative problems can in principle be transformed into technical ones (Amadae 2003, 2016). The important concept of economic agency is indeed technical (Ross 2012). But insofar as its attribution to a person is a normative complement, it celebrates a form of cognitive and professional achievement, not general wisdom of character.

There is an admirable tradition in the culture of economics that emphasises the modesty of economists' normative ambitions. Keynes (1936) urged economists to refrain from promoting sweeping normative programmes and to adopt the posture of 'humble, competent people, on a level with dentists'

(p. 373). Keynes is explicit that his intended force of 'humble' is to exclude promotion – *or* blockage – of sweeping programmes for reforming human values. This attitude followed the example of one of Keynes's principal mentors, Marshall, who emphasised that an economist's normative opinions *qua* economist concern 'the ordinary business of life', as contrasted with the deep moral and historicist quandaries assessed by Aristotelian philosophers (Backhouse 2002, pp. 180–181). More recently, Colander and Su (2018) argue for precisely the Keynesian vision of humbleness, stressing that even with respect to considerations of practical efficiency economists should not derive advice for actual people *directly from* theory that applies to economic agents.[9] Economic theory should not be seen as designed to formally characterise whole people (Ross 2005). That is why, when it is applied to the problems of whole people, the understanding it facilitates must be blended with knowledge of history, political psychology, demographics, analytical sociology, and artistic assessment. Keynes said roughly the same thing.

There have been cultural moments in which economists' rhetoric suggesting that technical utility analysis is a superior substitute for philosophical assessment of Aristotelian rationality has been based in earnest on technocratic hubris. However, my sense is that contemporary expressions of the sentiment much more frequently reflect reaction by economists, after having been lectured by their critics and their own heroes to manifest humbleness,[10] against the audacity of philosophers' claims to expertise about general normative wisdom. Again, we can distinguish between a view of philosophers' ambitions as being grandiose, and a view of their claim to special expertise as being presumptuous. Either view, and obviously both held together, can motivate impatience with or indeed hostility to the Aristotelian project with respect to normative rationality.

It would take us far beyond the scope of this essay to engage in meta-philosophical *evaluation* of the extent of grandiosity and presumptuousness among philosophers.[11] My personal opinion, for what it is worth, is that grand questions will be posed regardless of whether they can be thought to have timeless best answers, that we should therefore prefer them to be addressed by careful thinkers who rigorously immerse themselves in deep scholarly traditions, and that skilled practitioners can be objectively identified. My limited aim to this point has been to defend the claim that when economists model people or other natural choosers as economic agents, they are not engaged in a project that competes with, or even has any particularly close relationship with, philosophical reflection on rationality as an over-arching criterion for assessing whole human lives.

As a critical target, this is far from a straw person. A major scholarly industry, philosophical decision theory, has devoted itself to the project of building a general account of practical rationality on the basis of models of utility maximisation. I think that this enterprise rests on confusion, in the sense that its aim is Quixotic: pursuit of an unachievable objective that would not be worth having if we could get it.

I will demonstrate the grounds for this fundamental scepticism about a whole province of analytic philosophy by considering a recent example that meets a high standard of technical accuracy – that, indeed, is sound economic methodology if, contrary to its author's stated purpose, it is read as such. Lara Buchak (2013) frames her work as inquiry into general practical rationality. She asks whether, to earn designation as generally rational, an agent's choices should be captured by a utility function such that the choices optimise their subjective expected utility (SEU) as per Savage (1954). The direct critical target can be regarded as Savage himself, who famously responded to Allais's putative 'paradox' by revising his original preference across the two Allais choice contexts so as to conform to SEU theory and preserve what he charac- terised as his commitment to his own rationality. Buchak argues that Savage's revision, rather than his first response, was his site of error: the rational agent, she argues, will not be generally constrained by Savage's trade-off consist- ency axioms (the sure-thing principle [STP] and the independence axiom), or the reduction-of-compound lotteries axiom (ROCL). Such agents thus shouldn't be judged to be irrational if they violate SEU in these specific ways. However, their choices must, Buchak contends, be representable as optimising some member of the family of rank-dependent utility (RDU) functions (Quiggin 1982, 1993). Buchak develops axioms for what she calls a 'Risk-Weighted Expected Utility' (REU) theory of the rational agent. The economic substance of REU is identical to that of generalised RDU; the difference is simply that RDU is descriptive whereas REU is explicitly nor- mative. SEU is formally nested in RDU, so Buchak's rational agent will conform their choice behaviour to SEU in some contexts but will depart from it in others. Choices among insurance policies, she argues, provide the clearest test cases for these different contexts.

Through her first three chapters, Buchak explicitly stalks the usual target of normative decision theory: the agent who deserves to be congratulated for general rationality thanks to making choices that respect appropriate consist- ency axioms. The standard seems to be an a priori ideal: we begin knowing what rationality conceptually demands, and we stress-test some axioms to see if they capture this conception.

However, to steal a nice joke from Ken Binmore (1998), in Chapter 4 Buchak effectively de-Kants the operation when she narrows her focus to what she says is the basis for the *importance* of practical rationality. This is that we care whether the agent (i) tends to realize consequences that are aligned in expectation with her goals and (ii) manifests choice patterns that allow error to be distinguished from bad luck. This is just what an economist practicing NSPE aims to do when she applies the intentional stance to behaviour that is sensitive to incentives defined by reference to consequences. Every hypothet- ical test case of a choice that she considers in her extended defence of REU can be reinterpreted directly as an instance of standard welfare comparison. Thus the economist who might feel like a visitor to a foreign land in the early chapters can settle in comfortably for the later ones. If REU were supposed to replace SEU as an account of welfare optimisation across the board (rather than of rationality, as Buchak intends), then most economists would want to hold out for a richer range of evidence and argument. But the economist reader need not accept REU to assess Buchak's analyses of cases as welfare assessment. Indeed, Buchak argues in her Chapters 6 and 7 that when we consider decisions in diachronic contexts – precisely the contexts that the neo-Samuelsonian requires in order to characterise stochastic choice patterns as revealed preference – it's best to have *both* SEU and REU in the tool-box for her normative analysis. This is no casual concession: the second half of Buchak's book is devoted to chasing down the answer to what she regards as a live question, whether SEU *ever* does *normative* work that REU by itself does not. Ultimately, she concludes that it does: the REU agent, she shows, will be ambivalent about some insurance offers where the SEU agent should rationally decline them. Insurance issues, Buchak maintains, provide deep test cases for normative assessments, and she is explicit that one should not try to settle them in general by dogmatically imposing REU as a *general* prior. In the end, REU wins as the general account of rationality because even in the cases where SEU delivers more specific insight, REU as a general policy minimises risk from fine errors of risk calculation.

Some existing economic literature echoes Buchak's conclusion as an insight about welfare evaluation rather than rationality. Harrison and Ng (2016) analyse an experimental insurance product market in terms closely aligned with Buchak's intuitions, though using structural estimation of real choice data rather than hypothetical toy problems that require no econometrics. Harrison and Ng also reach the kind of conclusion Buchak expects: optimal individual choices of insurance are sensitive to whether subjects are descriptively better classified as expected utility maximisers or RDU maximisers, but this distinction does *not* distinguish the subjects whose choices imply welfare losses from those whose choices realise available consumer surplus. In another experimental setting, Harrison and Ross (2018) argue against any general programme, such as that constructed by Bleichrodt et al. (2001), for paternalistically over-riding risk attitudes estimated as revealed preferences under RDU in favour of what agents would choose if they conformed to EUT.[12] We nevertheless offered policy advice in the specific real-world problem context we analysed (choices of household investment portfolios from a particular fixed menu, with specified information provision about the options) based on optimisation under EUT. As humble economists, in Keynes's sense, we based this on our empirical findings, along with knowledge we had about our clients' exogenous value context (wanting households' expected retirement resources to be maximised), not on any general theory of rationality. The key point is that Buchak does not advocate appealing, on a priori grounds, to REU (or SEU) in this kind of application either. Economists may therefore doubt that if their tool-box includes RDU, adding REU to it can bring any additional value with respect to their purposes.

But what other purpose is there? There is *only* Buchak's original, stated purpose of deciding who deserves to be called 'rational'. By virtue precisely of the sensible arguments about (hypothetical) cases to which she turns after her third chapter, and her solid understanding of the relevant economics, she reaches what at least some economists consider sound theoretical conclusions – thereby demonstrating that the philosophical framing is redundant. Philosophers who conceive of general rationality in Aristotle's sense are apt to be no more convinced of the project's importance.

The defender of philosophical decision theory might, however, here try to turn the tables by arguing that defenders of NSPE could read Buchak as throwing a life preserver to save us from the other challenge arising in Hands's critique, that of saying what differing descriptive models of choice have to do with welfare. That is, my reconstruction of her overall argument could be read as showing that if the NSPE advocate can somehow salvage the claim that rationalisability under the intentional stance delivers a theory of normative rationality, then analyses like Buchak's show us that we can derive intuitive welfare consequences from the kinds of empirical methods we favour. However, the price of this strategy is too high. Use of the intentional stance is indeed normative, but in itself it holds the bar of rationality very low. Merely applying the intentional stance can't tell us that welfare is what we should focus on for policy analysis. Additional grounds must be sought.

Welfare

Economic policy advice is for humans and human institutions, not non-existent 'inner rational agents' (Infante et al. 2016; Sugden 2018), and also not, according to my argument above, to humans who aspire to be called 'rational' by making their discrete choices consistent. The goal of the policy maker, one might then think, is to try to create conditions in which as many people as possible, given decent luck, can enjoy lives that combine psychological peace with earned pride in judgements well made and mistakes well managed and learned from. Thus it might be supposed from what I have said that the policy maker should seek advice on how to help people be generally rational in Aristotle's sense. And I have just argued that general rationality is not connected in any direct sense with maximising economic utility.[13]

But in fact economists, in offering policy recommendations, do not try to promote general rationality. Economists whose methodology is accurately characterised by NSPE give advice to agents about how to make future choices, and current choices with future consequences, consistent with more efficiently achieving goals consistent with those revealed by the agents' own past patterns of choice. They refer to this as promoting 'welfare'. Hands's critical demand is for arguments, consistent with CRPT/NSPE, as to why economists expect that people should want to receive and follow such advice. More directly, given economists' main practical role, why should people be expected to want their civil servants, political representatives, and corporate managers to follow such advice on their behalf?

It follows from the disassociation I have urged between utility maximisation and general rationality that people should want *personal* advice from economists only when their well-being is significantly put at risk by choices that are inconsistent in the hard-to-monitor or hard-to-forecast ways that economists specialise in identifying. There are familiar such contexts in Marshall's 'ordinary business of life'. Most people's well-being will be seriously compromised if they fear being drastically consumption-constrained in the future relative to the present and will be still more seriously undermined if such fears turn out to be realised. In modern societies, avoiding such outcomes requires accumulating and maintaining at least minimum levels of wealth, and hard-to-identify inconsistent investments of existing wealth strongly tend to impede such accumulation and maintenance. Wise people look for such expert financial advice as they can find and afford, and such advice is economic advice regardless of whether those who provide it are economists strictly speaking. The best such advice, in general, is what would be given to a modelled economic agent who shared the advisee's future consumption aspirations and dynamic budget constraints.

This is the severely limited domain of economics as Aristotle understood it (Meikle 1995). In modern times economists have mainly delegated it to financial services professionals, though it is implied second-order advice when economists advise retail investment providers, as in Harrison and Ross (2018). An economist who ventures beyond it in the realm of personal advice – for example, telling a person that she should align her revealed preferences over health risk with her revealed preferences over education choice risk, even where she can't buy insurance policies that make these mutually fungible – should not be surprised to be asked by the advisee why this should matter to her. In the actual world, economists normally do not give unsolicited advice about personal choice patterns that cannot be financially mediated and thus transformed into advice about alternative investments. Perhaps this is just because economists don't try to supply non-existent demand, but perhaps the non-existence of 'personal economists' also reflects recognition that welfare is not the same thing as personal well-being, and economists are experts on the former. This point responds directly to an example used by Hands (2013, p. 1100) when he complains that economics based on CRPT doesn't help him improve his stock-picking.

Where economic advice and welfare maximisation meet, a domain Aristotle didn't imagine, is in policy for people whose choices constrain the options of other, generally anonymous, people. In standard cases, free of corruption, they don't give advice that would maximise the personal utility of the advisees, who are treated as agents, but advice that addresses the utility of the third parties with legitimate stakes in the outcomes of the choices, whom they thus effectively treat as principals. Since these principals usually have heterogeneous, and very often conflicting, utility functions over the potential outcomes, economists shape their advice by looking for aggregate-scale efficiencies in welfare. These are often very difficult to uncontroversially identify, but economists are the most reliable experts in identifying them, and agree about them relatively often. For a familiar example, they regularly remind governments that raising special cost barriers against imported products, if they are safe and not socially or environmentally harmful in themselves, is almost always welfare inefficient. This analysis is not always decisive; the argument against trade barriers is defeasible if institutional arrangements allow a special subset of the principals to hog almost all the welfare gains for themselves and another subset suffers losses.

This is of course the standard picture of applied economics. As raised at the outset, the critical question about it posed by Hands, following Hausman, is: what is the normative justification for advocating policies that target welfare improvement if, as per CRPT/NSPE, welfare is disassociated from subjective satisfaction in the folk-psychological sense – and, as I have now argued, also from well-being on its best considered philosophical interpretation? The economist's instinctive first answer might be: we have an efficiency measure for welfare but not for folk-psychological satisfaction or Aristotelian well-being. The standard retort to this occurs repeatedly in the critical literature about standard economic practice: that it is analogous to searching for dropped keys under the streetlight. A procedure, that is, is defended on the grounds that we know how to use it, rather than on the basis of an argument for its actual normative importance.

I think, however, that the economist's instinctive response is correct. NSPE, I contend, helps us see its justificatory logic better than older accounts of economic agency according to which economics idealises practical folk psychology or utilitarian theories of well-being.

A first gain in clarity from NSPE here is that it naturally separates criticisms based on concern for folk-psychological satisfaction from criticisms based on normative prioritisation of well-being. The externalist/Dennettian account of intentionality denies that the traditional, internalist model of psychological satisfaction captures anything that satisfies the criteria for acknowledgement as a real pattern. The closest real phenomena to the objects of the internalist account are relatively stable patterns of response that people give when they are asked to choose actions that reflect comparative evaluations of possible prospects. That is to say: they are the patterns we identify when we probe for revealed preferences using our most reliable methods, particularly incentivised experimentation.

That this reconceptualisation is not mere semantic footwork is shown if we ask whether these revealed preferences are 'subjective'. On the internalist account, the immediate affirmative answer derives from the assumption that they are privately experienced and reported on the basis of introspection or phenomenology, a person's reading of her own mind. The externalist, by contrast, grants them subjectivity only in the sense they reflect an individual's idiosyncratic social history, on which the individual in question has the greatest *pre-scientific* expertise because she has the densest record of observations. This expertise is limited in scope. Experiments might show, for example, that the person's choices over risky monetary prospects are best characterised by a concave utility function combined with an inverse-S shaped rank-dependent probability weighting function with particular parameter values in the flexible Prelec (1998) specification, and this is highly unlikely to be something the subject antecedently believed about herself on the basis of everyday observation (Harrison and Ross 2018). Furthermore, the revealed preferences are not primitive, fixed properties of the individual in the sense of being either innate or wholly self-constructed: they are products of social mindshaping, and they are labile.

The social origins of externally attributed preferences – along with the beliefs and other PAs that, as Hausman (2012) rightly stresses, are essential for predicting behaviour – partly explains their central importance in policy selection. People engage continuously and pervasively in mindshaping because most of their social behaviour involves cooperation and normatively or literally regulated competition. Mindshaping creates shared reference points that furnish enough structure for people to select strategies, divide labour in sensible ways, and stabilise descriptive and normative expectations (Ross 2005; Bicchieri 2006, 2017; Ross et al. 2021). Thus their revealed preferences literally *constitute* the normative elements around which social policies are conceptualised and bargained over (implicitly or institutionally; see Binmore 1994, 1998, 2005). Since, according to NSPE, welfare is nothing over and above the measurement system for comparatively assessing payoffs of social interactions, it comes close to being a tautology that welfare is the target of public policy (not just economic policy), and particularly of policies that are institutionally situated as 'official'.

Close to a tautology, but not quite.[14] In the previous section, I argued that general rationality applies, or fails to apply, to whole-life narratives, and that these are conceptually distinct from the kinds of preferences over which policies are coordinated. One crucial dimension of difference is that, as all of the leading philosophers in the Aristotelian tradition stress, general rationality revolves around integrating what Gibbard (1990) calls 'wise choices' with 'apt feelings'. The latter are richly particular and sensitive to distinctive personal history profiles, which is why general rationality is usually assessed through criticism of narratives. Administrative systems typically abstract away from aptness of feelings, precisely because these are so thick and particular. For one thing, this causes them to resist aggregation and quantitative representation and measurement. For another thing, public institutions often incorporate explicit mandates to handle similar claims to public resources similarly, which requires the construction of relatively wide equivalence classes of outcomes. If I favour a policy as a sad necessity while you favour the same policy as a splendid and progressive triumph, from the perspective of welfare analysis we both count as winners if the policy is adopted. But our intimates and our biographers will register our attitudes very differently when incorporating our respective emotions about the policy into their assessments of our general rationality.

On the modernist conception of the state that has dominated wealthy societies for about two centuries – the conception for which Hegel struggled to forge a descriptively adequate language (Herrmann-Pillath and Boldyrev 2014), and which was first fully articulated in empiricist-friendly terms by Max Weber (1922) – professional civil servants regard themselves as agents who are tasked by a public mandate to design and implement policies and regulations on behalf of an aggregated set of principals (roughly, citizens) by reference to the principals' welfare (Besley 2006; Dowding and Taylor 2019). Economists choose and analyse problems as if they are technical advisors to these agents. As Sugden (2018) rightly complains, they often generate such advice without any explicit commission, and with no attention to the limited power of *actual* such agents. That is, as Sugden puts it, they direct advice to hypothetical benevolent dictators. However, often enough economists receive genuine commissions to assess or design policies and combine broad practical awareness of solution constraints with Keynes's recommended normative humbleness (Ross and Townshend 2021).

My brief here is to defend the normative importance of welfare as understood in NSPE, not to argue that all is well in the world. *Exclusive* focus on welfare in public policy is open to criticism for ignoring dimensions of value that resist quantitative measurement (Alexandrova 2017). Another, particularly serious and consequential, problem is that economists are often not very loud about reminding governing elites that to be satisfied with mere Kaldor-Hicks efficiency, regardless of whether gains from policies are in fact used to compensate losers (Blinder 2018; Boix 2019), can generate the opposite of welfare improvement. Arguably, this recurrent failing has been an important contributing cause of the widely perceived crisis of trust in government and expertise, and associated surges of populism that threaten the legitimacy of elections, the rule of law, and public willingness to receive and respect technically informed advice (Nichols 2017; Tanzi 2017).

It is far from clear that, even in the absence of crisis-level strains in welfare-focused governance, most members of democratic societies genuinely assent to the role of principals who hire officials as agents to promote welfare. Expressive voting in electorates can be construed as reflecting an idea that political leaders should promote general well-being by exemplifying ideals of character, and citizens under the sway of this idea may display near-indifference to policy choices framed by reference to welfare (Caplan 2007; Achen and Bartels 2016). Demand for politics of this kind is energetically amplified by supply from political entrepreneurs.

The result tends to be disastrous for general well-being as philosophers understand it. In pluralistic societies, a politician whose central campaign theme is 'I am a representative of your generally rational ideal' can only give concrete policy content to this fantastic pretence by favouring some interest groups over others, with no obligation to address welfare efficiencies at all.

Worse, if a sub-population's interests are promoted on grounds that they are more generally rational than those of rival coalitions, then the tight entanglement of general rationality with deep moral commitments leads quickly to the moralisation of all disagreements, to elections that are existential crises for all sides, and to willingness to abandon constitutional rules and scruples because winning at all costs seems justified by higher morality. The situation just described is hardly hypothetical in current circumstances in many countries, especially larger ones, and its baleful effects on *both* general well-being and welfare can hardly be overstated. The situation is especially dire when extremely urgent and difficult threats, such as climate change, require widespread pragmatic bargaining over trade-offs on multiple intersecting margins. That task demands policies that target carefully estimated welfare effects.

Some critics of standard economic policy assessment, for example Sen (1999) and Nussbaum (2000), argue that economic development policy should directly target general well-being rather than welfare. Answering these criticisms of 'welfarism' extends beyond the response to Hands's and Hausman's concern, which requires only defending the claim that welfare as conceptualised according to NSPE is normatively significant. Neither Sen nor Nussbaum assert that welfare is normatively irrelevant. However, a few words should be said about their views in light of my use of the contrast between welfare and well-being in explaining why most applied economists focus on welfare.

Sen and Nussbaum seem to offer (slightly different) ways around the worry that political emphasis on general rationality leads to demagoguery. That is, they identify what they claim are measurable proxies for general well-being and argue that public policy should target these proxies. Claims I have defended here indicate lines of defence for the welfarist. Nussbaum agrees with my claim that the articulation of both general well-being and general rationality is essentially discursive and thus doesn't lead towards a measurable common currency for the many dimensions of general well-being. Consequently, her approach is open to Dasgupta's (2009) criticism that it offers no guidance about trade-offs given scarce resources. (The scarcest resource in question is likely to be political rather than material capital.) Similar comments apply to Sen's approach, along with the additional problem that he defends so many proxies for good development policy that almost any official agent will always be able to claim success along some measure his account promotes. Given that accountability is arguably the single greatest real barrier to sustained development promotion, I think this is a decisive objection. Sen also does not rigorously address the question of how his proxy measures dynamically cross-predict one another empirically. If, as seems probable, household consumption expenditure predicts the others better than they predict themselves (Ravallion 1992), then we could preserve accountability by demanding that development policies improve that. And household consumption expenditure seems closer to what economists aim to capture in welfare theory than to what philosophers aim to characterise when inquiring into general well-being.

The reach of NSPE

Hands (2013, p. 1103) concludes his criticism of CRPT/NSPE by suggesting that empirical evidence for its success is restricted to a particular corner of economics, applied demand analysis, but that as yet we have no grounds to believe 'that it would be possible, and better, to do all of choice-theoretic economics – in macroeconomics, finance, industrial organization, law and economics, cost-benefit analysis, and all of the other things that modern economists do – by merely projecting patterns gleaned from GARP-consistent choice data onto new sets of parameters'. Thus Hands doubts that CRPT can yet be sold as the basis for a general philosophy of economics, as NSPE promises. He is clear, however, that the main basis for regarding the general extension of CRPT as far-fetched is his reading of it as a form of instrumentalism about choice. He diagnoses 'a notorious problem with instrumentalism – it doesn't travel well from domain to domain and must prove its robustness in each new application'.

This complaint exposes the point that the crucial foundation of NSPE is its identification of a version of RPT consistent with stochastic choice with the realistic interpretation of the intentional stance wobbily defended by Dennett (1991a) and formulated more categorically by Ross (2000) and Ladyman and Ross (2007). The intentional stance is a theory of choice as responsiveness to incentives, because it is to begin with a theory of what it is to be an agent, according to which the extensions of 'agent' and 'incentive-influenced entity' are identical. NSPE's central claim is that CRPT is simply the theory of the quantitative application of the intentional stance. Because the intentional stance is a kind of realism (dubbed 'rainforest realism' by Ladyman and Ross), not instrumentalism, Hands's general philosophical basis for doubting its reach is rejected.

Of course, it must be conceded that NSPE will need to prove itself in empirical applications. That applies to every philosophical theory of anything. A survey of applications from across the empire of economics would necessarily be a monograph-length enterprise. Here, I will indicate just a couple of signposts, aligned with Hands's list of candidates above. Ross (2014) cites Frydman and Goldberg (2007, 2011) as a programme for macroeconomics that is naturally interpreted as applied NSPE (though it needs to be dissociated from spurious connection by its authors to prospect theory, when the established high frequency of rank-dependent preferences suffices as an assumption for their modelling). As for industrial organisation, for decades theory in that area has been almost exclusively developed using non-cooperative game theory, thus depending on assignment of utility functions to individual agents that are typically firms. NSPE, in dissociating preferences from internal psychological states, licenses first-order ascription of real utility functions to firms, as opposed to taking them to be second-order approximations based on constructed representative agents.

All of microeconomics concerns choices of agents. NSPE, in incorporating a theory of choice and agency, thus applies to microeconomics without restriction. The same goes for macroeconomics *if* it is thought to depend on microfoundations.[15]

Conclusion

Hands is correct that CRPT is primarily motivated by interest in connecting utility theory with described empirical behaviour. NSPE, the philosophical generalisation of this methodology, is still more explicit in aiming to ground a *realist* interpretation of descriptive economic models. This furnishes its defender with straightforward resources for responding to those elements of Hands's criticism that depend on reading CRPT as instrumentalism. However, Hands puts useful pressure on an incomplete aspect of NSPE: the scope it provides for justifying normative economics. To the extent that theories of rationality and welfare rest on folk-psychological conceptions of human reasoning and well-being, NSPE's abandonment of folk psychology presents a challenge.

I have argued that the challenge should be met by conceding that economists are not in the business of assessing general rationality. Casual references to rationality that litter meta-textual commentary across the discipline obscure this. More directly, the wholescale borrowing of theoretical structures from the foundations of microeconomics in the project of philosophical decision theory encourages the idea that there should be a rigorous bridge between economists' interest in technical choice consistency and philosophers' interest in general rationality. NSPE implies that this approach to bridge-building is misguided. Dynamic rationality in a whole person is essentially a distinct normative issue from descriptive consistency across discrete choices by economic agents. This would be a serious problem if economists, like decision theorists, were in the business of giving general advice to individual people. But they are not. Economics is a policy science, but the policy domains to which it aims to be relevant are public and corporate. Once this is recognised, NSPE actually provides clearer insight than alternative philosophies of economics as to why economists concentrate on welfare, rather than well-being, as their primary normative target. As welfare is not the only valuable dimension of social life, let alone personal life, economists offering contributions to social guidance should read their Keynes and be humble about their role.

Notes

1. Chater (2018) argues that *all* outputs of mindreading efforts are errors, because the view that there is anything to be read is false: all that is internal, he argues, are brain states, and these have no stable interpretations in terms of propositional content.

This is consistent with Dennett's (1991b) account of consciousness, though not, I would argue, with Dennett's account of PAs. Chater, in my view, exaggerates the empirical instability of PAs because he focuses on psychological experiments that isolate subjects from social scaffolds, the primary force for their stabilisation.

2. I assume an externalist understanding of the belief, so this attribution does not commit me to the hypothesis that your brain performed some unsound computation. My judgment is that patterns in your behaviour, including what you say, are summarised by saying that you have this (false) belief.

3. Obliviousness to risk does not, of course, mean risk neutrality, a property I expect to be observed by the financial agents I hire.

4. It should be noted that rhetoric here is unstable. For example, Pennesi (2021) refers to a parameter for limiting Fechner error as a 'rationality measure'.

5. This applies to the champions of ubiquitous framing effects in real people, nudgers.

6. Kahneman and Tversky took a fateful step when they moved from the purely psychological context of original prospect theory (Kahneman and Tversky 1979) to the economic theory of cumulative prospect theory (CPT) (Tversky and Kahneman 1992) which was intended to allow for advice about improving rational decisions.

7. I do not mean to suggest that my mother was typical of Alzheimer's patients in this respect. The majority die before their agency vanishes.

8. These assumptions do not divide economists from philosophers *in general*. Hume was among the forgers of economists' working professional value system, and there are today at least as many Humean philosophers as broadly Aristotelian ones.

9. Duflo (2017) superficially seems to echo Keynes when she sketches a role for development economists as 'plumbers'. By this, she refers to the value of attention to local-scale features that accommodate or resist *installation* of policy ideas, as opposed to just intended inputs and desired outputs. However, Duflo emphatically fails to follow Keynes in urging humbleness upon economists. She thinks that while some economists engage in plumbing, *other* economists ('engineers') should be entrusted with formal mechanism design and still others ('scientists') should develop and test relevant generalisations. This amounts to assigning economists *all* of the primary roles in shaping and promoting public policy!

10. I am not claiming that economists who give policy advice generally *are* humble. Many are, but many others are obviously not. My claim is rather that a norm of humbleness now prevails, such that un-humble economists are expected to at least pay lip service to that attitude. Such signalling was a trope in the rhetoric even of Samuelson, during the era of maximal technocratic confidence (Backhouse 2017).

11. Setting out to evaluate such presumed presumptuousness would perhaps be more presumptuous than the work to be evaluated! On the other hand, see Eklund (2017).

12. I refer here to EUT rather than SEU to emphasise that we have descended from Buchak's philosophical heights to the ground of descriptive economic identification, paralleling reference to RDU instead of REU. A further complication here is that Bleichrodt et al. say they compare analysis of observed choices conditional on EUT with analysis of the same choices conditional on CPT. But as they consider data in which subjects encounter no loss frames, they cannot empirically pin down CPT's special λ parameter for loss aversion and should be properly interpreted as talking about an RDU model.

13. As conceded above, general rationality plausibly excludes economic *insanity* – being oblivious to relative prices and relative risks – but economists don't give advice against this because it is never an actual problem.

14. There would not be a basis for objection here if it were entirely a tautology. Theories that specify identification restrictions are not empirical hypotheses.

15. In fact, I am sceptical of that widely held view, for reasons given in Hoover (2009) and Ross (2014). Macroeconomists aim to identify real patterns, but these might abstract away from reference to agents' choices. I thus think that details of relationships between macroeconomic theory and NSPE remain unresolved. This is hardly surprising, given the current absence of consensus on the foundations of macroeconomic theory in general.

References

Achen, C., & Bartels, L. (2016). *Democracy for Realists*. Princeton University Press.

Afriat, S. (1967). The construction of utility functions from expenditure data. *International Economic Review* 8: 67–77.

Alexandrova, A. (2017). *A Philosophy for the Science of Well Being*. Oxford University Press.

Alekseev, A., Harrison, G., Lau, M., & Ross, D. (2018). Deciphering the noise: The welfare costs of noisy behavior. Center for the Economic Analysis of Risk Working Paper 2018-01. https://cear.gsu.edu/wp-2018-01-deciphering-the-noise-the-welfare-costs-of-noisy-behavior/.

Amadae, S. (2003). *Rationalizing Capitalist Democracy*. University of Chicago Press.

Amadae, S. (2016). *Prisoners of Reason*. Cambridge University Press.

Andersen, S., Harrison, G., Lau, M., & Rutström, E. (2008). Eliciting risk and time preferences. *Econometrica* 76: 583–618.

Backhouse, R. (2002). *The Ordinary Business of Life*. Princeton University Press.

Backhouse, R. (2017). *Founder of Modern Economics: Paul A. Samuelson* (Volume 1). Oxford University Press.

Bernheim, B.D. (2016). The good, the bad, and the ugly: A unified approach to behavioral welfare economics. *Journal of Benefit Cost Analysis* 7: 12–68.

Bernheim, B.D., & Rangel, A. (2008). Choice-theoretic foundations for behavioral welfare economics. In A. Caplin & A. Schotter, eds., *The Foundations of Positive and Normative Economics: A Handbook*, pp. 155–192. Oxford University Press.

Besley, T. (2006). *Principled Agents: The Political Economy of Good Government*. Oxford University Press.

Bicchieri, C. (2006). *The Grammar of Society*. Cambridge University Press.

Bicchieri, C. (2017). *Norms in the Wild*. Oxford University Press.

Binmore, K. (1994). *Game Theory and the Social Contract, Volume 1: Playing Fair*. MIT Press.

Binmore, K. (1998). *Game Theory and the Social Contract, Volume 2: Just Playing*. MIT Press.

Binmore, K. (2005). *Natural Justice*. Oxford University Press.

Binmore, K. (2009a). *Rational Decisions*. Princeton University Press.

Binmore, K. (2009b). Interpersonal comparisons of utility. In H. Kincaid & D. Ross, eds., *The Oxford Handbook of Philosophy of Economics*, pp. 540–559. Oxford University Press.

Bleichrodt, H., Pinto, J., & Wakker, P. (2001). Using descriptive findings of prospect theory to improve the prescriptive use of expected utility. *Management Science* 47: 1498–1514.

Blinder, A. (2018). *Advice and Dissent*. Basic Books.

Bogdan, R. (1997). *Interpreting Minds*. MIT Press.

Bogdan, R. (2000). *Minding Minds*. MIT Press.

Bogdan, R. (2009). *Predicative Minds*. MIT Press.

Bogdan, R. (2010). *Our Own Minds*. MIT Press.

Bogdan, R. (2013). *Mindvaults*. MIT Press.

Boix, C. (2019). *Democratic Capitalism at the Crossroads*. Princeton University Press.

Bourgeois-Gironde, S. (2020). *The Mind under the Axioms*. Academic Press.

Buchak, L. (2013). *Risk and Rationality*. Oxford University Press.

Burge, T. (1986). Individualism and psychology. *Philosophical Review* 95: 3–45.

Camerer, C., Loewenstein, G., & Prelec, D. (2005). Neuroeconomics: How neuroscience can inform economics. *Journal of Economic Literature* 43: 9–64.

Caplan, B. (2007). *The Myth of the Rational Voter*. Princeton University Press.

Chater, N. (2018). *The Mind is Flat*. Allen Lane.

Clark, A. (1997). *Being There*. MIT Press.

Colander, D., & Su, H.-C. (2018). *How Economics Should Be Done*. Edward Elgar.

Dasgupta, P. (2009). Facts and values in modern economics. In H. Kincaid & D. Ross, eds., *The Oxford Handbook of Philosophy of Economics*, pp. 580–640. Oxford University Press.

Dennett, D. (1987). *The Intentional Stance*. MIT Press.

Dennett, D. (1991a). Real patterns. *Journal of Philosophy* 88: 27–51.

Dennett, D. (1991b). *Consciousness Explained*. Little, Brown.

Dennett, D. (1991c). Two contrasts: Folk craft versus folk science, and belief versus opinion. In J. Greenwood, ed., *The Future of Folk Psychology*, pp. 135–175. Cambridge University Press.

Dowding, K., & Taylor, B. (2019). *Economic Perspectives on Government*. Palgrave Macmillan.

Duflo, E. (2017). The economist as plumber. *American Economic Review* 107: 1–26.

Eklund, M. (2017). *Choosing Normative Concepts*. Oxford University Press.

Fodor, J. (1978). Propositional attitudes. *The Monist* 61: 501–524.

Frydman, R., & Goldberg, M. (2007). *Imperfect Knowledge Economics: Exchange Rates and Risk*. Princeton University Press.

Frydman, R., & Goldberg, M. (2011). *Beyond Mechanical Markets*. Princeton University Press.

Gibbard, A. (1990). *Wise Choices, Apt Feelings*. Harvard University Press.

Gul, F., & Pesendorfer, W (2001). Temptation and self-control. *Econometrica* 69: 1403–1435.

Gul, F., & Pesendorfer, W. (2008). The case for mindless economics. In A. Caplin & A. Schotter, eds., *The Foundations of Positive and Normative Economics: A Handbook*, pp. 3–39. Oxford University Press.

Hands, W. (2013). Foundations of contemporary revealed preference theory. *Erkenntnis* 78: 1081–1108.

Harrison, G., & Ng, J.-M. (2016). Evaluating the expected welfare gain from insurance. *Journal of Risk and Insurance* 83: 91–120.

Harrison, G., & Ross, D. (2018). Varieties of paternalism and the heterogeneity of utility structures. *Journal of Economic Methodology* 25: 42–67.

Harrison, G., & Rutström, E. (2008). Risk aversion in the laboratory. In J. Cox & G. Harrison, eds., *Risk Aversion in Experiments*, pp. 41–196. Emerald.

Hausman, D. (1992). *The Inexact and Separate Science of Economics*. Cambridge University Press.

Hausman, D. (1995). Rational choice and social theory: A comment. *Journal of Philosophy* 92: 96–102.

Hausman, D. (2000). Revealed preference, belief, and game theory. *Economics and Philosophy* 16: 99–115.

Hausman, D. (2008). Mindless or mindful economics: A methodological evaluation. In A. Caplin & A. Schotter, eds., *The Foundations of Positive and Normative Economics: A Handbook*, pp. 125–151. Oxford University Press.

Hausman, D. (2012). *Preferences, Value, Choice, and Welfare*. Cambridge University Press.

Herrmann-Pillath, C., & Boldyrev, I. (2014). *Hegel, Institutions, and Economics*. Routledge.

Hoover, K. (2009). Microfoundations and the ontology of macroeconomics. In H. Kincaid & D. Ross, eds., *The Oxford Handbook of Philosophy of Economics*, pp. 386–409. Oxford University Press.

Infante, G., Lecouteux, G., & Sugden, R. (2016). Preference purification and the inner rational agent: A critique of the conventional wisdom of behavioural welfare economics. *Journal of Economic Methodology* 23: 1–25.

Kahneman, D., & Tversky, A. (1979). Prospect theory: An analysis of decision under risk. *Econometrica* 47: 263–292.

Keynes, J.M. (1936). Economic possibilities for our grand-children. Re-printed in Keynes, *Essays in Persuasion*, pp. 358–373. Norton (1963).

Ladyman, J., & Ross, D. (2007). *Every Thing Must Go: Metaphysics Naturalised*. Oxford University Press.

McClamrock, R. (1995). *Existential Cognition*. University of Chicago Press.

Meikle, S. (1995). *Aristotle's Economic Thought*. Oxford University Press.

Nichols, S., & Stich, S. (2003). *Mindreading*. Oxford University Press.

Nichols, T. (2017). *The Death of Expertise*. Oxford University Press.

Nussbaum, M. (1997). *Cultivating Humanity*. Cambridge University Press.

Nussbaum, M. (2000). The costs of tragedy: Some moral limits of cost-benefit analysis. *Journal of Legal Studies* 29: 1005–1036.

Pennesi, D. (2021). Intertemporal discrete choice. *Journal of Economic Behavior and Organization* 186: 690–706.

Prelec, D. (1998). The probability weighting function. *Econometrica* 66: 95–113.

Putnam, H. (1975). *Mind, Language, and Reality*. Cambridge University Press.

Quiggin, J. (1982). A theory of anticipated utility. *Journal of Economic Behavior and Organization* 3: 323–343.

Quiggin, J. (1993). *Generalized Expected Utility Theory. The Rank-Dependent Model*. Kluwer.

Ravallion, M. (1992). Poverty comparisons: A guide to concepts and methods. World Bank Living Standards Measurement Study Working Paper 88.

Ross, D. (2000). Rainforest realism: A Dennettian theory of existence. In D. Ross, A. Brook, & D. Thompson, eds., *Dennett's Philosophy: A Comprehensive Assessment*, pp. 147–168. MIT Press.

Ross, D. (2005). *Economic Theory and Cognitive Science: Microexplanation*. MIT Press.

Ross, D. (2008). Ontic structural realism and economics. *Philosophy of Science* 75: 732–743.

Ross, D. (2011). Estranged parents and a schizophrenic child: Choice in economics, psychology, and neuroscience. *Journal of Economic Methodology* 18: 217–231.

Ross, D. (2012). The economic agent: Not human, but important. In U. Mäki, ed., *Handbook of the Philosophy of Science, Volume 13: Economics*, pp. 691–735. Elsevier.

Ross, D. (2014). *Philosophy of Economics*. Palgrave Macmillan.

Ross, D., & Stirling, W. (2021). Economics, social neuroscience, and mindshaping. In J. Herbecke & C. Herrmann-Pillath, eds., *Social Neuroeconomics*, pp. 174–201. Routledge.

Ross, D., Stirling, W., & Tummolini, L. (2021). Strategic theory of norms for empirical applications in political science and political economy. In H. Kincaid & J. Van Bouwel, eds., *The Oxford Handbook of Philosophy of Empirical Political Science*. Oxford University Press.

Ross, D., & Townshend, M. (2021). Everyday economics. In H. Kincaid & D. Ross, eds., *Modern Guide to Philosophy of Economics, pp. 344-370*. Edward Elgar.

Savage, L. (1954). *The Foundations of Statistics*. Wiley.

Sen, A. (1973). Behaviour and the concept of preference. *Economica* 40: 241–259.

Sen, A. (1999). *Development as Freedom*. Oxford University Press.

Smith, V. (2008). *Rationality in Economics*. Cambridge: Cambridge University Press.

Sugden, R. (2018). *The Community of Advantage*. Oxford University Press.

Tanzi, V. (2017). *Termites of the State*. Cambridge University Press.

Thaler, R. (1992). *The Winner's Curse*. Free Press.

Tiberius, V. (2010). *The Reflective Life*. Oxford University Press.

Tversky, A., & Kahneman, D. (1992). Advances in prospect theory: Cumulative representation of uncertainty. *Journal of Risk and Uncertainty* 5: 297–323.

Weber, M. (1922). *Wirtschaft und Gesellschaft*. Mohr Siebeck.

Wilcox, N. (2008). Stochastic models for binary discrete choice under risk: A critical primer and econometric comparison. In J. Cox & G. Harrison, eds., *Risk Aversion in Experiments*, pp. 197–292. Emerald.

Wilcox, N. (2021). Utility measurement: Some contemporary concerns. In H. Kincaid & D. Ross, eds., *Modern Guide to Philosophy of Economics*, pp. 14–27. Edward Elgar.

Williams, B. (1981). *Moral Luck*. Cambridge University Press.

Williams, B. (2006). *Philosophy as a Humanistic Discipline*. Princeton University Press.

Zawidzki, T. (2013). *Mindshaping*. MIT Press.

Part III

Pragmatism

7 Models, Truth, and Analytic Inference in Economics

Kevin D. Hoover

Piecemeal Empirical Models

The period since the Second World War can be well described as the age of models in science – not only in the natural sciences, but also in economics and, perhaps to a lesser degree, in other social sciences. While philosophers of science and philosophers of economics are alert to the importance of models, they have little noticed how much quantitative empirical research dominates economics. Influential philosophical discussions of economic models have focused on making sense of how theoretical models that are "caricatures" or "unrealistic" can nonetheless be informative about the real world (Gibbard and Varian 1978, pp. 665–666, Sugden 2000, p. 3). They explicitly eschew consideration of quantitative empirical models or address them only at the level of "casual empiricism" (Gibbard and Varian 1978, p. 665, Sugden 2000, p. 6).[1]

In the wider philosophy of science, there is a vision of how models should relate to the world that Paul Teller (2001) refers to as the Perfect Model Model. The perfect model would tell us everything about everything. An example of perfect-model thinking is Pierre Laplace's famous claim that given a complete set of initial conditions and the laws of physics, one could, in principle, write the history of the world in detail in advance. A similar vision is implicit in the economics of his compatriot, Leon Walras (1874[1954]), whose general equilibrium model aims at a comprehensive account of the interdependence among all economic agents. Walras's theory is, even more than Laplace's, a schema, but the idea in both cases is to fill in the missing pieces completely, and the measure of success is how far current models deviate from the ideal perfect model.

An alternative vision – and the one that I shall argue for – measures our scientific achievement not against the inaccessible perfect model at the end of the scientific journey, but against the history of that journey. Success is counted in additions to the stock of facts and explanations. Herbert Simon and Nicholas Rescher (1966) present an alternative to the Laplace/Walras vision of a comprehensive perfect model embodying universal laws. The function of the scientific model in their vision is to articulate the causal

DOI: 10.4324/9781003266051-11

structure of the world. Simon and Rescher would readily concede that, in principle, everything is connected to everything else. Yet the actual acquisition of causal knowledge cannot proceed on that basis. Rather, it must set aside many potential causal connections in order to effectively uncover the most important ones. A causal understanding of the world can be constructed only on the basis of the Empty World Postulate, which posits that causal connections are not so dense that the investigator cannot isolate subsystems, and the Postulate of Prepotence, which states that subsystems can be isolated in which causal relationships internal to the subsystem are strong relative to those between the subsystem and the world external to the subsystem (see also Simon 1996, ch. 8). These two postulates amount to a methodological vision that knowledge can be effectively acquired in a piecemeal fashion.[2] In a world of piecemeal acquisition of knowledge, models are esteemed when they prove to be powerful instruments both of fact gathering and explanation.

As instruments or tools, models are a puzzle to philosophers. Models are generally thought to represent the world. Yet the world is too complex to be represented completely, so that models, at best, incompletely achieve their task. Worse still, in practice some features of models seem to *misrepresent* the world. Much of the discussion of models as idealizations or fictions addresses the implied puzzles: how can models that are false be part of good science? How can mispresentation be useful? The statistician George Box frequently wrote variants on a favorite theme: "All models are wrong, but some are useful" (Box and Draper 1987, p. 424). My thesis is that Box is wrong: *All useful models are* essentially *true*.[3]

Truth and Knowledge

The puzzles about how models that appear to misrepresent or to trade in fictions arise from a peculiarly philosophical treatment of truth and knowledge. (Note that I say a *philosophical* treatment and not a *philosopher's* treatment; for it is a mode of thinking that is also found among economists and other practitioners when they reflect on their own activities.) Philosophical treatments often link knowledge not only to truth, but to perfect truth: "the truth, the whole truth, and nothing but the truth." The standard is impossibly high and very far from the kind of truth that we demand of our children, our friends, and our fellow citizens. Truth in ordinary language really is thought of as something like Tarski's (1944) famous deflationary formulation "'snow it white' is true if, and only if, snow is white." The expectation for truth telling that we typically demand of others credits them with telling the truth if the propositions that they assert reliably correspond to the relevant feature of the world and conform to a rhetorical rule – "do not express such propositions in a manner that is calculated to mislead." Even in an American court, where one swears to tell "the truth, the whole truth, and nothing but the truth, so help you God," judges and lawyers limit the scope of one's testimony: the whole truth is not, legally speaking, truth without any omission and even statements that do not fully conform to the Tarskian standard are problematic only if they intend to mislead.

I take knowledge to be the stock of truths. A venerable philosophical account of *knowledge* defines it as *justified, true belief.* The definition has, of course, been a source of paradox and the subject of criticism. The focus of both the paradoxes and the criticism has typically been on justification: is a proposition an element of knowledge when its truth is adventitious, because its justification is defective? I would criticize it from a different angle: if knowledge is justified, true belief and knowledge must be of truth that is final and indefeasible, then the conception of truth is so pure that nothing could ever warrant our belief. We might actually possess such a final truth and, indeed, we might have justification for our belief, but that justification will always fall short of indefeasibility; we cannot know with certainty that we know what is true on such an extreme conception of truth and of the requirements of knowledge. It is this problem that ultimately lies behind such anti-scientific-realist views such as Laudan's (1981) "pessimistic induction" and instrumentalism more generally. Knowledge on such a view becomes an empty category.

Again, philosophical thinking carries us far from ordinary people's understanding. When I was a child, we owned an encyclopedia called *The Book of Knowledge.* It was old, even when I began using it, and, no doubt, many facts and explanations recorded in it were not seen as correct by advanced opinion even in my childhood, much less today. Yet, ordinary usage would not, for that reason, reject the encyclopedia's title as pernicious. The common phrase "to the best of our knowledge" conveys both that the target of knowledge is truth and that what is regarded today as knowledge may prove to be defeasible and supplanted tomorrow. We commonly assert that we know something and yet admit that being wrong is not beyond *all* possibility. To say that we "know" is to vouch strongly for our belief, our justification, or both. We can also say, "we thought that we knew, but it turned out that we were wrong." If run through the mill of a severe logic, the ordinary usage of "truth" and "knowledge" is rife with tensions and contradictions. Such tensions and contradictions signal that knowledge in ordinary language – and also in science itself – while it aims at truth and aims at strong justification, nonetheless cannot live with the notion that knowledge consists only of indefeasible truth.

We need to understand the relationship among past, present, and future knowledge, accounting for the growth of knowledge without taking each revision in our beliefs as wiping the slate clean. We need to account for the piecemeal manner in which knowledge is acquired. Modeling practices make sense only with respect to that kind of account.

Models as Instruments for Telling the Truth

It is not uncommon to say that a model is wrong or not true; but strictly speaking, models are not true or false, because propositions are the bearers of truth and models are not propositions. Models are objects and may be used or referred to in propositions to represent other objects, processes, events, and so forth. Models are possibly physical objects – e.g., wind-tunnel models or A.W. H. Phillips's famous hydraulic model of the economy (1950). Many scientific models are abstract – for example, they are embodied in interpreted systems of equations. (Even abstract models are frequently physically embodied in marks on paper or physical states and processes on a computer.) The properties of models are not intrinsic. An object becomes a model only when it is used to represent, and representation involves constraints imposed both by its author and by its receiver or interpreter.

How does a model get its representational grip on the world? The relationship between model and world is not typically anything so strict as isomorphism, as some older, formalist accounts of scientific theories suggest. Ronald Giere (1999, ch. 7, Section 3) likens models to complex predicates. A *classical particle system* is a model of behavior that obeys the Newton's laws and the law of gravity for interacting point masses. We can take "is a classical particle system" to be a predicate, and we can predicate it of our solar system on Giere's account, just as the predicate "is red" can be predicated of a rose. "The rose is red" is true, if, and only if, the rose is red; "the solar system is a classical particle system" is true, if, and only if, the solar system is a classical particle system. To say that our solar system is a classical particle system is to make a claim that this model can be predicated of the solar system or that the solar system is a member of the same type as the model (Giere 1979, ch. 5, also Giere 1999, pp. 98–100, 122 and 2006, p. 65, cf. Hausman 1992, p. 74). Some economic examples of theoretical models that might fit the models-as-predicates view might include the prisoners' dilemma or Akerlof's market for lemons.

Epistemically, the Tarskian formulation is an empty shell. If we actually want to check whether the rose is red, we must implicitly or explicitly appeal to a standard. We might hold up a red color sample against the rose and ask whether they look alike. Even, so simple a model as a color sample points to some of the complexity of models in general: we still have to abstract from the materials and shape and other properties of the color sample and concentrate only on its color if the model is to do its work. Weisberg (2015), among others, argues that the relationship of model to target is one of similarity. In the case of models more complex than color samples, the relationship might be better described as one of analogy.

We can think of analogies as structured similarities. The American pragmatist philosopher, mathematician, and scientist Charles S. Peirce (1.69) defined *analogy* as "the inference that a not very large collection of objects which agree in various respects may very likely agree in another respect."[4] The emphasis on "respects" points to the fact that we do not expect analogies to be complete. We should not expect them to stand in a one-to-one relationship on dimensions of similarity nor on degree of match on any particular dimension. Analogies are *apt* when they broker a satisfactory match of dimensions and a satisfactory degree of match on those dimensions for our particular purposes.

In an account of the role of analogies in science, Mary Hesse (1966, pp. 8–9) distinguished among positive, negative, and neutral analogies (see, also Morgan 1997, pp. S304–S305). Many philosophers have explicated models through the example of maps (e.g., Giere 2006, ch. 4, Hoover 2012). Roman Frigg (2010, pp. 276–280) is particularly illuminating on the required rules for reading maps in relationship to both analogical features and conventions embodied in scales, legends, keys, and so forth. Maps set up both positive and negative analogies. A map that is to scale for measuring distances between points may fail to draw the width of the lines representing roads on the same scale (or, indeed, on any fixed scale) relative to the actual roads, and the colors of different roads on the map may correspond to a fact about the actual road (e.g., main road or secondary road) but probably not to the color of the road surface.

Models are similar. Many claims that some feature of a model is a fiction or a misrepresentation result either from misunderstood or underspecified rules or from a dispute over the implicit rules of reading the model. A map employing a Mercator projection of the Earth is sometimes treated as a false representation of scale. Properly, it is false only if it is supposed to represent scale in a particular linear way rather than to be used exclusively for representing compass headings. In fact, many Mercator maps *do* represent scale by including a continuously graduated nonlinear key to the scale that varies by latitude. A map or a model trades neither in fiction nor in misrepresentation when the rules for reading imply a negative analogy.

The same objects, events, or phenomena are describable from multiple perspectives using distinct models drawing on different analogies (Hoover 2012). Through a judicious choice of negative analogies, such differing perspectives and models need not conflict. Teller (2008, p. 245) points out that water is usefully analogized to a continuous, incompressible medium when analyzing its fluid properties but must be analogized to a collection of discrete particles when analyzing the diffusion of a drop of ink.

Even perspicacious friends of perspectival and piecemeal knowledge often cannot resist the rhetoric of fiction and misrepresentation, despite their awareness that models, like maps, are read according to rules that treat some aspects as positive analogies and others as negative analogies that are meant to be ignored. It is "unfortunate," Giere (2006, p. 78) writes that "Mercator's map ... presents a quite distorted picture of the geography of the Earth." But of course it does not present a distorted picture, except when we insist on reading it differently than it was intended.

Similarly, Teller (2008, p. 239) argues that "generally an idealization involves some radical misdescription." More specifically, he takes his own example of treating water as a continuous medium as "a mistake": water "is not a continuous medium"; yet, he points out scientists "continue to use Euler's equations [that seem to treat water as a continuous medium] in a wide range of applications" (p. 245). Therein lies one of the major philosophical puzzles surrounding scientific models. How can modeling moves that are radical misdescriptions, mistakes, or distortions be so useful? I suggest that this is a puzzle of the philosophers' own making that result from misapprehending the nature of the model and its relationship to its target. No analogy is complete or exact. If "my love is like a red, red rose that's newly sprung in June," I still don't think that planting her in a bed fertilized with fish meal would be the key to her flourishing. The analogical power of models – whether of Euler's equations of fluid dynamics or of a simple paint sample on cardboard – rests on distinguishing between dimensions of similarity that are to be used and dimensions of dissimiliarity that are to be ignored.

The temptation to fall into the trap of treating models as if they are deficient when not every feature is similar or similar to the highest degree points toward a more subtle account of the functioning of analogies between models and their targets. Models are often constructed to meet certain positive desiderata, and we may know some of the negative analogies from the first formulation of the model (e.g., idealizations are often made at the outset). Some negative analogies may simply be forced upon us, owing to the fact that models are objects with lives of their own (Morgan and Morrison 1999). Scale effects provide physical examples. It is impossible to maintain proportional linear outlines of countries and their areas and true compass headings when a roughly spherical Earth is projected onto the flat plane of a map (Boumans 2005, ch. 6). Either one has to give up proportionality for some of the features or one has to provide a complicated nonlinear key to guide the reading. Similarly, it is impossible in the case of a wind-tunnel model to maintain the proportionality of linear, area, and volume measurements at the same time. In each case, either some features must be regarded as negative analogies or compromises must be reached among conflicting desiderata or more subtle rules must be developed for reading the models. Even abstract models may be similarly constrained. Models using differential calculus may be forced to treat variables as continuous, which may be a positive or negative analogy.

Some features of a model may be classified in advance into positive (determining whether the analogy is apt) or negative (staking out the features that are to be set aside). Others may not be known in advance. These are the *neutral analogies* – that is, those aspects of the analogical object (e.g., the model) for which we do not know at the point of formulating the analogy whether to classify as positive or negative. The "may very likely" in Peirce's definition of analogy ("agree in some respects *may very likely* agree in another respect") highlights the possibility of a neutral analogy and explains why he regards analogy as a form of inference.[5]

Neutral analogies can be illustrated through the textbook supply-and-demand model. The model consists of two curves and conventions for operating with them: a price change represents a movement along a curve; a change in any other factor is a shift right or left of the curve. The analogy is drawn when the modeler identifies actors to which the curves apply and classifies various real world factors into those shifting supply and those shifting demand. These are positive analogies. Depending on what version of the supply-and-demand model we choose, there may also be negative analogies, such as only qualitative and not quantitative relationships should be considered. We cannot read any of the desired results from the model unless we decide at what point on the diagram we should read prices and quantities. It may seem obvious that the point at which the curves cross is the point to read.[6] Yet, even if we read it at that point, there is a question about the nature of the analogy. Yes, we take it to be a positive analogy that price and quantity in the model correspond to price and quantity in the world; but if we have analogized the supply and demand curves to the conjectural responses of market participants in the world, to what do we analogize the crossing point?[7]

Consider three interpretations: first, the crossing point may not be analogized to anything at all. It may simply be a requirement of making the diagram yield a definite result that we pick the crossing point. We would then regard it as a material condition of making the model work – similar to the supports that hold up a wind-tunnel model or to the pump that drives the colored liquid through the perspex tubes of the Phillips machine, each of which is a negative analogy, in that nothing in the world corresponds to that particular feature of the model and each of which is required to make the model function in a way that makes the positive analogies possible. Arbitrage models in finance, which take as their starting points that prices are aligned such that no profit opportunities are available, while not containing any element that corresponds to the mechanism that keeps them aligned, make precisely the same kind of interpretation.

Second, we could equally propose the interpretation that the crossing point corresponds to the behavior of an auctioneer. If the market that we are modeling actually has an auctioneer, the analogy is positive, and we have precisified the connection of the model to the world. Third, on the other hand, if the market that we are modeling does not have an auctioneer and, yet, the model still seems to capture the behavior of prices and quantities as if it did, then another response would be to ask, what is it in the world that serves the function of an auctioneer? It is not, then, that the model has a missing piece, so much as it provides a characterization of what any piece needs to look like to fill the auctioneer-shaped hole.

Models are a powerful resource to science in part because they frame our ignorance; but in part because they frame it in such a way that they supply guidance about how to resolve it, not unlike the way that the geometry of a hole in a jigsaw puzzle and the visual patterns adjacent to the hole provide guidance for sorting the remaining unplaced pieces and identifying the missing piece.[8] One way to understand the role of story-telling in model building or the exploration of fictional or credible worlds is either as a way of characterizing specific missing pieces or, more generically, as a building up of sets of potential positive analogies that could be called upon where appropriate (e.g., Frigg 2010, Morgan 2001, Sugden 2000, Teller 2001).[9]

Again, it is important to recall that propositions, and not models, are the bearers of truth values. The proposition that some aspect of the world is captured in a model is the assertion that there is an apt analogy with the appropriate similarity relationships. When the asserted relationships hold positively, then the proposition is true – even when there are, as always, negative analogies as well. No fiction or falsehood is involved when a model contains a negative analogy, even when that feature is needed for the positive functioning of the model; for the point of stipulating that an analogy is negative or, in the case of empirical exploration of neutral analogies, the point of resolving a neutral analogy into a negative analogy is to define a rule of reading for model that forbids us to assess the truth of a proposition involving the model by any correspondence to a real-world counterpart to that feature. The observation that some parts of the model do not correspond to parts of the world really amounts to no more than the noting that a negative analogy is not a positive analogy. Since no correspondence is asserted, nothing is said about the world that is untrue. Of course, a model in which negative analogies outweigh positive ones will not be especially informative about the world.

To illustrate, consider my quartz watch as a model of the *time-keeping* of my mechanical clock. The only positive analogy that I wish to assert is between the times indicated on their dials. When I assert that the watch is a model, I perfectly correctly claim that I can track the movement of the hands of the clock by the movement of the hands of the watch, notwithstanding the negative analogy of vastly different internal mechanisms, each of which is necessary to its time-keeping function. There is nothing the least fictional or untrue in my claim – no radical misdescription, no mistake, no distortion. Of course, if I asserted that I could understand *how* my clock tracked the time using my watch as a model, I would be asserting a very different proposition and one that would in fact be untrue, which, if followed through, would thwart any would-be clockmaker who sought to use my watch as a guide to repairing the clock.

Quantitative, empirical models require more than the coarse classification into positive, negative, and neutral analogies. It is useful to draw a clear distinction between accuracy and precision. By *accuracy* I want to indicate whether a particular positive analogy, a particular correspondence between the model and the world holds. By *precision* I want to indicate a measure of fineness of the standard by which that correspondence is judged. Precision may have a qualitative aspect defined, in part, by the nature and number of the negative analogies a model involves and, in part, by the scope of the model – the ambition to apply it to a narrower or wider domain. Nonetheless, I will here confine attention to the quantitative aspects of precision. A model can be used to assert something true about the world when it contains features that are accurately positively analogous to a feature of the world at a particular level of precision.

One of the propositions for which Nicholas Kaldor (1961) first coined the term *stylized fact* states that labor's share in GDP is constant. Here Kaldor implicitly employed a wide standard of precision. It is accurate to assert that labor's share in GDP in the post-World War II United States stood at a constant 0.7 with a precision of ±0.1. The statement is true, not nearly true or approximately true, but simply true. Yet, it would not be accurate to say that it stood at a constant 0.7 with a precision of ±0.01. The point of calling a fact "stylized" is either to assert that it is accurate at a coarse level of precision but would not be accurate at a finer level of precision that is readily available to us or to assert that it is not accurate at our usual level of precision for such matters but would be accurate at a coarser level of precision that is good enough for present purposes. The possibility of stylization (of facts or of features of models) or of degrees of precision finer than those that we have chosen to employ do not automatically render stylizations inaccurate or false or fictional.

What is more, stylizations do not trade in approximation. Approximation is a distinct notion from stylization or degree of precision. Properly speaking – though loose speaking on this point abounds – *approximations* should be asserted only when there is a clearly characterizable standard against which to measure the approximation. Thus, if there is a complex function, it might be approximated through a much simpler function, and how good the approximation is can be assessed either through explicit or implicit measures of the deviation or through setting bounds on the limits of the deviation. This is the sense in which a higher order polynomial can be approximated by a linear function at a point.

Approximation has important scientific uses; but too often the term is used even in cases for which we do not have a clear characterization of the target of approximation. Frequently, it is asserted that a model is a good one if it approximates the ultimate truth about the world. That ultimate truth, however, is not available to us as a standard against which to judge the approximation. The use of the term, then, is not so much wrong as empty and useless.

One temptation is to change the target from the ultimate truth about the world to the observed data. If data are regarded as facts, transparently true of the world, then a model might be regarded as good if it approximates the data. It would still be false, but it would be "true enough" as a description of the data (Elgin 2004). A theoretical model might, then, explain those facts (e.g., provide reasons why the facts should come out in the way that they do). Such an understanding of the role of approximation promotes the idea that we might have models that become more and more precise until they eventually form the perfect match for their target. This is the lure of the perfect model. Catherine Elgin (2004, p. 116) gives an example of this way of thinking in her discussion of curve smoothing as a kind of fictionalization of the observed data. The problem with Elgin's view is that the target of theoretical models is not, in the first instance, to explain the observed data, but rather to explain the smoothed curves. Curve smoothing is an example of a model of data (see Suppes 1962). The goal of the scientist is more accurately described not as explaining the smooth curve but as reconciling a theoretical model with a model of the data.

Suppes' distinction between theoretical and data models aims to character-ize the complexity of empirical modeling in a manner related to Bogen and Woodward's (1988) distinction between *data* and *phenomena* (cf. Duarte and Hoover 2012, pp. 227, 244–246). Early statistical techniques (for example, Gauss's development of ordinary least squares estimators) aimed at isolating phenomena distinct from the data. The point was decidedly not (*pace* Elgin) to fit each observed point, but rather, in Gauss's case, to characterize the shape of an orbit with an empirical relationship that was truer than the osten-sibly raw observations. The goal was not only to describe the target more accurately but also more precisely as well.

Bogen and Woodward's distinction between phenomena and data is a rel-ative one, since recorded data are representations, and all representations say less than everything that can be said of their referents. What is more, most data should be seen as the product of a model, even if it is only as simple a model as a classification scheme or the taking of average values (such as price indices as models of the general price level). Some data are much more deeply theoretical than smoothing or averages or classification. For example, the U.S. Congressional Budget Office publishes "data" on potential output and the natural rate of unemployment that are created using a theoretical model – a particular expectations-augmented Phillips curve. These data are taken as a primary input into other empirical economic models and are treated in that context as "raw observations" (cf. Hoover and Juselius 2015, Section 4).

It might seem that the difference between Elgin's "true enough" and my insisting on "true" with an explicit or implicit standard of precision as the appropriate virtues for models is a merely semantic distinction. And, of course, I should acknowledge that Elgin, like Giere, Teller, and others, adopts views that are in large measure compatible with mine in that they oppose the Perfect Model Model or favor the piecemeal acquisition of knowledge. Yet, the distinction is not entirely semantic, as the semantics reveal an apologetic attitude, aimed more at parrying the perceived shortcomings of models than of explaining why they possess their positive virtues.

Some may read the notion of giving up the perfectly precise, perfectly accurate model as a target of scientific investigation in favor of the model that is perfectly accurate for a level of precision that is adequate to a particu-lar purpose as a kind of instrumentalism (Hands 2001, pp. 235–238). I have argued elsewhere that it is a kind of Peircean pragmatism that warrants a perspectival realism (Hoover 2012; see also Giere 2006). The problem with instrumentalism of a kind that requires only, as per van Fraassen (1980), that models save the phenomena or that holds that good models are not true, but they work, is that it makes understanding why they work (or why they sometimes do not work) into a mystery. The kind of realism that I wish to endorse says that models are good and they work when they accurately capture relevant features of the world (e.g., when they accurately articulate causal mechanisms) up to the levels of precision and from the points of view that are relevant for the particular problems that we wish to address.

This view of models suggests a natural answer to the pessimistic induction. When a model that is to some significant degree successful at achieving its purposes is supplanted on the same explanatory domain by apparently radically different models, it poses a scientific problem. The successor model may look radically different because it has adopted a different point of view and takes, in part, different aspects of reality as its target. To the degree that it aims to explain the same aspects of reality, it incurs an obligation to explain the success of the supplanted model, insofar as it was successful. The obligation arises because, if the supplanted model was in fact reliable on such matters, the only non-mysterious account of its reliability was that it actually did characterize some aspects of reality accurately from its point of view.[10]

The Analytical Method[11]

The vision of science as a system of a relatively few, relatively simple universal laws governing large domains of events is hardly adequate to the actual practice of most sciences – certainly not to economics – or to the nature of knowledge that is acquired in bits and pieces. We seem to know a lot, but what we know is clearly massively incomplete. Viewing science in terms of its disparate models rather than in terms of its comprehensive system of laws captures much better the actual practices of economics and of many other sciences. Greater attention needs to be paid to how models function in scientific inference. In line with my declared pragmatism, let me go back to the first pragmatist – Peirce (Hands 2001, p. 218).

Peirce famously rejected the division of inference into deductive and inductive, dividing it instead into deductive and ampliative and subdividing ampliative inference into induction and abduction. What is less well known is that Peirce argued that *analogy* constituted an important fourth form of inference. Analogy, he maintained, was a hybrid of abduction and induction.

The purest form of induction in Peirce's view is simply a kind of counting. Suppose that one wants to know the proportion of black and white beans in a bag. Naturally, one can count them all. Even such a count requires a *frame* (not Peirce's term) that determines how beans are to be classified as black or white, given variations in the colors of individuals. One might also learn the proportion – especially if the numbers are large or indefinite – using more elaborate frames. For example, one might thoroughly mix the beans (a process of *randomization*) and then draw a sample of say a cup of beans. Then classifying and counting the beans in the cup allows one to measure the proportions. The step of asserting that the proportions determined by the count are the proportions of the beans in the whole bag relies vitally on the frame. In this case, the frame consists in the classification standard and the assumption that the mixing in fact achieves randomization. In order to quantify the precision of the induction, additional elements are included in the frame, such as the assumption that the inferential setup is analogous to a particular probability model. It is on this basis that formal statistical procedures permit us to assign standard errors to inductive estimates.

Peirce was impressed that quantitative induction disciplined by a probabilistic frame was self-correcting in the sense that the more samples one drew (with replacement, as we are not considering an exhaustive count), the higher the precision of the measurement of the proportions. In that sense, induction was a self-correcting procedure that was bound to lead to the truth if pursued long enough. The self-correcting nature of induction is obviously conditional on the accuracy of the frame in which the induction is conducted. While Peirce would not reject Hume's objection that induction has no logical warrant if induction is taken to be unconditional, he argues that conditional on the frame, it is a deductive truth that induction has the self-correcting quality. Even some elements of the frame can be examined within the context of the frame itself. Are the samples actually random? Probability theory allows us to test randomness – not absolutely, but up to a level of precision that depends on sample size and other conditions. But again, such tests are conditional on other aspects of the frame itself. Nothing can rule out a radical mistake in the frame: if on the fifteenth sample, we discover a yellow bean, the black/white framing assumption is simply wrong and will have to be replaced.

The idea that there are frames that, while not rendering the induction itself into deductive truth, render its self-correcting properties into conditional truths is the fundamental idea behind diagnostic testing in econometrics and statistics. The coefficient estimates and standard errors of an ordinary-least-squares regression have very nice properties conditional on, for example, regressors being exogenous and errors being identically, independent, random errors. These properties are, themselves, testable within a conditional frame.

Where do frames come from? For Peirce, abduction is the supplier of frames. The abductions take the form:

> The surprising fact, C, is observed;
> But if A were true, C would be a matter of course,
> Hence, there is reason to suspect that A is true.
> (Peirce 5.188)

Put this way, abduction has been treated as a species of inference to the best explanation or a Popperian conjecture (Hands 2001, pp. 118–119). But a better interpretation is that an abductive inference amounts to the process of asserting a model, and modeling fits into a larger account of scientific method.

What has come to be thought of as modeling is a good example of what Peirce (1.64) referred to as the "Analytic Method to which modern physics owes all of its triumphs." Peirce also notes that it has "been applied with great success in the psychical sciences. (Thus, the classical political economist, especially Ricardo, pursued this method" – as, I would argue, they still do today. The analytical method is

> to substitute for those problems others much simpler, much more abstract, of which there is a good prospect of finding probable solutions. Then, the reasonably certain solutions of these last problems will throw a light more or less clear upon more concrete problems which are in certain respects more interesting.
>
> (Peirce 1.63)

In the analytical method, abduction supplies the frame in which induction does its work.

Abduction operates through analogical relations. Although Peirce does not use the term model, he does note that "analogy" is a translation of Aristotle's *paradeigma*, from which the word *paradigm* is derived. Peirce uses the term in its pre-Kuhnian sense, based on its Greek roots, *para*, meaning "parallel or going beyond," according to the *Oxford English Dictionary*, and *deigma*, meaning "a sample or pattern." The word itself aptly conveys the strategy of analogical reasoning that Peirce attributed both to physics and to classical political economy and maps very nicely onto modern practices in which stripped down or idealized root models are elaborated successively to come closer to empirical observations while maintaining their underlying basic character and tractability.

Peirce clarifies analogy as hybrid of abduction and induction with an extended analysis of Kepler's discovery of his laws of planetary motion (Peirce 1.72–74, especially 1.74). Kepler began with Copernicus's hypothesis of the planets in circular orbits around the sun and Tycho Brahe's and his own observations. The analogy was between Kepler's mathematical model (to use the modern term), with its precise orbits, and the actual observations. The analogy was not, at first a good one: the Copernican model fit the data rather badly. Out of keeping with Popper's later methodological pronouncements, Kepler did not simply scrap Copernicus's model. His procedure was not haphazard, but systematic and conservative, in the sense that, at each new abductive step, he tried to preserve his quantitative success hitherto – that is, to stay within the bounds of error already achieved – and to use the specific ways in which the hypothesis fell short to suggest the next abductive step. Kepler's own abductive contribution was to consider the dynamical implications of the sun, which he knew to be vastly larger than any of the planets and which he conjectured and exercised some vaguely-defined causal power over them. Alternating abductions to introduce modifications and inductions to characterize the nature and degree of the deviations between conjecture and data, Kepler refined the model:

> never modifying his theory capriciously, but always with a sound and rational motive for just the modification – of most striking simplicity

and rationality – which exactly satisfies the observations, it stands upon a totally different logical footing from what it would if it had been struck out at random, or the reader knows not how, and had been found to satisfy the observation.

(Peirce 1.74)

The analytical method for Peirce is largely the method of refining and precisifying analogies. The Copernican model relied not on detailed observation but on stylized facts. Kepler modified the analogy but also particularized and added precision to the facts. Economic laws, for Peirce, are truer on average than they are for any individual. Economics is thus the natural landscape for statistical refinement, for inductions that raise the precision of the models (Peirce quoted in Eisele 1979, p. 251).

Analogical reasoning represents a *constructive* interplay of abduction and induction. Any induction presupposes a prior abduction. A surprise or an inconsistency between the induction and the prior abduction provides the impetus for a new abduction. Such an abduction could be wholly novel or it could be, which is vastly more likely to be fruitful, a carefully selected variation on the original abduction.

In starting with a simple hypothesis and successively modifying it within a class of possible hypotheses that are obvious from the start, we are, Peirce believes, engaged in induction, not abduction: "induction adds nothing. At the very most it corrects the value of a ratio or slightly modifies a hypothesis in a way which had already been contemplated as possible" (Peirce 7.217). Peirce's idea seems to be that even a fairly specific hypothesis, such as that the data are quadratic, can be treated not as a precise claim but in a manner close to original meaning of "paradigm," as an instance or exemplar that can serve as an index for wider family of precise hypotheses. Thus, the quadratic hypothesis could be taken to be an index of the whole polynomial family; and, just as enumerative induction of a statistical kind results in a narrowing of the bounds on the value that a true ratio could take, inductions of a nonstatistical kind can be taken as a narrowing of the subset of family members compatible with the truth. The true abduction – the inference that might provide "unexpected additions to our knowledge" – is the replacement of one family of models by another.

The promise of both statistical and nonstatistical induction for Peirce is their property that, if we keep at it, they are bound to reveal the falsity of our hypothesis – even the falseness only beyond some limit of precision – in the fullness of time. There is no certainty of their success even in a negative sense: the falsifying observation may always lie just round the corner. And there is absolutely no certainty in the positive sense: an observation may tell us that we are entertaining entirely the wrong family of hypotheses; it requires luck or a natural affinity for the truth, an affinity which can be grounded only in hope and not in knowledge, to pick the right family (Peirce 1.121, 7.219).

Peirce holds up Ricardo's theory of rent as a prime example of analytical reasoning, not only for economics but also for all science. The manner in which he moves seamlessly in his exposition of the theory from the specific details of rent to the question of tax incidence, which involves demand analysis – quite new since Ricardo – suggests that he regards the theory as a starting point, an initial template, an index of a family of hypotheses whose members differ in their scope and complexity, which is ripe for inductive precisification and which, in the manner of Kepler's introduction of the causal powers of the sun, can be joined to novel abductions to build an empirically grounded economic model of real-world phenomena (Peirce 4.115).[12]

Macroeconometric Models

To take stock: I have argued that the function of models in economics and other sciences is to serve as instruments for telling the truth – that is, to portray the world accurately for a purpose and from a point of view up to an implicit or explicit degree of precision. Models operate through analogy, and analogy is based not on any notion of identity but on a complex of cases, divided into similar aspects (positive analogies), on which the working features of the model are based, dissimilar aspects (negative analogies), which must be bracketed off and ignored, and yet-to-be-classified aspects (neutral analogies), which represent the ground for scientific exploration. The practice of empirical scientific modeling can be seen as an application of Peirce's analytical inference – a progressive interplay of abduction and induction. Abduction supplies paradigmatic models that serve as indices to classes of models and provides the frames in which induction precisifies the models, both systematically selecting particular members out of a contemplated class of models and quantifying parameters of the model at increasing levels of precision.

There are many illustrations of using models in conformity to the analytical method in the history of economics. I will end by examining a little piece of the history of macroeconometric models (see Morgan 1990, ch. 4, Bodkin, Klein, and Marwah 1991). The earliest modern macroeconometric models were first developed in the 1930s by Jan Tinbergen for the Dutch and U.S. economies and were significantly advanced through the work of Lawrence Klein in the late 1940s. Subsequently, increasingly complex macroeconometric models were developed for many countries for use in economic research and for practical economic analysis by governments, central banks, and businesses. One might be tempted to view the increasing complexity of macroeconometric models between the 1930s and the 1970s as the relentless pursuit of the perfect model, but that would, I believe, misunderstand the actual practice of the macroeconometric modelers. Rather than attempt a methodological history of eight decades of macroeconometric modeling, I will focus on one early contribution – the family of three models examined in Klein's monograph *Economic Fluctuations in the United States, 1921–1941* (1950).

A singular feature of Klein's monograph is that, standing near the beginning of the macroeconometric program, it is both a methodological investigation of how to build and use macroeconometric models and an investigation into the nature of the American economy. Some of the issues of interest to the philosopher of science are, as a result, more explicitly brought to the fore than with later macroeconometric models.

Klein presents three models of the U.S. economy: Model II is the least complex, a three-equation model (one behavioral equation and two identities); Model I is a six-equation model (three behavioral relationships and three identities) that supports the estimation of a system of three equations; Model III is a "large," sixteen-equation model (eleven behavioral equations and five identities).[13] None of these models is partial in the sense of being confined to a subpart of the American economy; rather each models the whole economy with different degrees of articulation of important aspects. The situation is not unlike that of a realistic cityscape in which human figures appear in the distance, yet when examined at very closely the figures resolve into a few simple blotches of paint.

To cast this into the framework of Peirce's analytical inference, the fundamental abduction is that the economy can be described in a Keynesian framework of aggregate supply and aggregate demand. Aggregate demand is determined by the decisions of types of agents (consumers, firms, etc.), who must make decisions over the flows of their expenditure (consumption, investment, etc.), as well as decisions over their holdings of stocks of assets (money, bond, shares, real capital, etc.). Aggregate supply of goods and services is determined by production technology and the decisions to supply factors of production (labor and capital, etc.). Prices of goods and financial assets coordinate the whole system, though in a manner that permits some available factors of production to be less than fully employed. This is but a partial accounting of the basics Keynesian framework, but even when more fully specified, it characterizes, from a quantitative, empirical view, an extremely broad class of models that might be instantiated in a variety of ways. To call a model "Keynesian" is rather closer to calling it heliocentric than to calling it Copernican, where that term is taken to imply circular orbits.

Klein does not attempt a comprehensive search over every member of the class of Keynesian models. It is not even clear how such a search could be constructed. Rather he approaches the task much like Kepler in Peirce's characterization by starting with a very simple member of the class. Model II (Appendix 1) can be taken to be Klein's Copernican model – an extremely simply index of the class. It is essentially the textbook "Keynesian cross" model, used since the 1940s to teach undergraduates about the fundamental concepts behind Keynesian economics. As a textbook model, it could easily be thought of as a caricature model along the lines of Gibbard and Varian (1978). Yet, Klein solves out the identities to obtain a single equation, associates each of its theoretical variables with data collected by U.S. government statistics bureaux, and estimates the resulting equation (a "reduced form").

What is to be gained from the estimation – an induction conditional on a frame that, Klein himself regards as too coarse, to serve his ultimate purpose of a policy relevant model?

On the one hand, Klein is applying Simon and Rescher's Empty-World and Prepotence Postulates in assuming that many possible connections either do not exist or are sufficiently weak that, at a loose enough standard of precision, the model may nonetheless accurately characterize the economy. On the other hand, Klein is employing an idea similar to Peirce's that a model too simple to be accurate at a desired level of precision will reveal through the detailed ways in which it deviates from accuracy the direction in which the model would need to be modified (Peirce 7.221). One question that he poses to Model II is whether the analogy with the probability model of independent random errors is a good one. In particular, he looks at test statistics that are meant to be sensitive to the presence of serial correlation in the residuals, which that model presumes to be absent. He deems the model to be inadequate, though the level of precision is not, in fact, very high. For example, he calculates the government expenditure multiplier implied by his estimates and finds it to be implausibly high; but he notes that the confidence interval for the multiplier is very wide. Thus, while the model is not necessarily inaccurate in the sense in which I have defined there term, it also would not be precise enough to support policy analysis, which is Klein's ultimate purpose.

Klein also estimates another model within the class defined by his reduced-form equation. The model is suggested by the large standard error on the estimated parameter α_3 governing the strength of the connection between money and GDP. The imprecise estimate may either be that the effect is weak (lack of prepotence) or that it is nonexistent (empty world). While modern economists have turned significance tests into a nearly mechanical judgment, it is clear from the way in which Klein discusses this parameter estimate that the idea that an analogy is being drawn between the patterns of his data and a specific model of probability implied by the stochastic specification of his model is exactly what lies behind such tests. Given this signal, Klein specifies another model with money omitted ($\alpha_3 = 0$), and he finds that the simpler model is accurate to essentially the same degree of precision as the model with money. Since money appears in the theoretical model only in the consumption function (Equation (3.2.1)), Klein takes the lesson from Model II that more complex models, whatever other role they assign to money, can likely omit it from the consumption function – as, in fact, Models I and III do.

Once money is omitted from the consumption function, Model II is more or less nested in Models I (Appendix 2).[14] Like Model II, Model I is an exploration of a model intentionally simpler than any model that Klein would regard as adequate for his purposes. Its target, however, is still the whole economy. This is evident in the expenditure identities (Equations (3.1.19) and (3.1.20)) that cover GNP just as completely (now from an income, as well as an expenditure point of view), albeit with a finer breakdown into its components than the expenditure identity of Model II (Equation (3.2.2)).

To investigate the adequacy of the statistical model, Klein estimates it using both a full-information maximum likelihood (FIML) estimator and a limited-information maximum likelihood estimator (LIML). These draw somewhat different analogies to the probability model invoked in the statistical design. The advantage of LIML was that it permitted estimates of coefficient standard errors, while, with the statistical technology of 1950 (no longer a constraint today), FIML did not. In effect, while FIML provided quantitatively more precise estimates of the means of the probability distributions, LIML provided a qualitatively more precise estimate, in that it permitted an estimate of two moments of the probability distribution, but at the cost of some quantitative precision. Given the levels of precision, both methods provide accurate estimates of the theoretical model, conditional on both the underlying theoretical model and the probability model invoked by the statistics. In each case, Klein checks the adequacy of the statistical model using the same approach as with Model II.

Klein uses the LIML estimates as the key measure of adequacy of the theoretical model. Again, as with Peirce's Kepler, Klein takes the discrepancies on various dimensions not as rejections, but as invitations to explore the space of the subclass of models in the immediate vicinity of the initial version of Model I.

Models I and II can be seen principally as scouting expeditions. Neither is adequate to Klein's ultimate purpose, which is to construct models in which it would be possible to conduct policy-relevant counterfactual experiments. In part, Klein was simply using these models to learn how to integrate recent developments in econometric theory, guiding the statistical frame with theoretical models. In employing models that were members of the same broad class and were aimed at the same real world target, however, Klein engaged not only in a technical exercise of auto-pedagogic value, he also sought to learn from the inductive step of estimating the models statistically useful directions to develop the model into one that could represent accurately at a useful level of precision the causal relationship of policy instruments (e.g., government expenditure or taxes) to the targets of policy (e.g., GDP growth or labor demand). Model III is his first attempt at such a model. The investigation and development of this more complex model follows a similar strategy to the investigation of the simpler Models I and II. It offers us no particularly new insights into the process.

In the event, Klein did not regard Model III as either sufficiently accurate or sufficiently developed on the necessary dimensions to support the needs of policy. It too was a step in the iterative process of analytical inference (model building) that Peirce locates at the heart of quantitative sciences. The next step was an even larger macroeconometric model, the *Klein-Goldberger Model*, which proved to be the first macroeconometric model of the United States actually used for practical policy analysis (Klein and Goldberger 1955). The Klein-Goldberger model was the ancestor of a several generations of macroeconometric models – some still in use in the U.S. government and the

Federal Reserve system and the inspiration for a number of other models in the United States and many other countries (see Bodkin et al. 1991).

All Useful Models are Essentially True

Much of the attention to models in economics has focused on the activities of economic theorists, as opposed to empirical researchers. Theorists spend a good deal of time elaborating models and specializing and adapting them to particular targets. The goal of the theorist is often to highlight a surprising or overlooked phenomenon or to work out a mechanism that could operate in principle. Such perfectly creditable goals, I believe, account for the popularity of the notion that models in economics are caricatures or devices for exploring credible worlds or fictions of varying degrees of realisticness. Quantitative modeling receives far less attention. In explaining why their focus is on theoretical models as caricatures, Gibbard and Varian (1978, p. 665) "liken econometric models ... to photographs." They express the view that the representation of an economic phenomenon might "gradually evolve [from a caricature model] into an econometrically estimable model" – that is, from "a literal caricature" to a "photograph" of the economy (pp. 665, 666). The nature of empirical model building and of the process of evolution is, however, not their topic – it is mentioned merely to be set aside. The invocation of the photographic realism, however, suggests something like the Perfect Model Model.

That actual empirical models fall short of photographic realism probably explains the appeal of ideas such as instrumentalism ("all models are wrong, but some are useful"), and that models are approximations or "true enough." These ideas fail to explain how models work or why they are effective. The best explanation is that models somehow capture truths about the world. This point is implicitly understood by the philosophers and methodologists of purely theoretical models: caricatures contain truths that are exaggerated for emphasis; a credible world is a world that, while not the actual world, contains mechanisms of the actual world; realistic fiction, including realistic fictional models, is realistic because important aspects of their working corresponds to mechanisms in the actual world.

A model that aims to capture empirical truth about the economy at any reasonable level of quantitative precision needs to go further than the theorists. If they are not photographically realistic – and few would assert that they are – if they do not approach the perfect model, how do they succeed? Models work analogically, and analogies can be loose or tight, they can possess different degrees of articulation. Empirical models work when they are based in apt analogies with a degree of articulation adequate to the purposes and required precision of the modeler. When they succeed in this way, they are instruments for telling the truth.

The key point about Peirce's account of analytical inference is that accurate and quantitatively precise analogies must be shaped or molded. When we think of economics as a model-building science, it is precisely this shaping and molding with its interplay of abduction and induction that constitutes the ordinary life of the empirical economist. Importantly, abduction is not a haphazard activity; rather it is a directed activity in which new hypotheses build on the fate of old ones revealed and evaluated in the light of the inductions that the old abductions had framed.

Shaping or molding models seems to contravene methodological strictures to which economists pay frequent lip service. We are often taught that science is a sequence of hypothesize, test, accept or reject, and that it is bad science to tailor hypotheses to the data. Partly, this come from the fact that Popper's methodology of conjectures and refutations remains popular among practicing economists if not among philosophers and methodologists of economics, and Popper was strident about "immunizing strategies." Partly, it comes from an analogy with hypothesis testing in statistics, where it can be shown that certain kinds of specification search results in test statistics whose actual size (probability of type-I error) are much higher than their nominal size. One response is a general prejudice against anything that smacks of "data mining."

Elsewhere, I have answered the objection to data mining through statistical specification search.[15] That answer takes a similar form to the analysis in the current paper. Statistical estimation relies on an analogy between the data packaged in a certain way and a probability model. The first question for any analogy is, is it apt? Are the supposed analogical features actually similar? Estimation is the inductive step in Peirce's analytical inference at the level of the data model. Precision in such an induction is useful only *conditionally* on the analogy in fact being accurate. Specification search (aka data mining) amounts to the effort to mold an accurate analogy. If done right (and that is a big if), specification search adapts to constraints in the world, which produces a model that can be accurately predicated of the data and quantified through induction.

The focus of the current paper was not on data models, but on theoretical models that are quantified through their analogical relations to data models. Klein's macroeconometric models illustrate that the process of molding models sequentially is typical of the way economists actually work. If this contravenes methodological strictures, the account of model building that I am advocating locates the problem, not with the practices of Klein and other economists, but with the methodological strictures themselves.

Acknowledgements

My thanks to the organizers and participants in the Conference on "Explanation, Normativity, and Uncertainty in Economic Modelling," London School of Economics, 16–17 March 2016, for which an earlier version of this paper was delivered as the keynote lecture. I am also grateful to the organizers and participants at the Workshop on "The History of Modeling Practices in Macroeconomics," University of Lille, 13 October 2016 for comments and discussion.

Notes

1. There are exceptions: for a penetrating analysis of empirical models, see Boumans (2005).
2. The language of piecemeal knowledge has been adopted, especially by philosophers of biology (e.g., Wimsatt 2007).
3. While this paper was not originally motivated by Reiss's (2012) "explanation paradox," it can be seen as an argument we should dismiss the paradox altogether. Hands (2013, p. 235) summarizes the paradox as "the inconsistency of accepting the three statements: (i) economic models are false, (ii) economic models explain, and (iii) only truth explains." My argument accepts (ii) and (iii) and rejects (i), so that no paradox is in play.
4. Following the custom of Peirce scholarship, references to Peirce's *Collected Papers* (1933–1958) are by volume number and paragraph: e.g., 1.69 = volume 1, paragraph 69. For a brief account of Peirce's pragmatism, see Hands (2001, pp. 218–224) or Hoover (1994).
5. Hands (2001, p. 224) suggests that "abduction is a relatively loose notion of inference," which explains why it has been neglected in the Received View of the philosophy of science, which emphasized rigor and, therefore, deductive and "formulaic" inductive inference. Section IV below gives grounds to question Hands' notion that abduction is a loose form of inference.
6. It is, in fact, not obvious. There are supply-and-demand models in which prices and quantities are not read at the crossing point – e.g., cobweb models of price dynamics.
7. Arrow (1959) poses exactly this question with respect to the supply-and-demand model.
8. Reacting to such guidance results in a process that Boumans (2005, chs. 1 and 3) refers to as "mathematical molding"; see also Hoover (2013).
9. The "socialist calculation debate" of the 1930s hinged on the credibility of two fictional worlds. Both sides referred to a Walrasian general equilibrium model, which like the supply-and-demand model provides no mechanism for actually setting prices, though it shows where they must be set to clear the market. The socialist side suggested that the hole could be credibly filled with a computer, which had not yet been invented. Even now no computer would be adequate to the task. The Austrian, free-market side argued that the market itself was an effective computer.
10. The notion that distinct perspectives permit accurate representations that may used to make true claims and that science should find a way both to incorporate them into common perspectives when they conflict and to account for their successes, even when superseded, raises some of the issues of pluralism versus unificationism in science that are addressed in Hands (2021).
11. This section draws on draft material from a book in progress, joint with James Wible, on Peirce's engagement with economics.
12. Peirce's treatment of Ricardo is deeply consistent with Morgan's (2012, ch. 2) treatment of him, not only as a generic "modeler" but also as one who used the generic model as a template for quantitative refinement.
13. Here the models are discussed in their order of complexity. For reasons related principally to his investigation of estimation methods, Klein considers the simpler Model II after the more complex Model I.
14. "More or less" because variables in Model II, unlike Model I, are expressed in per-capita terms. Both Model I and Model III, which also does not use per-capita variables, aim to capture some of the same features through time trends.
15. See Hoover (1995, 2013) and Hoover and Perez (1999, 2000, 2004).

140   *Kevin Hoover*

References

Arrow, Kenneth J. (1959) "Toward a Theory of Price Adjustment", in Moses Abramovitz et al., *The Allocation of Economic Resources: Essays in Honor of Bernard Francis Haley.* Stanford, CA: Stanford University Press, pp. 41–51.

Bodkin, Ronald; Lawrence R. Klein, and Kanta Marwah. (1991) *A History of Macroeconometric Model-Building.* Cheltenham: Edward Elgar.

Bogen, James and James Woodward. (1988) "Saving the Phenomena," *Philosophical Review* 97(3):303–352.

Boumans, Marcel. (2005) *How Economists Model the World into Numbers.* Abingdon, Oxon: Routledge.

Box, George E. P. and Draper, Norman R. (1987). *Empirical Model Building and Response Surfaces.* New York, NY: Wiley.

Duarte, Pedro G. and Kevin D. Hoover. (2012) "Observing Shocks," in Harro Maas and Mary Morgan, editors. *Histories of Observation in Economics, History of Political Economy* 44(supplement), pp. 226–249. Durham, NC: Duke University Press, 2012.

Elgin, Catherine. (2004) "True Enough," *Philosophical Issues* 14(1):113–131.

Eisele, Carolyn. (1979) *Studies in the Scientific and Mathematical Philosophy of Charles S. Perice.* The Hague: Mouton.

Frigg, Roman. (2010) "Fiction in Science," in John Woods, editor. *Fiction and Models: New Essays.* Munich: Philosophia Verlag.

Gibbard, Allan and Hal R. Varian. (1978) "Economic Models," *Journal of Philosophy* 75(11):664–677.

Giere, Ronald N. (1979) *Understanding Scientific Reasoning.* New York, NY: Holt, Rinehart, and Winston.

Giere, Ronald N. (1999) *Science without Laws.* Chicago, IL: University of Chicago Press.

Giere, Ronald N. (2006) *Scientific Perspectivism.* Chicago, IL: University of Chicago Press.

Hands, D. Wade. (2001) *Reflection without Rules: Economic Methodology and Contemporary Science Theory.* Cambridge: Cambridge University Press.

Hands, D. Wade. (2013) "Introduction to Symposium on the Explanation Paradox," *Journal of Economic Methodology* 20(3):235–236.

Hands, D. Wade. (2021) "The Many Faces of Unification and Pluralism in Economics: The Case of Paul Samuelson's Foundations of Economic Analysis," *Erkenntnis* 88:209–219.

Hausman, Daniel M. (1992) *The Inexact and Separate Science of Economics.* Cambridge: Cambridge University Press

Hesse, Mary. (1966) *Models and Analogies in Science.* South Bend, IN: University of Notre Dame Press.

Hoover, Kevin D. (1994) "Pragmatism, Pragmaticism, and Economic Method," in Roger Backhouse, editor. *New Directions in Economic Methodology.* London: Routledge, pp. 286–315.

Hoover, Kevin D. (1995) "In Defense of Data Mining: Some Preliminary Thoughts," in Kevin D. Hoover and Steven M. Sheffrin, editors, *Monetarism and the Methodology of Empirical Economics: Essays in Honor of Thomas Mayer.* Aldershot: Edward Elgar, pp. 242–257.

Hoover, Kevin D. (2012) "Pragmatism, Perspectival Realism, and Econometrics," in Aki Lehtinen, Jaakko Kuorikoski and Petri Ylikoski, editors. *Economics for Real: Uskali Mäki and the Place of Truth in Economics* pp. 223–240. Abingdon, Oxon: Routledge.

Hoover, Kevin D. (2013) "The Role of Hypothesis Testing in the Molding of Econometric Models," *Erasmus Journal for the Philosophy of Economics* 6(2):42–65.

Hoover, Kevin D. and Katarina Juselius. (2015) "Trygve Haavelmo's Experimental Methodology and Scenario Analysis in a Cointegrated Vector Autoregression," *Econometric Theory* 31(2):249–274, 2015.

Hoover, Kevin D. and Stephen J. Perez. (1999) "Data Mining Reconsidered: Encompassing and the General-to-Specific Approach to Specification Search," *Econometrics Journal* 2(2):1–25.

Hoover, Kevin D. and Stephen J. Perez. (2000) "Three Attitudes towards Data-mining," *Journal of Economic Methodology* 7(2):195–210.

Hoover, Kevin D. and Stephen J. Perez. (2004) "Truth and Robustness in Cross-Country Growth Regressions," *Oxford Bulletin of Economics and Statistics* 66(5):765–798.

Kaldor, Nicholas. (1961) "Capital Accumulation and Economic Growth," in F.A. Lutz and D.C. Hague, editors. *The Theory of Capital* pp. 177–222. London: Macmillan.

Klein, Lawrence R. (1950) *Economic Fluctuations in the United States, 1921–1941* (Cowles Commission Monograph No. 11). New York, NY: Wiley.

Klein, Lawrence R. and Arthur S. Goldberger. (1955) *An Econometric Model of the United States 1929–1952*. Amsterdam: North-Holland Publishing Company, 1955.

Laudan, Larry. (1981) "A Confutation of Convergent Realism," *Philosophy of Science* 48(1):19–49.

Morgan, Mary S. (1990) *The History of Econometric Ideas*. Cambridge: Cambridge University Press.

Morgan, Mary S. (1997) "The Technology of Analogical Models: Irving Fisher's Monetary Worlds," *Philosophy of Science* 64(Supplement; Part II: Symposia Papers):S304–S314.

Morgan, Mary S. (2001) "Models, Stories and the Economic World," *Journal of Economic Methodology* 8(3):361–384.

Morgan, Mary S. (2012) *The World in the Model: How Economists Work and Think*. Cambridge: Cambridge University Press.

Morgan, Mary S. and Margaret Morrison. 1999. *Models as Mediators: Perspectives on Natural and Social Science*. Cambridge: Cambridge University Press.

Peirce, Charles S. (1933-1958) *Collected Papers of Charles Sanders Peirce*, vols. 1–8, Charles Hartshorne, Paul Weiss, and Arthur Burks, editors. Cambridge: Belknap Press.

Phillips, A.W.H (1950) "Mechanical Models in Economic Dynamics," *Economica NS* 17(67):283–305.

Reiss, Julian. (2012) "The Explanation Paradox," *Journal of Economic Methodology*, 19(1):43–62.

Simon, Herbert A. (1996) *The Sciences of the Artificial*, 3rd ed. Cambridge, MA: MIT Press.

Simon, Herbert and Nicholas Rescher. (1966) "Causes and Counterfactuals," *Philosophy of Science* 33(4):323–340.

Sugden, Robert. (2000) "Credibile Worlds: The Status of Theoretical Models in Economics," *Journal of Economic Perspectives* 7(1):1–31.

Suppes, Patrick. (1962) "Models of Data," in Ernest Nagel, Patrick Suppes and Alfred Tarski, editors. *Logic, Methodology and Philosophy of Science: Proceedings of the 1960 International Congress* pp. 252–261. Stanford, CA: Stanford University Press.

Tarski, Alfred. (1944) "The Semantic Conception of Truth: and the Foundations of Semantics," *Philosophy and Phenomenological Research* 4(3):341–376.

Teller, Paul. (2001) "Twilight of the Perfect Model Model," *Erkenntnis* 55(3):393–415.

142   *Kevin Hoover*

Teller, Paul. (2008) "Fictions, Fictionalization, and Truth in Science," in Mauricio Suárez, editor. *Fictions in Science: Philosophical Essays on Modeling and Idealization* pp. 235–247. London: Routledge.

van Fraassen, Bas C. (1980) *The Scientific Image.* Oxford: Oxford University Press.

Walras, Leon. (1874[1954]) *The Elements of Pure Economics*, William Jaffé, editor. London: George Allen & Unwin.

Weisberg, Michael. (2105) *Simulation and Similarity.* Oxford: Oxford University Press.

Wimsatt, William C. (2007) *Re-engineering Philosophy for Limited Beings: Piecewise Approximations to Reality.*

Appendix 1: Klein's Model II

Structural Model

$$\frac{C}{pN} = \alpha_0 + \alpha_1 \frac{Y}{pN} + \alpha_2 \left(\frac{Y}{pN}\right)_{-1} + \alpha_3 \left(\frac{M}{pN}\right)_{-1} + u \qquad (3.2.1)^1$$

$$GNP = C + I' + G \qquad (3.2.2)$$

$$GNP = Y + T \qquad (3.2.3)$$

Reduced Form

$$\frac{Y}{pN} = \frac{\alpha_0}{1-\alpha_1} + \frac{\alpha_2}{1-\alpha_1}\left(\frac{Y}{pN}\right)_{-1} + \frac{\alpha_3}{1-\alpha_1}\left(\frac{M}{pN}\right)_{-1}$$

$$+ \frac{1}{1-\alpha_1}\left(\frac{I'+G-T}{pN}\right) + \frac{1}{1-\alpha_1}u \qquad (3.2.5)$$

Reduced-Form Estimates

Estimates based on annual data for the United States 1921–1941.

$$\frac{Y}{pN} = 186.53 + 0.30_{(0.13)}\left(\frac{Y}{pN}\right)_{-1} + 0.13_{(0.10)}\left(\frac{M}{pN}\right)_{-1} + 2.36_{(0.35)}\left(\frac{I'+G-T}{pN}\right) + u' \qquad (3.2.1)$$

(Standard errors in parentheses below coefficient estimates.)

Variables

Current Dollar Variables:

   C = consumption;

Y = disposable income;

M = money supply;

I' = gross investment;

G = government expenditure;

GNP = gross national product;

T = government receipts.

Other Variables:

p = cost-of-living index;

N = population;

u = structural random disturbance

u' = reduced-form disturbance.

Statistics:

$\bar{S}$ = mean squared error of regression;

$\left(\dfrac{\delta^2}{S^2}\right)$ = measure of serial correlation for *j*th equation; 5 percent acceptance region for null of no serial correlation = 1.25–3.00.

Appendix 2 Klein's Model I

Structural Model

$$C = \alpha_0 + \alpha_1(W_1 + W_2) + \alpha_2 \Pi + u_1 \tag{3.1.16}$$

$$I = \beta_0 + \beta_1 \Pi + \beta_2 \Pi_{-1} + \beta_3 K_{-1} + u_2 \tag{3.1.17}$$

$$W_1 = \gamma_0 + \gamma_1(Y + T - W_2) + \gamma_2(Y + T - W_2)_{-1} + \gamma_3 t + u_3 \tag{3.1.18}$$

$$Y + T - W_2 \tag{3.1.19}$$

$$Y = W_1 + W_1 + \Pi \tag{3.1.20}$$

$$\Delta K = I \tag{3.1.21}$$

Structural Estimates (LIML)

Estimates based on annual data for the United States 1921–1941.

$$C = 17.71 + \underset{(0.04)}{0.87}(W_1 + W_2) + \underset{(0.07)}{0.02}\Pi + u_1'' \tag{3.1.31}$$

$$I = 22.59 + \underset{(0.23)}{0.08}\,\Pi + \underset{(0.21)}{0.68}\,\Pi_{-1} - \underset{(0.04)}{0.17}\,K_{-1} + u_2'' \qquad (3.1.32)$$

$$W_1 = 1.53 + \underset{(0.03)}{0.43}\,(Y + T - W_2) + \underset{(0.03)}{0.15}\,(Y + T - W_2)_{-1}$$

$$+ \underset{(0.02)}{0.13}\,(t - 1931) + u_3'' \qquad (3.1.33)$$

(Standard errors in parentheses below coefficient estimates.)

$$\bar{S}_1 = 1.30 \quad \bar{S}_2 = 1.43 \quad \bar{S}_3 = 0.77 \qquad (3.1.34)$$

$$\left(\frac{\delta^2}{S^2}\right)_1 = 0.98 \left(\frac{\delta^2}{S^2}\right)_2 = 2.18 \left(\frac{\delta^2}{S^2}\right)_3 = 2.10 \qquad (3.1.35)$$

Variables

Constant Dollar Variables:

  C = consumption;

  G = government expenditure;

  I = gross investment;

  K = capital stock;

  W_1 = private wage bill;

  W_2 = government wage bill;

  Y = gross national product income;

  Π = profits.

Other Variables:

  t = time trend;

  u_j'' = random disturbance (j = 1, 2, 3).

Statistics:

  $\bar{S}_j$ = mean squared error of regression for jth equation;

  $\left(\dfrac{\delta^2}{S^2}\right)_j$ = measure of serial correlation for jth equation; 5 percent acceptance region for null of no serial correlation = 1.25–3.00.

Note

1. Equation numbers refer to the numbers in Klein's original text.

8 Institutional Economics and John Dewey's Instrumentalism

Malcolm Rutherford

Introduction

As noted by Wade Hands "it is almost a cliché that any discussion of American institutionalism must include a reference to the 'impact' of pragmatic philosophy," but, with the exception of the very clear and obvious relationship between John Dewey and Clarence Ayres, Hands seems to regard most of the proposed connections between institutionalism and pragmatism to be "rather controversial" (Hands 2001, p. 231). The argument to be made here is that connections between institutionalism and pragmatism, and especially of John Dewey's pragmatic instrumentalism, during the period when both were at their peak, are not hard to see. This is less a matter of explicit references to Charles Peirce or Dewey, or to any writings in philosophy, but more a matter of the practice of institutional economists. Institutional economics in the interwar period can be seen as an attempt to carry out a research program along instrumentalist lines.

It must be said that Veblen is something of an exception to this characterization. Veblen's work does share a number of characteristics with Peirce and Dewey, but his basic view of science was not instrumental, so several aspects of the instrumental approach common to other institutionalists are not evident in Veblen's writings. This is a key factor in Veblen's relative lack of interest in practical reform efforts. Veblen did not subscribe to the enthusiasm for "social control" that was shared by Dewey and virtually all other institutionalists, as his view was that significant institutional change could only come from evolutionary processes that altered the "discipline" of life. A different issue concerns Clarence Ayres. Ayres clearly had a close relationship with Dewey and was strongly influenced by his ideas, but Ayres' training was in philosophy not economics, and his major works focused on questions of valuation and the definition of "progress" (Ayres 1944). What I want to focus on here is the *economic* research done by institutionalists, and Ayres did very little economics of the type done by other institutionalists.

DOI: 10.4324/9781003266051-12

Dewey's Instrumentalism

Dewey's view of science is that it consists of a process of *inquiry* that is ongoing and has no terminus. What gives rise to inquiry is, in the first instance, what Dewey calls an "indeterminate situation." This situation is one in which the constituent parts do not "hang together." The situation is "uncertain, unsettled, disturbed" and evokes doubt and questioning. These doubts are due to the indeterminate nature of the situation being faced and cannot be resolved by mental processes. Resolution requires an active and operational response (Dewey 1938, pp. 105–107).

The process of inquiry begins by transforming the indeterminate situation into a defined problematic situation or problem. The way in which the problem is conceptualized or defined will then determine how the resolution of the problem is approached, what data are selected for collection and examination, and what specific suggestions are entertained (Dewey 1938, pp. 107–108). As the process of inquiry proceeds it may become necessary to redefine the problem or reconceptualize it.

Starting from a problem situation, the next step is to search out its constituents, or as Dewey puts it "the facts of the case." These facts "constitute the terms of the problem because they are conditions that must be reckoned with or taken account of in any relevant solution that is proposed." Possible solutions are suggested by the "determination of factual conditions which are secured by observation" (Dewey 1938, p. 109). Proposed solutions are ideas, hypotheses, and involve both means and ends. The ends here are not to be seen as ultimate ends, but ends-in-view. The proposed solutions are sets of anticipated consequences, forecasts, or predictions. Observation and hypothesis making interact:

> Observation of facts and suggested meanings or ideas arise and develop in correspondence with each other. The more the facts of the case come to light in consequence of being subjected to observation, the clearer and more pertinent become the conceptions of the way the problem constituted by these facts is to be dealt with. On the other side, the clearer the idea, the more definite, as a truism, become the operations of observation and of execution that must be performed in order to resolve the situation.
>
> (Dewey 1938, p. 109)

The exact methods to be used in this process of inquiry are not tightly circumscribed, they are the methods of reason, intelligence, reflective thought, empirical investigation, theorizing, prediction, experiment, and appraisal of consequences. Dewey puts particular emphasis on what he calls experimental reasoning. This too is thought of in broad terms, but it breaks down the distinction between knowing and doing. Knowledge is gained by trying to do things in the material world. In terms of the physical sciences, Dewey argues that:

It came into being when men intentionally experimented, on the basis of ideas and hypotheses, with observed phenomena to modify them and disclose new observations. This process is self-corrective and self-developing. Imperfect and even wrong hypotheses when *acted upon,* brought to light significant phenomena which made improved ideas and improved experimentations possible.

(Dewey 1931, p. 276)

The attempt to solve a problem in practice will reveal new information which may result in a change to the proposed means or a re-evaluation of the ends themselves. Both means and ends are in a constant process of appraisal and re-appraisal. Science is fallible, but failures will result in attempts to find other solutions that work. Experience may also result in changes to underlying values, to the notion of what worthwhile goals consist of. In Dewey's work, values are subject to exactly the same processes of empirical scientific inquiry.

The fundamental purpose of inquiry is to arrive at solutions to problem situations, or, in other words, to make indeterminate situations determinate. The aim is to discover "what works in the solution of concrete problems and furthers or enhances human life" (Hands 2001, p. 227), or what is an effective *instrument* for the solution of the problem concerned. This is an active and ongoing process of discovery. The goal here is not truth in the sense of correspondence to some external reality, but instrumentally effective knowledge. In this philosophy what is "true" is what has been shown to work.

In terms of social science, Dewey was well aware of the particular difficulties presented in the social realm. The complexity of the subject matter, the dynamic and evolving nature of society, the social context within which problems have to be solved, and the need for democratic agreement on solutions, all make problem solving much more difficult. Furthermore, the traditional separation of theory from practice has retarded progress. Dewey argues that among "practical" people there is often an assumption that a problem is already well defined and just needs a solution. This ignores the need for "controlled *analytic* observation" to properly define the problem. In natural science, a great deal of technique is employed in determining the nature of the problem, obtaining data, determining the pertinence of that data as evidence, ensuring their accuracy, and arranging them in "the order in which past inquiry has shown to be most likely to indicate appropriate modes of procedure" (Dewey 1938, p. 494). On the other hand, "scientific" people sometimes argue along simple positivistic lines that arriving at valid generalizations just requires the collection of sufficient factual information. Dewey points out that hypotheses are required in the selection and ordering of factual information: "A generalization is quite as much an antecedent of observation and assemblage of facts as it is a consequence of observing and assembling them" (Dewey 1938, p. 498).

Dewey also confronts the idea that reference to practical affairs must be excluded from science, that a social science can be developed separate from practice or application. In contrast, he argues that any problem of scientific inquiry that does not grow out of an actual or practical problem is "factitious" and scientifically "dead," just a form of "intellectual busy work:"

> In social inquiry, genuine problems are set only by actual social situations which are themselves conflicting and confused. Social conflicts and confusions exist in fact before problems for inquiry exist. The latter are intellectualizations in inquiry of these "practical" troubles and difficulties.... In fine, problems with which inquiry into social subject-matter is concerned must, if they satisfy the conditions of scientific method, (1) grow out of actual social tensions, needs, "troubles"; (2) have their subject-matter determined by the conditions that are material means of bringing about a unified situation, and (3) be related to some hypothesis, which is a plan and policy for existential resolution of the conflicting social situation.
>
> (Dewey 1938, pp. 498–499)

Dewey also sharply criticizes the "conceptual" or deductive approach that has dominated the history of economics. Classical economics, in his view, rested its claims to scientific standing upon certain ultimate "first truths" and on the possibility of "rigorous 'deduction'" of actual economic phenomena from these truths. These conceptions were not regarded as hypotheses to be employed in observation and tested by their consequences; they were seen as unquestionable truths. They were framed neither by reference to problems existing at a particular time and place nor as methods of solving currently existing problems, but as universal principles. "In consequence, the three indispensable logical conditions of conceptual subject-matter in scientific method were ignored; namely, (1) the status of theoretical conceptions as hypotheses which (2) have a directive function in control of observation and ultimate practical transformation of antecedent phenomena, and which (3) are tested and continually revised on the ground of the consequences they produce in existential application" (Dewey 1938, pp. 504–506).

Dewey was a strong proponent of experiments in social science. These would take the form of experiments in "social control." For Dewey, such experiments in control should not wait upon the prior development of a social science. He argues that the "reverse is the case," that the "building up of social science, that is a body of knowledge in which facts are ascertained in their significant relations" is dependent upon attempts at social control. "If we want something to which the name 'social science' may be given, there is only one way to go about it, namely by entering upon the path of social planning and control" (Dewey 1931, pp. 276–277). The primary goal of social science endeavor, then, is not the development of some consistent body of general theory, but to solve problems. Dewey does not claim that an instrumental social science can become a science in the same sense as physics, given the particular nature of the social phenomena it deals with. Social science can, however, meet the logical conditions of scientific inquiry; it can be a science.

Institutional Economics

When one examines the institutionalist literature on economic research one finds certain terms and related concepts repeated frequently. In previous work, I have described the institutionalist program as one of "science and social control" (Rutherford 2011). The very term "social control" implies a central concern with problems and their solution, and the reference to "science" here can be seen as having a definite instrumentalist meaning. Institutional economists thought of a scientific approach to the discipline in terms of being *problem centered, investigational, experimental,* and aimed at effective *social control.* Economics is presented as consisting of (1) identifying significant economic problems; (2) investigating such problems empirically; (3) developing hypotheses and policy ideas; (4) implementing policy conceived of as an experiment; and (5) achieving social control of the problem in question. Examples of this approach to social science within institutionalism abound, but I will primarily focus here on some salient examples taken from the work of Wesley Mitchell, Walton Hamilton, and John R. Commons.

Wesley Mitchell

Wesley Mitchell had a great deal of contact with John Dewey, first as a student at the University of Chicago and later as a colleague at Columbia University and The New School. Mitchell and his wife, Lucy Sprague Mitchell, also founded an experimental nursery and teacher training school in New York (The Bureau of Educational Experiments) along the lines of Dewey's educational theories.

Mitchell's driving motivation was his desire to create the kind of social science research that "could provide the knowledge that would allow mankind to control social forces," develop social policies, and solve important economic and social problems (Biddle 1998, p. 43). Mitchell's scholarly reputation was established with his 1913 volume *Business Cycles* (Mitchell 1913). Mitchell had chosen to work on a problem of pressing social and economic importance, but also one for which a significant amount of data were available. Mitchell describes the book as offering an "'analytic description' of the complicated processes by which seasons of business prosperity, crisis, depression, and revival come about in the modern world" (Mitchell 1913, p. vii). The first part of the book is a review of then current business cycle theories, including those of Beveridge, May, Hobson, Aftalion, Bouniatian, Spiethoff, Lescure, Veblen, Sombart, Carver, Fisher, and Johannsen, and a setting out of the problem. Business cycles are seen not as occasional events due to special causes, but to some "inherent characteristic of economic organization or activity." The multiple different proposed explanations led Mitchell to believe that there was little point in trying to test each one in turn. What is required is "clear comprehension of the facts." The existing theories indicate "certain facts to be looked for, certain analyses to be made, certain arrangements to be tried" (Mitchell 1913, pp. 6, 20).

Part two of the book is made up of "the facts of the case:" statistical data dealing with cycles in the United States, England, France, and Germany between 1890 and 1911. The data include prices, wages, interest rates, share prices, business volumes, currency, the central banks, savings, investment, profits, and bankruptcies. This is followed by the third part: the "analytic description" of the "rhythm of business activity" that describes how each phase of the cycle leads into the next, based largely on the leads and lags in the movements of prices and wages, profit expectations on the part of businesspeople, and the behavior of the banking system. In order to improve the working of the system, Mitchell suggests changes to the banking system to prevent panics, countercyclical government and railway purchases, and Irving Fisher's plans for a stabilized dollar, but puts as much emphasis on improving methods of forecasting (Mitchell 1913, pp. 586–596).

Mitchell continued to work on the problem of business cycles. In 1921, a sharp downturn in the economy prompted the formation of a Committee on Business Cycles as part of the President's Conference. The Committee involved the then recently formed National Bureau under Mitchell's directorship to take on the job of reporting on the "facts of unemployment and the leading plans which have been suggested for preventing or mitigating it" (Mitchell 1923). The study was allowed only five months, a circumstance that Mitchell felt was "a reflection of an under-developed public appreciation of the social importance of careful study as the basis for social action." Despite the need for more research, Mitchell argued that attempts at forecasting cycles or engaging in policy were not premature:

> if forecasts are based upon the best analysis which can now be made of past business experience, they constitute a step in the process of winning more knowledge. No forecast is more instructive than one which proves wrong, provided the reason for its failure can be ascertained.
>
> (Mitchell 1923, p. 17)

Possible policies included "long-range planning of public works, a change in the policy of banks regarding credit ratios, or the establishment of a novel form of unemployment insurance." The results of such policies may be uncertain:

> But if we never act in social matters until we have perfect assurance regarding the consequences which will follow, we shall never act at all. Social experimentation, based on clearly thought out hypotheses and accompanied by careful record-keeping, is one of the essential processes in increasing social knowledge and gaining social control.
>
> (Mitchell 1923, p. 18)

In 1923, Mitchell launched a new attack on the problem of business cycles at the National Bureau. The first volume produced, *Business Cycles: The Problem and its Setting,* appeared in 1927. The book can be seen as an updating and considerable expansion of the first part of Mitchell's 1913 work. As the title suggests, the book is intended to provide a working definition of the problem, develop hypotheses to guide the factual investigation, and discuss the available sources of information: the "defining the problem" stage of Dewey's instrumental method. Again, Mitchell indicates his goal is to provide an "analytic description" of the cycle. In Mitchell's view, cycles do not have a single cause or set of causes: in the course of a cycle causes become effects that become causes. Mitchell also links this approach to the use of statistical methods as "what time series can be made to show are functional relationships" only. Causality is something that is read into the statistics, although neither does he suggest too "stiff" a refusal to employ causal expressions (Mitchell 1927, pp. 54–55). As a preliminary way of dealing with the maze of processes, Mitchell indicates that he will organize discussion around the effect of each factor on the current and prospective profits of businesses, but in the final analytic description "we shall concentrate attention on the net resultants of interrelated changes in many variables and relegate causal analysis to incidental uses" (Mitchell 1927, p. 471).

The working definition Mitchell arrives at is "Business cycles are a species of fluctuations in economic activities of organized communities. The adjective 'business' restricts the concept to fluctuations in activities which are systematically conducted on a commercial basis. The noun 'cycles' bars out fluctuations which do not recur with a measure of regularity" (Mitchell 1927, p. 468). The working plans include the use of existing theories, business annals, and statistical series in order to find what features have been characteristic of all or most cycles. Statistical investigations must be guided by rational hypotheses. The investigation aims at answering the question: "How do business cycles run their course?" rather than "What causes business cycles?" (Mitchell 1927, pp. 469–470).

In reply to a letter from J. M. Clark asking about his method, Mitchell argued that the behavior of economic agents is often more complex than it would appear from simply deducing behavior from simple assumptions such as the importance of profit for the businessperson: "There is much in the working of business technique which I should never think of if I were not always turning back to observation" (Mitchell 1928, p. 415). Scientific method for Mitchell consisted of "the patient processes of observation and testing—always critical testing—of the relations between the working hypotheses and the processes observed." This involves theorizing, but the place for theorizing is "*inside* the investigation," rather than thinking out "a deductive scheme and then verifying *that*" (Mitchell 1928, pp. 413–415).

Mitchell's project did eventually produce *Measuring Business Cycles* (Burns and Mitchell 1946). Here Mitchell extended his criticism of standard deductive methodologies. First, empirical testing may simply be neglected. Second,

the simplifying assumptions may give the theory only a "problematic relation" to real-world data and make it in practical terms untestable. Third,
even if it is testable, the researcher will focus on only those processes on
which it "centers attention," meaning that many other theories could be similarly verified. Finally, the researcher may suffer from a verification bias and
adduce only that evidence that supports his case (Burns and Mitchell 1946,
pp. 8–9). This book represents a vast expansion and updating of the second
part of the 1913 volume establishing "the facts of the case." The intent was to
follow this book with a final volume, expanding on the third part of the 1913
volume, and laying out the final analytic description of the rhythm of business activity. This work was not completed before Mitchell's death in 1948.
It would not have contained *a* theory of business cycles, but an attempt to
show "what cyclical behavior is characteristic of economic activities" (Burns
and Mitchell 1946, p.10).[1]

In the interim, the experience of the Great Depression led Mitchell to
develop his ideas concerning policy experimentation. Mitchell was clear in
his view that new forms of social control were necessary to deal with the
problem of business cycles and he suggested a form of national planning.
Previous efforts at planning he criticized as being either "piecemeal" and
overlooking the interdependencies of social processes, or "emergency planning in the face of impending disaster" done with too little time to "use
what wisdom we have." Mitchell suggests a National Planning Board with
advisory powers. The Board could conduct research through its own staff or
other agencies and advise on policy "proceeding in an experimental fashion"
(Mitchell 1935, pp. 99–102). Such a Board would have to be a continuing
one as "social problems are ever assuming new forms." It would also face the
problem of unclear or conflicting social purposes:

> In a democratic country national planners would have to serve as an
> agency for accomplishing what the majority desired. But by throwing
> light upon the consequences that different lines of action would pro-
> duce they could contribute much toward making social valuations more
> rational. Perhaps in the long run the chief gain from trying to plan
> national policies in the light of their probable consequences would be
> the attainment of a more valid scale of social values than now prevails
> among us.
>
> (Mitchell 1936, p. 135)

Walton Hamilton

Walton Hamilton was first exposed to Dewey's thinking by Charles H.
Cooley who had been a student of Dewey's and was Hamilton's teacher at
the University of Michigan. Later, Hamilton had "many years association
in the writings of Mr. Wesley C. Mitchell who had been very close to Mr.
Dewey."[2]

Hamilton was one of institutionalism's first and strongest advocates of the social control of industry. Hamilton's 1918 American Economic Association paper that first introduced the profession at large to what he called the "institutional approach to economic theory" takes the position that anything that "aspires to the name of economic theory" should be "relevant to the problem of control" (Hamilton 1919a, p. 311). This idea of social control involves an economics that concerns itself with "gathering facts and formulating principles necessary to an intelligent handing" of economic problems. The "problems" that Hamilton had in mind can be found in his text book *Current Economic Problems* (1919b) and include such items as business cycles, railway regulation, monopoly and unfair competition, unemployment and economic insecurity more generally, trade unions, industrial conflict, and labor law. The educational programs in economics that Hamilton developed, first at Amherst and then at the Robert Brookings Graduate School were heavily problem centered. The program at Brookings was described as being itself an "experimental" one. Hamilton's stated aim in these programs was to give attention to "problems rather than disciplines" and "relevant inquiries rather than academic categories." Hamilton intended his programs to "teach the art of handling problems" (Hamilton 1926a). Course titles included such as "Types of Industrial Control" and "The Ends and Means of Social Control." Hamilton talked of the economic system being subject to direction and control, and best directed "by knowledge of specific problems and the facts of the case" (Rutherford 2011, pp. 172–173). What he offered his students was "an invitation to detailed study" and participation in the "intelligent direction of social change" (Hamilton 1926a).[3] The mention of "detailed study" is noteworthy, as for Hamilton, the details of industrial and business practice mattered a great deal.

Over his career, Hamilton involved himself in numerous investigations of specific problems including irregular employment and low wages, the bituminous coal industry, medical care, the broadcasting industry, consumer protection, the price policies of large corporations, anti-trust, patents, and business regulation generally. His view was that the unregulated market was failing to provide acceptable results in these areas and more. His main concerns were with the welfare of workers and consumers, and of raising the standard of living.

Hamilton's work on the coal industry is an interesting case. It had been widely accepted for some time that the bituminous coal industry was a serious problem area, and issues surrounding the coal industry became a particular area of investigation at Brookings. Hamilton worked with his colleague Helen Wright to produce two books on the industry. The first book sought to outline the present state of the industry and the factors responsible for that state of affairs. They find the bituminous coal industry characterized by persistent excess capacity, irregular operation, unsafe working conditions, low wages, strikes, and labor unrest. Hamilton and Wright note that the industry is competitive, but competition has not brought about a stable equilibrium but a situation of "chaos." This state of affairs they attribute to technological changes increasing productivity combined with a cost structure of high overheads and bankruptcy laws that allow for reorganizations and that do not eliminate excess capacity from the industry. Individual mine operators are simply trying to survive as best they can, but the aggregate result is the "evil" of too much capacity and low profitability (Hamilton and Wright 1925; Hamilton 1926b).

Hamilton and Wright produced a follow up book in 1928 detailing a proposed solution. This solution is a modified version of a proposal made for the British coal industry by Henry Clay. Hamilton and Wright suggested the creation of a single United States Coal Corporation with control divided equally between representative bodies of workers and consumers. Shares in existing coal companies would be exchanged for bonds in the new, separating control from the right to income from capital. Hamilton and Wright were aware of the controversial nature of these proposals and of the difficulties of implementation, but their hypotheses did provoke discussion and it was quite widely accepted that centralization of the industry was required. The coal industry came under the National Recovery Administration codes during the New Deal, and Hamilton was himself a member of the Consumer's Advisory Board of the NRA. The negotiations over the coal code were extremely difficult and fraught, and the result was a relatively weak attempt at control of wages, prices, and production, but at the same time it embodied a move toward the treatment of the coal industry as a public utility (Johnson 1966). With the demise of the NRA code system as a result of the Supreme Court decision in the *Schechter* case, the regulation of the coal industry was continued with the passage of the Bituminous Coal Conservation Act of 1935 (Guffey Coal Act), described by one correspondent as "Hamilton's Coal Bill."[4] This Act created the Bituminous Coal Commission to regulate prices, wages, working conditions, allocate production, and create a code of competition. It also contained a provision for consumer representation. The bill levied a tax on coal but with all but one percent rebated for compliance. The bill has been described as "very neat: a bona fide panacea" (Watkinson 1987, p. 104), but it too ran into legal difficulty at the hands of the Supreme Court on the grounds that wages and working conditions were a result of local conditions. A replacement bill removing the contentious elements, but retaining the control of prices and production and the system of tax and tax rebate, was passed in 1937.

The Act cannot be said to have been entirely successful, given the complexities of the industry, but Hamilton responded to criticism of the Act by arguing that such criticisms indicated only the need for refinements and adjustments to the regulations, and not an abandonment of the effort while still in its "experimental stage." The Act is "an instrument fitted to an economic function," and while it has not "yet hit upon just that detail of policy through which its objective is to be gained" the experiment should be continued (Hamilton 1941). Hamilton's arguments for continuation were not successful, but the problems of the coal industry did not disappear.

A second example of Hamilton's investigations and experimental thinking is his work on price policies and anti-trust. The idea for the price policies work came initially in connection with a desire to study the working of the NRA codes[5] and was directed by Hamilton for the President's Cabinet Committee on Price Policy. The demise of the NRA codes caused a shift in plans, but the studies were continued (Hamilton and Associates 1938).

Hamilton's price studies are difficult to summarize or make generalizations about, but this is his point. Hamilton argues that industries are not alike, they have their own particular sets of practices, usages, and conventions that have grown up within the trade. They differ in the scale of enterprises, in the number of competitors, in the structure of costs, in the existence of joint products, in the arrangements made with suppliers and distributors, in the impacts of new technology or new regulations, in the methods of advertising and packaging, and in the particular methods used to confine or limit competition. Each industry's pattern is also undergoing continuous change (Hamilton and Associates 1938). Significantly, Hamilton argues that there is no sharp line of demarcation between competition and monopoly, "nor even a line running from perfect competition through monopolistic competition, oligopoly, duopoly, to pure monopoly on which particular cases may be set down." To do so is to make "hypothetical economic phenomena the subject of mathematical exercises." The "trick may be pulled off; but the result is not a picture of the pragmatic reality called industry" (Hamilton and Associates 1938, p. 23).

Right at the time of the publication of this work, Hamilton was appointed as Special Assistant to Thurman Arnold who had been put in charge of the Antitrust Division of the Department of Justice. Hamilton immediately saw a connection between his price studies and the direction he felt anti-trust enforcement should go. In Hamilton's view, the studies had two main purposes: (1) to help understand how prices are actually made in practice, to investigate "what lies back of a price—to make it high or low—to restrict or enlarge supply—to bring it within the reach of the few or the many" (Hamilton 1936), and (2) to provide a proper factual basis for the consideration of business regulation and anti-trust. On Arnold's appointment, he wrote to his publishers that Arnold "insists that the Department of Justice must get down to concretions, deal with each industry separately, and shape the Anti-Trust Acts in such a way as to bring them into accord with the web of industrial usage," an "application of the approach worked out in *Price and Price Policies.*"[6]

The road towards industrial government runs by way of authority and the particular. A proper freedom of collective action, within strict limits of public interest, must be accorded the agencies of business. The state in formulating public policy, must have a wide discretion, and statutes should be written in the broadest of terms. But a way of order and a program of control can be crowded into no set formula. The general standards of industrial code and legislative standard must be adapted to the shifting circumstances of particular industries. Since usage is forever on the make the exercise of authority must be grounded in a continuing exploration of industrial arrangements.

(Hamilton and Associates 1938, p. 555)

In line with Hamilton's hopes, Arnold did pursue a very active anti-trust policy and did adopt a case-by-case approach based on close study of conditions in each specific industry. Hamilton was involved in a number of cases some of which related to his previous work or the studies done in *Price and Price Policies*. For example, the cases against the automobile industry, the dairy industry, the oil industry, and the American Medical Association.[7] In addition, Hamilton was closely involved in the case against the motion picture industry and in the substantial investigation into the abuse of the patent system to limit competition.

Apart from his involvement in specific cases, Hamilton developed a series of proposals for the reform of the anti-trust system. He argued for a shift from a legalistic to an administrative basis, and for a development of the advisory opinion and consent decree to allow for a "code of industrial behavior to be approved in advance." Government and industry would cooperate in developing "a line of business activity which is believed to accord with public policy" (Hamilton and Till 1940b, p. 19). Such agreements would be subject to change with changing conditions. Hamilton realized that such a system could not come into force "full blown" but "must begin as a cautiously experimental power" (Hamilton and Till 1940a, p. 108).

Hamilton's proposals went further than Arnold was willing to go, particularly as Arnold thought retaining the threat of prosecution was important, and was not keen on a wholesale shift to an administrative system. But Arnold did utilize consent decrees where "defendants proposed industry-wide relief that fully restored competition beyond what could be achieved through a successful prosecution or civil action by the government and the defendants permitted meaningful monitoring by the government" (Waller 2004, pp. 580–581). He also instituted a policy "by which businesses interested in ascertaining the legality of future action could seek the opinion of the Antitrust Division regarding its enforcement intentions toward the proposed conduct. In return, the business could count on not being charged criminally, even if the government ultimately opposed the conduct" (Waller 2004, p. 581), exactly as Hamilton had suggested.

Hamilton's *Price and Price Policies* was critically reviewed by Vernon Mund for its failure to utilize standard theoretical categories. For Mund, the theories of competition and monopoly are abstractions from the concrete (Mund 1939). For Hamilton, nothing like perfect competition or pure monopoly can be found in practice, and to impose such categories on the data is to engage in dogma not industrial inquiry.

In the social studies there is a host of honest workers who are willing to don overalls, do exciting drudgery, and shape findings to reality. Their emergent work, from tentative hypothesis to tentative hypothesis, is at once descriptive and analytical, factual as well as theoretical. But in the philosophy of Mr. Mund and his kind there is no place for such things as another set of postulates, concepts fashioned out of concretions, the joyous ride into the winds, the story of how it all came about, the mores of industries, the usage that becomes an institution, the spirited inquiry that raises more questions than ever it answers. A study of industrial folk-ways is taboo because the folk-ways of a fundamentalist faith forbid.

(Hamilton 1939, p. 104)

John R. Commons

John R. Commons seems to have come to the pragmatism of Charles Peirce and John Dewey through his own reading. Part of his education was at Johns Hopkins, but he did not overlap with Peirce. From Peirce, Commons took the concept of the "active mind," and from Peirce's essay "How to Make Our Ideas Clear" his notion of "scientific pragmatism" as a method of investigation. Peirce's meaning was "if a *theory* 'works' when tested by experiments and verified by others, then the *theory* is true and right, so far as present knowledge is concerned and all the known facts are included." Dewey's inclusion of the ethical element of "*desirable social* consequences" Commons called "social pragmatism:" the "pragmatism of human beings—the subject matter of the science of economics" (Commons 1934a, pp. 150–151).[8]

Commons and his students[9] did huge amounts of investigation into issues involving labor unions and labor issues in general. This work, however, was always directed toward a practical end involving such issues as collective bargaining, unemployment, minimum wages, hours of labor, health and safety, social insurance, and the administration of labor law (see Commons and Andrews 1916). Paul and Elizabeth Raushenbush describe Commons' appeal to students as being due to his interest in "applying academic insights to the problems of the day," and trying to "use his brains, and enlist the brains of his students too, in seeking solutions of economic problems." Students were attracted as they "were being invited to participate in an attempt to deal with difficult problems on an intelligent and practical basis," and to engage in what they called "action research" (Raushenbush and Raushenbush 1979, pp. 3–9). In the introductory chapter to his *Institutional Economics* (1934), Commons himself described his active involvement in labor and other policy issues, from immigration to monetary policy—beginning in 1883 with his first membership in a labor union—as fifty years of participation in experiments (Commons 1934a, pp. 3, 9). Commons and his students had considerable success in developing legislation on such matters as civil service reform, public utility regulation, workman's compensation, unemployment insurance, and social security. His experimentalist point of view, derived from his efforts at deciding disputes and reconciling conflicting interests, principles, and purposes, was also the source of his investigational framework of transactions, going concerns, working rules, and reasonable values. All of these concepts came out of his investigations and attempts to implement policy.

Commons' efforts concerning workmen's compensation provide one example. It was widely recognized at the time that the old common law method of dealing with workplace accidents was failing. The Courts' interpretation of contributory negligence resulted in claims for compensation for injury being denied or substantially reduced. Wisconsin did have safety legislation but it was not effective. Commons found that in 1911 well over a million dollars was paid in insurance premiums by employers, ten thousand accidents occurred, 100 being fatal and the rest causing disability of seven days or more, and yet barely $300,000 reached only ten percent of the injured employees or their dependents (Commons 1913). Commons told his students that he regarded the existing law as inadequate and wanted to have a proposal on "what to do about safety" ready for the upcoming legislative session. He and his students researched the legislation passed in European and other countries. According to Commons' autobiography, he had fifty undergraduates speaking half a dozen languages, supervised in groups by graduates "charting up, in large sheets hung on the walls the labor laws of all countries" (Commons 1934b, p. 129). Commons also conducted a great deal of legal research on the characteristics the legislation would have to have in order to gain sufficient support to be passed by the State legislature and withstand legal challenge in the courts.

The Wisconsin legislation set up the Industrial Commission of Wisconsin which was to both administer and enforce factory safety. Instead of attempting to specify a detailed list of safety requirements the act simply stated that the employer had a responsibility to protect the life, safety, health, and welfare of employees, the Commission being authorized to draw up specific rules. The Commission put a great deal of emphasis on accident prevention, so that inspectors could work with employers to improve safety, rather than simply search for violations. This is an example of the mutuality Commons always sought in his solutions to problems.

Commons thought of commissions such as the Wisconsin Industrial Commission as a "fourth branch of government." It is administrative, but it also has functions of "investigation and research." The research and investigation it undertakes is neither academic nor journalistic, it is "constructive investigation" and should lead to "such administration of the law that those enjoined to obey it would respect and support it." As a part of his effort to write a bill that would allow the Commission to be able to experiment with rules and, at the same time be acceptable to the legislature and courts, Commons developed his ideas of "reasonable regulation through constructive investigation" and made the key step of defining reasonable as "best practice" (Commons 1913, pp. 251–253; Brandeis 1972, p. 128).

A further example is the work done by Commons on unemployment. He begins by discussing different types of unemployment, turnover, seasonal, and cyclical, with his focus on the last two. His attack on the issue was similarly two-fold: to attempt to pass unemployment compensation legislation of a type that would contain incentives for employers to stabilize their own employment, and to work on measures that would operate through the Federal Reserve System to stabilize the "credit cycle." Commons' aim was always to make employment constant, and not to accept unemployment as inevitable, or to simply provide a dole. Commons' unemployment compensation bill (the Huber bill of 1921) was worked out after a careful examination of European experience with unemployment insurance schemes (Commons 1921). Commons' scheme was modeled on his workman's compensation law: a mutual insurance fund is created operated by employers with contributions from employers only. Contribution rates would be set on the basis of claims experience giving an incentive to employers to maintain steady employment. In addition, bankers would be incentivized to be more cautious in their lending during inflationary times, in the knowledge that lay-offs would be expensive. The bill failed on the opposition of employers, but "Commons and his students made unemployment insurance a biennial issue in the Wisconsin legislature." The continued reintroduction of the Huber bill was itself an achievement in keeping the issue alive (Nelson 1967/1968, p. 119–120). On the side of the "credit cycle," Commons did a great deal of work in support of the Strong bill that proposed giving the Federal Reserve an explicit responsibility for the stabilization of prices. Commons developed statistical information, discussed the, then still recent, discovery and use of open market operations, and gave testimony (Commons 1927). The bill failed, but the mandate of the Federal Reserve was eventually expanded to include explicit recognition of price stability as a goal in the Federal Reserve Reform Act of 1977.

A renewed effort was made in 1931–1932 by Commons' students and colleagues Elizabeth Brandeis, Paul Raushenbush, and Harold Groves. The Huber bill system was amended to provide for separated reserves for each employer, so that each employer was responsible only for his own employees. If an employer provided steady work for his employees and his fund reached $75 per-worker he could cease further contributions (Raushenbush 1932). With the unemployment problem worsening, this bill (the Groves bill) passed the Wisconsin legislature early in 1932. The Wisconsin system also established an Advisory Committee initially to advise on administration. The Committee, however, was soon "advising about desirable legislative changes" and was later given a mandate to do so (Raushenbush and Raushenbush 1979, p. 73).

Commons himself continued his advocacy of commissions as agencies for investigation and experiment. Writing in 1939, he argued that the "pragmatic application" of the social sciences is to be found in the new field of administration: "Administration is pragmatic social philosophy. It brings together again, this time by methods of scientific investigation, the separated fields of economics, ethics and jurisprudence" (Commons 1939, p. 523). Commons argued that such commissions could fit within the American constitutional system, supplementing but not usurping the authority of legislatures or courts. This "fourth branch" of government "is an investigational branch" but its investigations are not "the mere search for truth, they are designed to improve conditions within the field assigned." They are investigational and inventive bodies but are themselves at the "experimental and debatable stage" and subject to "alarmed attacks." For Commons, this was "all the more reason" for the social sciences to "focus their investigations, and train their investigators within, this fourth department of the American experiment in government" (Commons 1939, pp. 529–531).

In his last book, *The Economics of Collective Action* (1950), Commons comes closest to laying out his investigational methods. He begins by defining economic activity in terms of collective action, individual action, transactions, and capitalism. Within this system of economic activity problems arise frequently in terms of conflicts of interest. Problems are approached initially in terms of the various aspects of economic activity, what Commons calls "simplified assumptions:" sovereignty, scarcity, efficiency, futurity, and custom. This step works to define the problem and organize further investigation. In this investigation, the units of the transaction and going concern are key, but also certain *relativities* have to be kept in mind: similarities and differences between cases, working rules, part-whole relations, and historical developments. Solutions to problems generally involve the creation of institutions capable of generating a reconciliation of conflicting interests, relating to Commons' theory of reasonable value. It is noteworthy that the early drafts of *Collective Action* were called *Investigational Economics* (Commons 1998).

Some Others

Hamilton, Mitchell, and Commons do not nearly exhaust the list of institutionalists who adopted pragmatic and instrumentalist ideas. Hamilton's colleague, Walter Stewart, spent a summer at Columbia to take courses from Dewey. Likewise, Rexford Tugwell, once at Columbia, took courses from Dewy and developed his ideas concerning the experimental method in economics, a notion he took to his own work in the New Deal (Tugwell 1924; Rutherford 2011, p. 235). Of course, many involved with the New Deal characterized it in experimental terms. Jerome Frank spoke of the New Deal as "an elaborate series of experiments which will seek to ascertain whether a social economy can be made to work for human welfare" undertaken by "experimentalist" lawyers and economists.[10] Morris Copeland, a student of Hamilton and J. M. Clark's wrote a long appendix to his PhD thesis on pragmatism with many references to Dewey and to the idea of "thinking as an instrument in the solution of a problematic situation."[11] Commons' student Edwin Witte defined institutional economics as based on problem solving and using a pragmatic approach (Witte 1954). Even J. M. Clark who was less empirical in his methods than most institutionalists called his approach a pragmatic one (Clark 1924). Clark always attempted to keep his theorizing as close to the facts as possible[12] and argued for an economics "actively relevant to the issues of its time" (Clark 1919). Clark's book *The Social Control of Business* (Clark 1926) was a major contribution to the institutionalist literature on social control. Many other examples could be given.

An Appraisal

The institutionalist emphasis on problem solving, investigation, experiment, and social control should be more than clear. If it is taken that the institutionalist notion of science in the interwar period was based on an interpretation of Dewey's instrumentalism, then it is apparent that many of the standard critiques of institutionalist work, made both then and since, are misconceived. The criticism of institutionalism as overly descriptive, lacking theory, or even anti-theoretical are all based on the application of logical positivist ideas to institutionalism. Institutionalists did do large amounts of empirical work but this was done not with the idea that generalizations would magically appear from masses of undirected data collectiôn, but that they would emerge from inquiries directed toward specific problems and guided by hypotheses as to the data of relevance for the problem concerned. If institutionalism is seen as the application of instrumentalist methods, then its successes and failures might be better seen as relating to the strengths and weaknesses of the Deweyian methodological program it adopted. This has added significance given the argument by Wade Hands that pragmatic and instrumental ideas are making a return to discussions concerning the philosophy of science (Hands 2001, p. 251, 2004).

The institutionalist program was aimed at the solution of economic problems or at successful social control. At the time the major issues facing economics and policy makers were matters of public utility regulation, monopoly, imperfect competition, business cycles, unemployment, and labor law. In terms of solutions to these problems, it would be hard to be critical of institutionalists as they were often successful, and many of their failures were not in their suggested solutions but in the political will to implement the policy "experiment" they proposed. Institutionalist work aimed at problem solving produced a vast array of legislation aimed at dealing with various perceived shortcomings of the market. It also produced a great deal of practical knowledge concerning the techniques of regulation and the work of commissions.

Moreover, the applied and practical work they did formed the basis for many further developments. Commons and Hamilton charted the interrelations of law and economics, contributing to what has become known as the first law and economics movement. Commons developed his own theoretical framework based on the transaction, an idea that has become part of transaction cost economics. Hamilton was one of the first to warn of the problems of agency capture, long before Stigler (Hamilton and Till 1940b, p. 25), an issue that, for Hamilton, was at least partly due to the lack of proper representation of the consumer interest on commissions. The tension between Hamilton's empirical price studies and Chamberlin's untestable monopolistic competition models resulted in the structure, conduct, performance approach to industrial organization (Rutherford 2011, pp. 317–319). Simon Kuznets' work at the NBER included the development of national income accounts, and Copeland later added flow of funds accounts. Mitchell's work on business cycles inspired J. M. Clark's accelerator theory and F. C. Mills' statistical work on price inflexibility. Mills' work, in turn, fed into the views of Rexford Tugwell and others in the New Deal that anticipated Keynes in a number of ways (Rutherford 2011, pp. 292–295). Institutionalists such as J. M. Clark also produced some very prescient criticisms of Keynesian models.

This is a considerable record of achievement, but thinking about Dewey's idea of social policy experiment in the light of institutionalist experience, and considering carefully the difficulties of social experimentation, does raise a number of issues. Mitchell pointed out that experimentation would require well thought out hypotheses and careful record keeping. He "held no brief" for experiments based on "emotional reaction to social ills" for "experimenters who do not count costs, proceed with caution, provide for recording results, or anticipate modifications" (Mitchell 1923, p. 18). Economic policies, however, even if initiated with an experimental intent may not live up to even Mitchell's conditions. Experiments get adopted, adjusted, or abandoned for political reasons, the carry through of the experiment over time may be lacking or become neglected, other conditions may change in ways hard to measure or even comprehend, and the complexity of the social world may confound the interpretation of results. Dewey himself argued:

> Wherever purposes are employed deliberately and systematically for the sake of a certain desired social results, there it is possible, within limits, to determine the connection between the human factor and the actual occurrence, and thus to get a complete social fact, namely the actual external occurrence in its human relationships. Prohibition, whether noble or not, is not an experiment in any intelligent scientific sense of the term. For it was undertaken without any effort to obtain the conditions of control which are essential to any experimental determination of fact. The Five Year Plan of Russia, on the other hand, whether noble or the reverse, has many of the traits of a social experiment, for it is an attempt to obtain certain specified social results by the use of specified definite measures, exercised under conditions of considerable, if not complete, control.
> (Dewey 1931, p. 276)

This sets an extraordinarily difficult standard for proper social experiments. It is also a point of view that may well be related to Dewey's extreme criticism of the market system. If one requires at least considerable control of experimental conditions for social experimentation to be valid, then anything less than "social planning" will not do. According to Dewey, if the social situation out of which facts emerge "is itself confused and chaotic" because it expresses "unregulated purpose and haphazard private intent" we shall "only add intellectual confusion to practical disorder" (Dewey 1931, p. 277).

As Wade Hands has noted, Dewey's political economy implies the desirability of a form of social democratic economic planning, and there is a clear tension between Dewey's pragmatic instrumentalism "with its fallibilism, context sensitivity, and anti-teleology," and his promotion of the idea that "it is possible to engage in wide scale social engineering and economic planning" (Hands 2004, p. 265). Some institutionalists, such as Rexford Tugwell, also endorsed economic planning, and Mitchell advocated an "advisory" National Planning Board, but none of them argued that national planning was a *prerequisite* to the experimental method. Rather, some form of planning (and there were many varieties suggested) was discussed in terms of it being a potential *solution* to macroeconomic problems. Similarly, most institutionalists, with the exceptions of Veblen and Ayres, accepted the instrumental importance of markets and saw their proposed social controls as supplementing and regulating the market, not replacing it. As Mitchell put it: the question is "how to make production for profit turn out a larger supply of useful goods under conditions more conducive to welfare?" (Mitchell 1922, p. 149).

This then raises a further question. If experimental conditions cannot be controlled in the way Dewey suggested, then does the experimental method hold the same promise in social science as in the natural sciences? If the answer is in the negative then the relative lack of "systematic theory" in the institutionalist literature may be due to this reason. My argument would be that the empirical and policy strengths of institutionalism as well as its relative theoretical weakness are alike the result of the methodological approach borrowed from Dewey.

This raises two final points. First, and despite what has been called Dewey's "latitudinarian" view of science, it is easy to agree with Hands that Dewey was not pluralistic enough (Hands 2004, p. 266). Not all problems in social science can be approached via the experimental method due to an inability to sufficiently control the experimental situation, or because the questions or problems involved may simply not be solvable by instrumental means. This is particularly the case where questions of fundamental values are involved. This suggests that social science will of necessity consist of a mix of methods both theoretical and empirical, non-experimental and experimental. Second, if, as Hands argues, ideas about scientific knowledge have moved in a direction more conducive to pragmatic ideas, it is to be hoped that the effect on economic practice will be to encourage both experimentalism and pluralism, and, just possibly, to taking the efforts of Dewey's earlier followers in economics as worthy of more serious attention.

Notes

1. A final volume *What Happens During Business Cycles* (Mitchell 1951) was produced after Mitchell's death based on a "progress report" he had produced.
2. Address was given by Walton Hamilton on the occasion of John Dewey's 80th birthday. Walton Hamilton Papers, Box 69, Folder 3.
3. These programs are discussed in more detail in Rutherford (2011).
4. Letter to Walton Hamilton from a correspondent at Yale Law School, signature page missing, 19 May 1933, Hamilton papers Box 66, Folder 6.
5. There was an increasing concern that the codes were aiding cartels and leading to higher prices.
6. Letter from Hamilton to Hugh Kelley, McGraw Hill, 11 May 1938. Hamilton Papers, Box 72, Folder 2.
7. Hamilton had been closely involved in the discussions surrounding the NRA Code for the petroleum industry, on the side of the consumer interest. Hamilton's previous involvement in the debates about medical care was substantial. He was a member of the Committee on the Costs of Medical Care and supported compulsory insurance and group practices. See Rutherford (2011, pp. 70–72; 79–80). Automobiles and milk were included in the price studies.
8. Aspects of Common's pragmatic instrumentalism are discussed by Biddle (1990, 1991).
9. It is really not possible to separate Commons' work from that of his students.
10. Except from an address given by Jerome N. Frank, General Counsel of the AAA, to the Association of American Law Schools, December 30, 1933. Walton Hamilton Papers, Box7, Folder 8.
11. Morris Copeland Papers, Box 8.
12. A good example would be Clark's book on overhead costs (Clark 1923). Writing to Mitchell, Clark said, "I sometimes think 'theory,' of the abstract sort, is a device for converting usefully-enlightening ideas about behavior and motivation into paper mechanisms whereby armchair theorists can grind out misleading results." Wesley Mitchell papers, Box 8, J. M. Clark Folder.

References

Archive Collections

Brookings Institution Archives, Brookings Institution, Washington DC.
Morris A. Copeland Papers, Butler Library, Columbia University, New York.
University of Wisconsin-Madison Archives, Oral History Project.
Walton Hamilton Papers, Tarlton Law Library, University of Texas, Austin.
Wesley Mitchell Papers, Butler Library, Columbia University, New York.

Books and Articles

Ayres, Clarence E. 1944. *The Theory of Economic Progress*. Chapel Hill, NC: University of North Carolina.
Biddle, Jeff. E. 1990. The Role of Negotiational Psychology in J. R. Commons's Proposed Reconstruction of Political Economy. *Review of Political Economy*, 2 (March): 1–25.
———. 1991. The Ideas of the Past as Tools for the Present: The Instrumental Presentism of John R. Commons. In JoAnne Brown and David Van Keuren, eds., *The Estate of Social Knowledge*. Baltimore, MD: Johns Hopkins.

————. 1998. Social Science and the Making of Social Policy: Wesley Mitchell's Vision. In Malcolm Rutherford, ed., *The Economic Mind in America: Essays in the History of American Economics*. London: Routledge.

Brandeis, Elizabeth. 1972. Interview #011 by Donna Taylor. University of Wisconsin-Madison Archives, Oral History Project.

Burns, Arthur F., and Wesley C. Mitchell. 1946. *Measuring Business Cycles*. New York, NY: NBER.

Clark, John M. 1919. Economic Theory in an Era of Social Readjustment. *American Economic Review*, 9 (March): 280–290.

————. 1923. *Studies in the Economics of Overhead Costs*. Chicago, IL: University of Chicago Press.

————. 1924. The Socializing of Theoretical Economics. In Rexford G. Tugwell, ed., *The Trend of Economics*. Port Washington: Kennikat Press (1971): 73–102.

————. 1926. *The Social Control of Business*. Chicago, IL: University of Chicago Press.

Commons, John R. 1913. Constructive Investigation and the Industrial Commission of Wisconsin. Reprinted in Malcolm Rutherford and Warren Samuels, eds., *John R. Commons: Selected Essays*. London: Routledge (1996): 251–267.

————. 1921. Unemployment: Compensation and Prevention. Reprinted in Malcolm Rutherford and Warren Samuels, eds., *John R. Commons: Selected Essays*. London: Routledge (1996): 288–298.

————. 1927. Price Stabilization and the Federal Reserve System. Reprinted in Malcolm Rutherford and Warren Samuels, eds., *John R. Commons: Selected Essays*. London: Routledge (1996): 386–396.

————. 1934a. *Institutional Economics: Its Place in Political Economy*. New York, NY: Macmillan.

————. 1934b. *Myself*. New York: Macmillan.

————. 1939. Twentieth Century Economics. Reprinted in Malcolm Rutherford and Warren Samuels, eds., *John R. Commons: Selected Essays*. London: Routledge (1996): 520–531.

————. 1950. *The Economics of Collective Action*. New York, NY: Macmillan.

————. 1998. "Investigational Economics." Edited and with an introduction by Warren J. Samuels. *Research in the History of Economic Thought and Methodology*, Archival Supplement 7.

Commons, John R. and John B. Andrews. 1916. *Principles of Labor Legislation*. New York, NY: Harper and Brothers.

Dewey, John. 1931. Social Science and Social Control. *New Republic*, 67 (July 29): 276–277.

————. 1938. *Logic: The Theory of Inquiry*. New York, NY: Henry Holt.

Hands, D. Wade. 2001. *Reflection Without Rules: Economic Methodology and Contemporary Science Theory*. Cambridge: Cambridge University Press.

————. 2004. Pragmatism, Knowledge, and Economic Science: Deweyan Pragmatic Philosophy and Contemporary Economic Methodology. In E. L. Khali, ed., *Dewey, Pragmatism, and Economic Knowledge*. London: Routledge: 255–270.

Hamilton, Walton H. 1919a. The Institutional Approach to Economic Theory. *American Economic Review*, 9 (March): 309–318.

————, ed. 1919b. *Current Economic Problems*, revised edition. Chicago, IL: University of Chicago.

————. 1926a. Report to the Board of Trustees, The Robert Brookings Graduate School of Economics and Government, April 30, 1926. Appendix 3 to Harold G.

Moulton, The History of the Organization of the Brookings Institution, June 1928. Brookings Institution Archives, Item 17, Formal and Informal Histories of the Brookings Institution, 1928-1966, Box 1, File: Memoranda on the Early History of the Brookings Institution.

———. 1926b. The Problem of Bituminous Coal. *American Labor Legislation Review*, 16: 217–229.

———. 1936. Why the Price Studies? *The Consumer*, 1 (January 15): 6–9.

———. 1939. Industrial Inquiry and Sectarian Dogma. *American Economic Review*, 29 (March): 102–106.

———. 1941. Coal and the Economy—A Demurrer. *Yale Law Journal*, 50 (February): 595–621.

Hamilton, Walton H. and Associates. 1938. *Price and Price Policies*. New York, NY: McGraw Hill.

Hamilton, Walton H. and Irene Till. 1940a. *Antitrust in Action*. Temporary National Economic Committee, Monograph No. 16. Washington, DC: Government Printing Office.

———. 1940b. Antitrust—The Reach After New Weapons. *Washington University Law Quarterly*, 26 (December): 1–26.

Hamilton, Walton H. and Helen R. Wright. 1925. *The Case of Bituminous Coal*. New York, NY: Macmillan.

———. 1928. *A Way of Order for Bituminous Coal*. New York, NY: Macmillan.

Johnson, James P. 1966. Drafting the NRA Code of Fair Competition for the Bituminous Coal Industry. *Journal of American History*, 53 (December): 521–541.

Mitchell, Wesley C. 1913. *Business Cycles*. Berkeley, CA: University of California.

———. 1922. Making Goods and Making Money. Reprinted in Wesley C. Mitchell, *The Backward Art of Spending Money*. New York, NY: Augustus Kelley (1950): 137–148.

———. 1923. Unemployment and Business Fluctuations. *American Labor Legislation Review*, 13 (March): 15–22.

———. 1927. *Business Cycles: The Problem and its Setting*. New York, NY: NBER.

———. 1928. Letter to John M. Clark. Reprinted in John M. Clark, *Preface to Social Economics*. New York, NY: Farrar and Rinehart (1936): 410–416.

———. 1935. The Social Sciences and National Planning. Reprinted in Wesley C. Mitchell, *The Backward Art of Spending Money*. New York, NY: Augustus Kelley (1950): 83–102.

———. 1936. Intelligence and the Guidance of Economic Evolution. Reprinted in Wesley C. Mitchell, *The Backward Art of Spending Money*. New York, NY: Augustus Kelley (1950): 103–136.

———. 1951. *What Happens During Business Cycles*. New York, NY: NBER.

Mund, Vernon. 1939. Comment by Professor Mund. *American Economic Review*, 29 (March): 106.

Nelson, Daniel. 1967/1968. The Origins of Unemployment Insurance in Wisconsin. *The Wisconsin Magazine of History*, 51 (Winter): 109–121.

Raushenbush, Paul A. 1932. Wisconsin's Unemployment Compensation Act. *American Labor Legislation Review*, 22 (March): 11–18.

Raushenbush, Paul A. and Elizabeth Brandeis Raushenbush. 1979. *Our "U. C." Story*. Madison: np.

Rutherford, Malcolm. 2011. *The Institutionalist Movement in American Economics, 1918-1947: Science and Social Control*. Cambridge: Cambridge University Press.

Tugwell, Rexford G. 1924. Experimental Economics. In Rexford G. Tugwell, ed., *The Trend of Economics*. Port Washington: Kennikat Press (1971): 371–422.

Waller, Spencer Weber. 2004. The Antitrust Legacy of Thurman Arnold. *St. John's Law Review*, 78 (Summer): 569–613.

Watkinson, James D. 1987. An Exercise in Futility: The Guffey Coal Act of 1935. *Pennsylvania History: A Journal of Mid-Atlantic Studies*, 54 (April): 103–114.

Witte, Edwin E. 1954. Institutional Economics as Seen by an Institutional Economist. *Southern Economic Journal*, 21 (October): 131–140.

9 E. F. Schumacher's *Metanoia*

Rejecting *Homo* Oeconomicus, 1950–1977

Robert Leonard[1]

Introduction

In 1972, at the invitation of Joan Robinson, the sixty-one-year-old E. F. Schumacher made a foray into the field of economic methodology: "Does Economics Help? – An Exploration of Meta-economics".[2] Presented at the annual meetings of Section F (Economics) of the British Association at Leicester, it was a quietly blistering attack on the economics discipline, criticising its assumptions and methods. Not only were economists impotent before the world's developmental and ecological problems, he said, but they were actually exacerbating them. In their commitment to economic growth and "modernisation", he implied, the high priests of the "dismal science" were destroyers of tradition and purveyors of cultural and environmental upheaval. As intended, his talk provoked consternation.

Some thirty years earlier, when Schumacher and Robinson (1903–1983) had previously shared the stage, things had been rather different. That was in May 1943, in the middle of the war, at a "Full Employment Conference" at the Royal Hotel in London where, amongst other speakers, Robinson asked, "What is a Planned Economy?", and Schumacher spoke about "Full Employment. The Problem in its International Setting".[3] At that time, both were ardent Keynesians, lying well to the left of centre, close to Michal Kaleçki, committed to economic growth and the establishment of the welfare state. Part of the "brains trust" assembled by Wm. Beveridge, and working in tandem with Nicholas Kaldor and Frank Pakenham, they acted as ghost-writers for *Full Employment for a Free Society* (1944).

During those three decades, therefore, Schumacher had undergone a considerable transformation: from being a conventional, and, indeed, highly capable, economist to becoming a disciplinary heretic and outsider. By the time he arrived at Leicester, the former Fabian, once committed to growth and international trade, had turned against not only the world of commerce and consumption but also, in large measure, the economics discipline itself. A year later, 1973, he published his *Small is Beautiful*, with its pregnant subtitle, *A Study of Economics as if People Mattered*, and found himself becoming a figurehead of a growing counter-cultural and environmental movement.[4]

DOI: 10.4324/9781003266051-13

In the following pages, we consider the evolution in Schumacher's think-ing between the 1950s and the 1970s, thereby illuminating his critical stance at the British Association. We will see that, while environmental and cul-tural considerations played a part in his change, the fundamental cause was a deep transformation of the *self* that took place in Schumacher over these years. Beginning in or around 1950, he entered a troubled phase of self-examination and began to pose existential questions of the deepest kind, concerning man and his place in the universe. Gradually, and indirectly, he went from being the hardened atheist of his wartime years to ultimately becoming the religious man that accepted Robinson's invitation in 1972. In turn, this personal transformation radically affected his view of the field of economics, making him increasingly critical of both its underlying con-ception of man, *homo oeconomicus*, and the role it exerted in the modern world.

In Part I, we consider the 1950s, when turning inward, Schumacher became seriously immersed in Buddhism, yoga and the esoteric teachings of G. I. Gurdjieff and P. D. Ouspensky. These interests carried him to Burma in 1955, where he spent a life-changing three-month sojourn. By the close of the fifties, still involved in Gurdjieff-Ouspensky, but now engaged with Traditionalist authors such as R. Guénon, F. Schuon and A. Coomaraswamy, Schumacher was speaking about his "double-life" – feeling the dissonance between his professional obligations as hard-nosed Coal Board economist and his growing ethical misgivings about modern society.

Part II concerns the next decade and opens with the tragic loss of Schumacher's still-young wife to cancer in 1960. Reinforced by his reading of R. H. Tawney and Dorothy Sayers, this change nudged him closer to Christianity and hardened his criticism of modern industrial and commer-cial life. By the mid-sixties, he had learned to see economics as an analytic approach that, far from being universally valid, was historically contingent and corrosive, promoting a particularly narrow view of man and overem-phasizing the economic aspect of life in society. Pursuing a reassessment catalysed by his time in Burma, he increasingly viewed economists, in their acquiescence in the pursuit of comfort, efficiency and material gain, as enemies of the belief-systems that were traditionally central to the lives of men. By 1972, when he stood before his former brethren at Joan Robinson's conference, it was as a changed man: *homo oeconomicus* had become *homo viator*, concerned with destiny and salvation.

The Epilogue briefly considers Schumacher's writings after 1972 in the light of his great change. While *Small is Beautiful* was the collection of essays that captured the public's attention, the work he regarded as his most impor-tant was, in fact, *A Guide for the Perplexed* (1977), which was begun on his return from Burma but published only posthumously, after twenty years in the making. Its allusive description of his life journey provides fitting closure for our account.

The 1950s: *Homo Oeconomicus* or Higher Consciousness?

Son of economics mandarin, Hermann Schumacher (1868–1952), Fritz Schumacher originally arrived at Oxford from Germany in 1930, as a Rhodes Scholar, to study economics and politics. Following two years there, he spent a period at Columbia University, New York, as researcher and lecturer. Returning to Germany from mid-1934 to early 1937, he considered pursuing doctoral studies but worked primarily in finance and trade in the private sector. In 1937, no longer able to tolerate the climate under Nazism, he chose to return to Britain, where he worked in the City. Upon the outbreak of World War II, Schumacher's situation changed radically, when he found himself without a job and confined, as an enemy alien, and farm labourer, to an estate in Northamptonshire. Persisting nonetheless with evening and weekend writings on international economics, he came into contact with Keynes and, in 1943, was taken on as a researcher at the Oxford Institute of Statistics. There, under Michal Kaleçki, he worked with immigrés Thomas Balogh, Frank Burchardt and Kurt Mandelbaum on wartime economics, his own specialty being international monetary affairs. Looking back on those years decades later, his Beveridge Plan collaborator, Joan Robinson, recalled the conventional outlook of her younger economist colleague. Although he was not anti-human, she said, at the time "his attitude of mind was very much to get the leaders to make society efficient. He had a beautifully clear mind".[5]

Throughout the mid-forties, Schumacher engaged critically with Keynes' work on international financial arrangements, including the Plan later presented at Bretton Woods, and when Keynes died in 1946 it was he who wrote his obituary in *The Times*. Following a 1945 stint with the Strategic Bombing Survey, again with Kaldor, and also J. K. Galbraith and Tibor Scitovsky, Schumacher spent a further four years in Germany working on post-war reconstruction, with the British section of the Allied Control Commission. In 1950, he resettled in England, joining the National Coal Board. Then four years old, it was a symbolic organisation in Beveridge's Britain, overseeing the mining and ancillary activities at hundreds of previously private collieries.

The two decades Schumacher spent with the Coal Board were marked by a twofold development. On the one hand, he went from being initially neglected by his employer in the early years to becoming increasingly involved in defending the British coal industry. By the mid-sixties, as the NCB struggled to brake its decline in the face of competition from Middle Eastern oil, Schumacher had become a veritable *Man Friday* to the company's embattled director, Alfred Robens. He was important, not only for the public defence of continued coal production but also for the NCB's continued internal "rationalisation" of operations, through mechanisation of mining and careful coalface selection. So close and valuable was Schumacher to the Coal Board management that he was mockingly described as the "court jester" by the company's Director of Research, one Jacob Bronowski.[6]

On the other hand, however, Schumacher's inner life evolved in a direction that put him increasingly at odds with the world of economics and ultimately serve to undermine his relationship with the discipline. This began in the early fifties when, underutilised at the office and somewhat adrift personally, he was drawn into the "Fourth Way", the esoteric teachings of Greek-Armenian mystic, Gyorgy Gurdjieff (1866–1949), and his Russian disciple, Pyotr Ouspensky (1878–1947).[7] The Fourth Way was about self-improvement: it suggested that one's ordinary personality was little other than the expression of one's automatic, unthinking responses to external stimuli. Such behaviour was conditioned and machine-like, and not a reflection of the authentic, or essential, self. Only through an austere programme of self-observation, or "self-remembering", could one hope to achieve a higher form of consciousness, and come in contact with one's integral, or essential, "I". To embark upon such a training was to do the "Work".

In 1922, Gurdjieff had settled at Le Prieuré, a villa near Fontainebleau, where he attracted foreign visitors to his Institute for the Harmonious Development of Man. His erstwhile follower, Ouspensky, settled in London in 1921, where he too established a "Work" community. Among the well-known early Gurdjieffians were A. E. Orage, influential editor of the *New English Weekly*, who, like many others, for a while "gave up everything" in order to follow the Fourth Way, becoming Gurdjieff's emissary in New York; Katherine Mansfield, the New Zealand-born author, who actually died of TB at Le Prieuré, and Ogilvanna Lazovic, who in 1928 would marry architect Frank Lloyd Wright, on whom Gurdjieff became a significant influence.[8]

In the early 1950s, Schumacher avidly read Ouspensky – his *Tertium Organum* (1920), *A New Model of the Universe* (1931), *In Search of the Miraculous* (1947) and *The Psychology of Man's Possible Evolution* (1950).[9] However, with the Russian teacher having died in 1947, he entered a London "Work" scene dominated by two of his followers, Maurice Nicoll (1884–1954) and John G. Bennett (1897–1974). Nicoll was a Scottish-born neurologist and psychiatrist, who had studied with Carl Jung in 1912 and become an important English disciple. During World War I, he was a medic in the British army, treating the wounded at both Gallipoli and the Siege of Kut, in what is now Iraq. Under the pen-name, Martin Swayne, Nicoll wrote several books and novels, including *In Mesopotamia* (1918). In 1921, he met Ouspensky and, breaking off all relations with Jung, sold his Harley St. practice and moved to Le Prieuré in order to devote himself to Gurdjieff and the Work. Returning to London in 1923, he followed Ouspensky for the rest of the decade, before setting up his own study groups as of 1931. These he conducted in London and, for the last years of his life, at Great Amwell, his rambling home in Hertfordshire.

Schumacher appears to have read everything by Nicoll: the five volumes of his *Psychological Commentaries on the Teachings of Gurdjieff and Ouspensky* (1952–1956); *The New Man* (1950), which Schumacher and his mother even translated into German in 1953; *Living Time and the Integration of Life* (1952) and *The Mark* (1954).[10] In time, he would also read various works on Nicoll, including the 1961 portrait by his follower and private secretary, Beryl Pogson, and her own continuation of the Fourth Way teachings.[11] While it is unclear whether or not he attended Nicoll's "Work" weekends at Great Amwell, he did attend those organised by John Bennett at nearby Coombe Springs, in Surrey. In fact, Bennett and Schumacher shared a "coal" connection, with the former being involved in the British Coal Utilisation Association, which was devoted to finding more efficient ways of utilising the fossil fuel and was located at Coombe Springs.[12]

Some insight into the methods of the Fourth Way can be had from Nicoll's (1998 [1940]) "Simple Explanation of Work Ideas". The starting point is the distinction between the person one is, "oneself", and the person one can hope to become. This transformation is made possible through self-observation, or "self-remembering", i.e., learning to scrutinise oneself, as it were, from the outside. Through observation, one discovers that one is not the permanent, fully conscious and unchanging "I" that one thought oneself to be, but, rather, quite fragmented and dispersed. Within the individual, there are "thinking", "emotional", "moving" and "instinctive" centres, each acting independently and determining what is presented to the outside world: it is as if one were "four people with different minds" or a "house in disorder, with the Master away and the servants doing what they like". Only through discipline and work can these various centres be brought into harmony and the true self-consciousness of the "Balanced Man" achieved. It is a process of overcoming the mere "personality" that is produced by life experience, in order to re-achieve the "essence" with which one was born. To overcome the suffering attendant upon living through mere personality, one must discard "negative emotions", i.e., cease believing that one is owed something by the world and develop, instead of self-pity, a spirit of gratitude.

Nicoll expresses an idea that would become central to Schumacher's thinking, namely the conviction that "Man is . . . unfinished", incomplete, imperfect. He has the possibility of completing himself, perfecting himself, and all that is necessary for this lies in him". He is "an experiment in self-evolution. As he is mechanically, he is incomplete and undeveloped but is capable of a further inner development. For this reason, it is said that man is a self-developing organism". This assertion of the possibility of personal change and improvement, which, of course, resonates with the theme of "salvation" common to most religious doctrines, would undermine Schumacher's belief in the "baser" conception of man found in orthodox economics. Moreover, the Gurdjieffian influence was permanent: till the end of his life, long after he had embraced Christianity, he would reiterate the Work themes of "man's incompleteness", "self-remembering" and getting one's "house in order".

His letters to his wife of the early fifties testify to his absorption in the Ouspenkian teachings. "'Personality' in the Work sense", he writes, "is derived from the outside world and depends on other people's reaction. But there is also 'Essence' with its possibility of growth, and that, we are told, comes 'from the stars' – from a higher level. I have tried to explain this to

[Edith] and she has taken it very well" (EFS to Anna Maria Schumacher, Aug. 24, 1952, SPKG).[13] In February 1954, he could write of a group-meeting at Bennett's, where he reported on having had "a taste of the meaning of 'Void', 'All', 'Mother', 'Nirvana' of whatever it may be called... But I cannot recapture it, and its value is simply that it enables me to feel complete conviction that the Work-Teaching is true and effective. For this I am profoundly grateful" (EFS to Anna Maria Schumacher, Feb. 7, 1954, SPKG).

Offering his work as fragments of the "hidden teachings" of the East, Ouspensky's writings contain much discussion of yoga and Buddhism. Thus Schumacher began to attend lectures at the Buddhist Society in London and began to practice yoga.[14] By 1954, enticed by the lure of the East, he was planning to spend the first three months of the following year in Buddhist Burma, on secondment as a consultant to the UN.

While in Rangoon, Schumacher examined the country's plans for economic and social development and immersed himself in a Buddhist society. Observing all from the perspective of the Fourth Way, he took classes in Vipassana meditation with renowned teacher, U Ba Khin, and spent time with the Burmese and with expatriate German converts to Buddhism.[15] Unlike in England, where his private philosophical interests were kept separate from the professional realm, Burma demanded a reconciliation of the two. The economic plan under consideration, which had been prepared largely by American consultants, promised to not only expand production and consumption but also encourage rural-urban migration, inculcate a stronger work ethic in the people, and intensify agricultural methods using mechanisation and chemicals. From Schumacher's perspective, the initiative was nothing short of a Western materialist threat to the East, and his response was to write a private essay, "Economics in a Buddhist Country", later revised as "Buddhist Economics" (1965). In it, he warned against such cultural encroachment and recommended that the Burmans adopt a "Middle Way" in development, free of the Western traps of consumerism and productivism. The Burmese experience had a catalytic effect on Schumacher, confirming him on his new path and reinforcing his misgivings about what he had come to regard as the "desert of today's civilization".

Returning to his Surrey garden, he pursued his explorations with intensity and began writing what would eventually become, some twenty years later, *A Guide for the Perplexed*.[16]

> I need some map, some guide-book for my life. Where do I find it? Religion tells me one thing; Science tells me another. What is more, Science tells me that religion is a superstition, that only 'scientific' knowledge can be trusted. Yet I cannot find in scientific knowledge any answer to my questions – what am I to do with my life? Why am I here? etc. Shall I then turn to philosophy? But there are dozens of philosophies. Perhaps the latest is the best: so I turn to Logical Positivism. This does not help me at all, for everything I want to know, I am told, is meaningless.[17]

He took meditation classes, continued yoga and plunged further into the work of a group of writers that would remain important for him for the rest of his life. These were the Traditionalists René Guénon (1886–1951), Frithjof Schuon (1907–1998) and Ananda Coomaraswamy (1887–1947).

Regarded as the spiritual father of Traditionalism, Guénon emerged from Catholic conservative circles in France in the 1920s before emigrating to Cairo, where he converted to Islam and died some twenty years later.[18] His foundational book, *The Crisis of the Modern World* (1942), provides a scathing critique of Western modernity. According to Guénon, prior to the advent of science and technology in the 17th century, most peoples had been in possession of a Perennial Wisdom, or *Sophia perennis*, a belief, common to all religions, in the supremacy of a divine realm. This acknowledgement of the essential, timeless order of things found expression in not only religious doctrine and rite but also in allied traditional arts and crafts. The abandonment by Western humanity of this worldview, for the pursuit of science and technology represented, not "progress" as the Enlightenment would have it, but a great *deviation* from the natural order of things: materialism rather than wisdom; the profane rather than the sacred; egalitarianism and democracy rather than natural hierarchy. Modernity, for Guénon, was characterised by fragmentation, chaos and multiplicity. Schumacher read many of Guénon's books, including *The Crisis*; the 1945 translation of the (1921) *The Introduction to the Study of the Hindu Doctrines* and *The Reign of Quantity and the Signs of the Times* (1953). He accepted Guénon's fundamental diagnosis of modernity as being a deviation from the natural order.

He encountered a similar message in the work of F. Schuon, the Swiss disciple of Guénon and leader of a Maryamiyya Sufi sect.[19] He read Schuon's (1954) *Spiritual Perspectives and Human Facts*, with its critique of the machine civilization of modernity, and, at some point later, visited Schuon in Switzerland. As for Ananda Coomaraswamy, an Anglo-Indian, he was the Traditionalist most directly linked to Schumacher's experience in India. Trained as a geologist but active in Gandhian nationalist circles at the beginning of the century, Coomaraswamy became an authority on Indian arts and crafts and went on to spent most of his career as keeper at the Boston Museum of Fine Art.[20] Amongst Coomaraswamy's astonishing output, Schumacher read *Art and Swadeshi* (1912); *The Transformation of Nature in Art* (1936); *The Bugbear of Literacy* (1949) and *Buddha and the Gospel of Buddhism* (1956). So taken was Schumacher by Traditionalism that, by the end of the decade, he would teach adult-education courses based on the theme of the Perennial Philosophy at London University.

Reading Radhakrishnan's (1953) *History of Philosophy, Eastern and Western*, he concluded that the Western physics to which the current era was committed had nothing to tell him about "value, meaning, purpose, aim or such" (op. cit., p. 4).[21] Taking notes on Guénon's *Hindu Doctrines*, he wrote that Western civilization lacked any unifying principle; indeed, it was devoted to "the service of an 'absence of principle'" and thus "condemned... to a hopeless state of intellectual endeavour". The domain of metaphysics, on the other hand, lay beyond external investigation: "*Cannot be subject to the influences of time & space*"; represented a "*Permanent and changeless attitude*".[22]

A book by which he was particularly captivated in the late fifties was G. N. M. Tyrrell's (1951) *Homo Faber*. A British mathematician and engineer who had been influential in the development of radio but thereafter devoted himself to the study of the paranormal; Tyrrell (1879–1952) became a long-time member of the Society for Psychical Research. *Homo Faber* asserts that through the accomplishment of instrumental tasks in the world, culminating in the development of science and technology, man had developed an "adapted mind", i.e., that part of the mind most suited to the execution of well-defined tasks. The effect of this growing instrumental efficacy was to reinforce the belief that everything that mattered in the functioning of the world could be grasped by the human intellect via the senses alone. This attitude had become dominant at the expense of other, non-scientific, perspectives, such as those involving extra-sensory, spiritual and religious phenomena. *Homo Faber* had prevailed, so to speak.

In his book, Tyrrell emphasises a distinction between two kinds of problems faced by humans. Put briefly, "convergent" problems are those that can be expressed precisely, and for which there exist obtainable, well-defined answers. Their solutions can be easily communicated between people. Most problems in the natural sciences and engineering are of the convergent kind. "Divergent" problems, on the other hand, are difficult to formulate precisely. They require existential solutions, which, sometimes, can only be evoked rather than stated explicitly, and cannot be easily communicated between people. Most problems in the realm of philosophy and religion are of the "divergent" kind. Science has progressed, and the "adapted mind" has prevailed, says Tyrrell, through the systematic elimination of all "divergent" elements.

Schumacher saw in Tyrrell confirmation of both the limitations of economics and the possibility of human advancement and perfectibility. The realm of the "convergent", of science and technique, called on man's lower, or "animal", level, on his relatively mundane problem-solving abilities. The philosophical or spiritual realm, on the other hand, appealed to a higher, or "angelic", level in man, to his capacity for confronting existential problems and contradictions to which there were simply no clear-cut answers.

> Science makes divergent problems into convergent ones by eliminating one of the two levels... It achieves 'convergence' by adopting a theory of man which is untrue (e.g. homo oeconomicus) and destructive of man himself.
>
> (Schumacher in "Tyrrell", p. 4, in Very early beginnings)

> Convergent problems "are not really human. They 'collapse' man into one level only. Scientific method is designed for c-problems. Hence it is useless for problems that concern the WHOLE MAN. It creates offensive

abstractions like homo oeconomicus; or treats man simply as either a mechanism or an animal".

(Ibid, emphasis in original)

Tyrrell's influence may be seen in "Economics and the Coal Industry", which Schumacher submitted to the *Review of Economics and Statistics* in late 1958 to early 1959. Against a background of increased imports of "cheaper" oil, and the consequent winding-down of the coal industry, he criticises the attempts to make economics supposedly more scientific.[23] By adopting a strategy of simplification similar to that adopted in the sciences, namely concentrating on appearances or "form" (i.e., the "market"), and by attending to quanti-tative measures only (i.e., "price"), economics was treating coal policy as a convergent problem whereas, in fact, it was divergent.

In contrast to consumption goods or renewable resources, obtaining coal was not "production" but, rather, capital consumption. The decision to take the easiest coal now, leaving the more difficult stuff for later generations, was an *ethical*, not an economic, decision. The choice to close a colliery was, in most cases, permanent, because of the ensuing flooding, with consequences for future coal production, when oil ceased to be cheap. Thus, to say that all that mattered was the current *price* of a ton of coal, just like any other good, was to treat as similar goods that were different *in kind*. Given the expected growth of global energy consumption, the availability of oil reserves, and the likelihood of renewed future demand for coal, he said, it would be wrong to conclude from the current market price that coal had become simply redun-dant. While it might be legitimate for the consumer to be "irresponsible" and focus on price only, the responsible economist needed to move beyond the surface of things and take other factors into consideration. There was no more urgent task for economists than to work out an economics of non-re-newable primary goods – "the very life-blood and substance of our present civilisation" (p. 9).[24]

In the autumn of 1959, he began to give a series of evening or weekend adult-education lectures at University College London loosely devoted to the theme of the Perennial Philosophy: "'Philosophical' or 'crucial' problems of modern living i.e., looking at life from the point of view of Meaning & Purpose".[25] The fundamental question was "What is Man?" A creature of God or of evolution? Imbued with transcendental meaning or lacking any meaning? Guided by values that were to be discovered or to be invented? Intended to guide his students towards a Traditionalist understanding of man, his lectures covered a remarkable range of subjects, including Kierkegaard, Hume, Sartre, St. Thomas Aquinas, scales of being (stone, plant, animal, man), Ruskin ("Industry without art is brutality")[26], Chesterton and the structure of myths and tales in Dante and Shakespeare.

Lecture No. 24, on March 23, 1960, spoke of the use of spiritual means for worldly ends, namely learning to live without war and how to live on income rather than capital ("exhaustion of fossil fuels etc."). "Machiavellianism;

Scientism; Modern Economics" belonged to the realm of materialism and violence and stood in contrast with the non-violent, spiritual means open to man: "If we want to preserve human civilisation we must learn 'non-violence' in <u>all</u> activities – not only politics but also economics, medicine, agriculture, horticulture, industry, etc. This really <u>needs to be worked out</u>. Task of conscious development. Pacifism is <u>not possible</u> if you permit any kind of violence against all parts of creation except man".

In keeping with his own inward turn, Schumacher advocated, not the collective action of Labour Party politics, but taking "yourself in hand", finding a "method". Unlike the Church, he said, which offered no precise instruction other than to "have the Faith", the "oriental creeds" of Buddhism, Hinduism (Vedanta), Yoga and even Sufism, all gave precise guidelines. Referring to the work of French cardiologist, Thérèse Brosse, he said that the methods of Yoga had all been scientifically shown to result in control of heartbeat and respiration and the stimulation of brainwaves that were congruent with greater openness in the individual and inclination towards altruism. Outlining the various approaches to Yoga, he noted that similar methods existed in the West, in the form of the *Hesychasm* of Orthodox prayer, the methods of St. Ignatius of Loyola, and the teachings of Gurdjieff/Ouspensky and Subud. The choice of method was not important: what was crucial was to take oneself in hand.

In two classes, Schumacher took the opportunity to speak about his own discipline in the context of his evolving ideas. In Lecture No. 18, "The Philosophy of Economics", he indicated his continued distancing from the field of "normal" politics, affirming that in both capitalism and socialism the crucial matter was "the religion of economics" – that the "material instinct is made dominant instead of subservient, independent instead of dependent, an end instead of a means". From this "poisonous root" stemmed three noxious consequences: "Degradation of the Higher; Contempt of the person – Misuse and alienation; Misuse of Nature". The fundamental error was to treat the "particular, conditional and relative activity" of economics and commerce as "a thing by itself ... absolutely independent and self-contained". To do so could result only in "disaster and sin". Here, he singles out Keynes for his endorsement, in "Economic Possibilities for our Grandchildren", of the sin of materialism, by advocating the continued need of "avarice and usury". Schumacher would repeat the condemnation several times during the decade. As he changed, so did Keynes cease to be his intellectual hero.

To his students, Schumacher described the "lamentable metaphysical ignorance of economists, political and social scientists", which led them to consider economics as a science, with its own laws, which were to be respected "irrespective of their human consequences". Economics, as currently taught, was concerned with neither the laws of nature nor Natural Law but was either "model building. Homo economicus" or merely descriptive economic history. "Neither approach can lead to anything because man is not homo oeconomicus and if he is treated as if he were he will go to pieces. But to the extent that he becomes homo oeconomicus, economics becomes true & scientific and man ceases to be man". Adam Smith's claim that "private material interest" or consumption was the purpose of labour was the "original sin" of economics, and it had led to "universal discord and destruction". This was the "bourgeois spirit" that gave us capitalism, with its "universal degradation of life". Referring to Erich Fromm's *The Sane Society*, Schumacher notes that the main critique of early capitalism concerned not the material welfare of the workers but, rather <u>man</u>, and what happens to him in the industrial system. As emphasised by "Owen and Proudhon, Tolstoy and Bakunin, Durkheim and Marx, Einstein and Schweizer", man lost his central place and was made "an instrument for the purposes of economic aims". The disease was one "of the spirit (idolatry), not just one of system or institutions". It was no longer possible to ignore the question of Natural Law: "what kind of economic life is appropriate and proper for human beings?". Schumacher's reply can be usefully regarded as a précis of what was to become his abiding standpoint:

- so-called economic necessities "do not exist apart from our own wishes";
- super-states are not politico-economic necessities, as alleged; they are a manifestation of the "reign of quantity";
- our way of life is "utterly impoverished": it is in no way desirable to spread it to the underdeveloped countries;
- the present way of life, whether in the United States. or as aspired to in the USSR, is against Natural Law: destroys culture and therefore its own intellectual basis; destroys its own moral laws; destroys its own material basis, through the use of non-renewable resources[27];
- the present system is "most dangerous where it is most successful": productivity and growth: physical exhaustion; ever more science: mental impoverishment; ever larger organisation: slavery; peaceful use of atomic energy: death; health and population increase: death;
- the "pill" was a poor alibi;
- the only hope: humility vis à vis the higher; pity for our fellow man; loving care for the world of nature.

In a witty, confessional class several weeks later, "The Double Life of a Post-Modern Economist", he began by humorously warning his students that they were on no account to use anything he told them in an exam. The "post-modern" economist, he said, was one who had escaped the grip of modernity and seen the historically contingent discipline for what it was: founded on an erroneous philosophy derived from 19th-century science and destined to bring the whole of society crashing down upon itself. "Modern man (homo occidentalis mechanicus, neo-barbarus, ridiculous) needs a total re-education at once, or he becomes tragicus". Economics was founded upon a picture of man in the universe that was derived from the natural sciences of the last 250 years. It contained no trace of Christian Faith, Hope and

Charity; or of the Greek Good, True and Beautiful; or of Roman Justice and Splendour; or of Islamic Manliness, Poetry and Devotion.

However, he claimed, it was time to realise that the age of the dominance of science was over. "The modern age – the age of evolutionism, determinism, mechanism, materialism, countless variations of idealism, and finally unlimited relativism – thought it had erected all these bizarre and uncomfortable structures on the unshakeable foundations of 'exact science', experimentally verified". But the best scientists were now admitting the limitation of their work, and their inability to say anything about "reality as a whole, about its meaning, or purpose, about the place & the role of Man in the World".

What had all this to do with the economist? His discipline, too, said Schumacher, was a reflection of the philosophy of the age. If the latter accepted that there was "no god, no purpose of life, no obligation on man", anthropology would see man as "homo oeconomicus" – "the consumer, the customer, fundamentally concerned with nothing but comfort, and from this the economist will derive his own notions of what is economic and what is not". However, were that philosophy to change, and were it be acknowledged "that life had a very profound meaning for every man, that there was a definite task to be accomplished for which each one of us had only a limited amount of time – and that the task was not maximum consumption! – then the starting notions of the economist would be completely changed: many things now considered 'economic' would, with impeccable logic, be shown as intolerably 'wasteful' and vice versa".

Referring clearly to himself, he says that the post-modern economist has "escaped from the thralldom of modern philosophy which had created a topsy-turvy world of values. So he is in very great difficulties – hence his double life. His primary difficulty is that he finds most propositions neither right nor wrong, but either meaningless or beside the point. (Always the sign of an end of an era!)".

The 1960s: Economic Calculus or Spiritual Discernment?

While Schumacher's wife, Anna Maria, was alive, it was she, not he, who brought the children to church. A devout Christian, during the 1950s, she had watched his esoteric explorations with a certain degree of apprehension, and, consequently, several of his letters show him keen to reassure her. For example, from Rangoon, he wrote: "You say for instance that my interest in Buddhism is imposing a new strain upon you, but please, Muschilein, there is no conceivable cause of strain in this. My sole motive and interest in Buddhism is in getting rid of all sorts of weaknesses and defilements in my character – of all the things that that really could impose strain upon you and others" (EFS to Anna Maria Schumacher, Feb. 26, 1955, Schumacher Family Papers, London; hereafter SFPL). Whenever the opportunity arose to find common religious ground with his wife, he appears to have done so. Thus, again from Burma, where, in addition to practicing Yoga and Satipatthana meditation, he was reading the Gospels: "I am very pleased indeed that you have discovered Meister Eckhardt. A master, indeed, as you say" (EFS to Anna Maria Schumacher, Mar. 2, 1955, SFPL).

By the summer of 1960, however, it was clear that Anna Maria was seriously ill. That August, she returned to her German family, while he took the children on holiday in the Swiss Alps. From a chalet at La Comballaz, near Vésey, he wrote: "I hear from everyone... that you are doing very well and that your strength seems to be returning. I do hope that you are cheerful and confident. How you would have enjoyed the holiday here" (EFS to Anna Maria Schumacher, Aug. 23, 1960, SFPL). By mid-September, he was back at the Coal Board and, to his satisfaction, increasingly busy, but she was still in Reinbek. "Are you sticking to ultra-light, raw-vegetable, raw-fruit, sour milk etc. diet?", he wrote. "I can't help feeling that it is most important" (EFS to Anna Maria Schumacher, Sept. 18th, 1960, SFPL). Two days later, he sent her a prayer he had found in an anthology. By October, he had joined her at her hospital bedside, where he remained with her until she passed away on the 26th.

According to friends, the tragedy made Schumacher a more compassionate and humane person. George McRobie (1926–2016), who was brought to the Coal Board by him and would later work with him in Intermediate Technology, said that, after his wife's death, Schumacher became less intellectually austere than before: "he began to talk about people, become involved in people". At Hobart House, he became a "kind of father confessor to all and sundry". According to Julia Porter (1926–1992), who also worked with him in Intermediate Technology and knew him well, the weeks Schumacher spent sitting and talking with his dying wife were the most important of his life. Thereafter, he would spend hours simply sitting in the churches of central London, such as Westminster Cathedral and St. Peter's, Eaton Square.[28] Her death was also a pivotal moment insofar as it reinforced the idea that he was on a quest or pilgrimage. A few weeks after the event, writing to his mother-in-law, he noted the "great spiritual strength that flowed through" his dying wife, casting her as the Beatrice to his Dante in the *Divine Comedy*.[29]

By 1961, his family situation had calmed somewhat with the decision of the family's Swiss *au pair*, Verena Rosenberger, to remain in the Surrey house for another while. This allowed Schumacher a short visit to Poona in India in January of that year, at the invitation of J. P. Narayan (1902–1979), the popular Gandhian and government critic who had published his Burma paper, "Economics in a Buddhist Country". There he gave a series of lectures, including, in addition to the Burma paper, "Nonviolent Economics", an *Observer* article from the previous year, "Paths to Economic Growth", "Help to Those who need it most", "Notes on Indian Development Problems" and "Levels of Technology".[30] It was here that he laid out what was to become his position on the role of technology in development: namely that developing countries could not hope to pass quickly from the "bullock-cart" to the "jet engine". Such hasty development involved the introduction of technological projects that were not only inaccessible to the vast majority of the population but also highly disruptive of traditional ways of life and patterns of settlement.

Schumacher's opposition to this undermining of traditional civilizations had been catalysed by his time in Burma and reinforced by his reading of Guénon and Schuon. For the Traditionalists, while the modern, explosive development of science and technology had brought increased human mastery of nature and greater comfort, it had served to distract humanity from metaphysical truths concerning its position in the cosmos. Thus Schuon:

> In a certain outward sense, the great social and political evil of the West is mechanization; it is the machine that gives rise most directly to the great evils from which the world today is suffering. The machine is characterized *grosso modo* by the use of iron, fire, and invisible forces. Nothing is more fanciful than to speak of the wise use of machines, of their serving the human spirit, for it is in the very nature of mechanization to reduce men to slavery and devour them utterly, leaving them with nothing human, nothing beyond the animal, nothing beyond the collective. The reign of the machine has succeeded that of iron, or rather it has given iron its most sinister expression: man, who created the machine, ends by becoming its creature.
>
> (2007 [1954], p. 17)

While Schumacher, as economist, could not simply dismiss machinery completely, he was acutely sensitive to the disruptive effect of imported technologies and sophisticated projects on traditional communities. He was also aware that behind the development and adoption of machinery and the improvement of efficiency lay the questionable motive of human "appetite".

In August 1961, he returned, for the third time in four years, to Clarens, Switzerland, to a conference at which he spoke about "Determinants of Peace", with abundant reference to "Mater et Magistra", Pope John XXIII's encyclical of the previous May.[31] He agreed with the Vatican's claim that man, while dominating the material sphere, had become "a pygmy in the supernatural and eternal world". The search for peace could not be based on fixed assumptions concerning the predominance of economics, power or ownership of the means of production, or the belief that the natural sciences were the key to everything. There was a need to establish a hierarchy of values, he said. Scientific and technical progress were good only insofar as they promoted the "spiritual perfection of mankind, both in the natural & the supernatural order". Service and sacrifice were greater than egotism: the recognition that "pure selfishness cannot and does not fulfill human nature, because man has within himself a supernatural element – must lead up to the recognition of God". On the specific matter of economic development, things were generally left up to economists and engineers, he said, who chose "the most ruthless way", with the result that the rest of society "goes to pieces". This way of proceeding, with its immoral undermining of consciousness, was a danger to civilisation, an "insidious poison". Among the culpable were Eugene Black, then President of the World Bank, and Andrew Schonfield, a British-economist contemporary of Schumacher. Such economists, he implied, were, "quite uneducated" as human beings, lacking a proper understanding of man. "The universal tradition of mankind sees man as *homo viator* or *homo in statu viatoris*, as a traveller whose destination is not simply in this world".

Returning to England, he continued to juggle his two careers: as coal economist, on the one hand, and as unorthodox, Gandhian development advisor, on the other. NCB Chairman, Alfred Robens, relied on him increasingly in order to help defend the coal industry and to rationalise operations through greater mechanisation of coal extraction and judicious coalface selection. Years later, looking back, and most probably unaware of the "double-life" of his employee, Robens recalled Schumacher's emphasis on the need to minimise the stoppage time of the coal-cutting machinery, so that "within a year or two, the whole situation changed and [the mining engineers] were eagerly seeking his advice on specific pits and specific performances".[32] Since Robens attached particular importance to Schumacher's advice, he had no trouble providing him with the flexibility and periods of leave required for his external work, which sometimes involved long periods overseas.

In September 1964, Schumacher spoke at the Cambridge Conference on Development, where he presented his minority view on the role of technology.[33] A purely quantitative concept of economic growth, he said, devoid of qualitative considerations, was unacceptable as a policy objective. The problems of mass unemployment and mass migration into cities, which economists regarded as merely temporary setbacks, were, in fact, steadily worsening. Fresh thinking was required. Only by providing capital that was relatively cheap and aimed at creating employment in the small towns and villages, could the task of development be tackled. It was pointless to introduce highly developed, Western labour-saving machinery in countries where manpower was in abundance. The developed countries had advanced through successive stages, without relying on massive injections of inappropriate technology from abroad, and without suffering the mass misery now evident in the developing countries. Only when people started to make their own tools and other equipment would the circle be closed and genuine development occur. He took pains to reassure those present that his argument was not "anti-science": it was about using scientific discoveries intelligently. However, what was missing in modern development was not sophisticated science: it was local materials and traditional knowledge; green manure and organic methods; wooden construction, not poured concrete:

> Tree planting, indeed, deserves to be singled out for special emphasis in this context, because the world is full of cases where the neglect of trees is one of the chief causes of misery and helplessness, while the recovery of a realistic sense of man's dependence on trees would be a most fruitful

move in the right direction. No high technology or foreign aid is needed
for planting and looking after trees; every able-bodied person can make
his contribution and benefit from it; a wide range of useful materials can
be obtained from trees – some species being very fast growers in tropical
and even semi-tropical climates – and these materials lend themselves
exceptionally well for utilisation by 'intermediate technology'. Yet there
are few 'developing' countries where trees do not suffer from heedless
neglect.

(pp. 140–141)

The presentation duly led to what organiser Ronald Robinson described as a
"memorable encounter" between Schumacher, on the other side, and, on the
other, his old wartime colleague, Nicholas Kaldor, and V. K. Ramaswami,
advisor to the Indian Ministry of Finance. Advanced projects were a more
efficient use of capital, they retorted, and could, in principle, release public
funds for subsequent aid to the countryside. To which Schumacher replied
that the political and human costs in the meantime were so great as to threaten
social disintegration.

According to one report, the interventions in favour of rapid industrialisation effectively swept Schumacher's arguments aside, as far as most of the
conference participants were concerned.[34] However, reviewing the literature
at the end of decade, Robinson said that, despite the conference consensus,
subsequent contributions on rural development had shifted the balance of the
argument towards Schumacher.[35] As for Kaldor himself, looking back in the
early 1980s, he admitted that he had disagreed with Schumacher at the time,
but that he now felt more open-minded about the matter.[36]

Undaunted by his Cambridge experience, Schumacher returned to the
question of economic development and Buddhism early the following year,
in a BBC broadcast to Burma and India.[37] Western plans to transform entire
societies by encouraging work, consumption and growth were a form of
"social engineering" with which he fundamentally disagreed. The way of
life in traditional civilizations was to be defended, not dismantled: it was
the product of "wisdom", not of science and could "never be constructed
by scientists – economists, sociologists and other so-called experts – at all"
(First talk, p. 1). The Buddhist teachings on the achievement of freedom
through liberation from craving were fundamentally opposed to the teachings of modern economics, which:

> treats material goods and services as the only 'value' to reckoned with;
> and even material goods and services are treated as being without value
> when they are freely available to everyone, like sun and air; it is only
> their scarcity and man's craving after scarce things that makes them val-
> uable. This way of looking at the world, giving rise to a science which
> meticulously studies how the 'values' stemming from scarcity and crav-
> ing can be increased – occasionally by causing scarcities and invariably

by stimulating craving – this way of looking at the world, of course, is the outlook of Materialism in its crudest form... [To] question whether economic growth and development make people better, happier, or more beautiful is not permissible; these are treated as treasonable questions which should never, never be asked. In short, modern economics is the systematic theory of an unbridled idolatry of material wealth, and most of the development plans in the world today are the offspring of that idolatry.

(p. 3)

Quoting Ruskin – "industry without art is brutality" – Schumacher painted a bleak picture of life in modern technological society, where specialisation forced the person to "lose contact with the reality of life, as a whole ... [and] be satisfied with completely meaningless and mechanical work" (Second talk, p. 3).

On the particular question of *transport*, his Gandhian position represented a complete reversal of the pro-trade and development views of his Fabian years.[38] Addressing the Indians, he said that the deliberate limitation of transport offered regions a kind of protective isolation from external competition. As a result:

The local population develops many ingenious methods to make local raw materials serve essential human needs. The basis of the economy is local production for local use, and long-distance trade plays only a very minor part. The result is that village life is colourful and interesting, because a large number of crafts and trades is there represented; traditional knowledge and wisdom of a highly practical kind is passed on from generation to generation. The resilience of such communities is enormous.

(Talk 8, p. 2)

The modern economist, on the other hand, convinced that industrial development required foreign advice and techniques "knows nothing of the marvellous culture of the Indian craftsman, or the grace and dignity of rural life in South-East Asia a hundred years ago" (Talk 8, p. 3).[39]

The following year, in a talk to the Church of England Men's Society, he contrasted the current "Religion of Economics", not with Buddhism this time, but with the Christian teachings.[40] With its fragmentary picture of man as a production and consumption machine, economics ran counter to key Christian edicts such as "'See ye first the Kingdom of God, and his righteousness, and all these things' – all these other things which you also need, the economic things – 'shall be added unto you'" (p. 2). As he would increasingly throughout the decade, he here turned to the work of Christian Socialist, R. H. Tawney, whose books *The Acquisitive Society* (1920) and *Religion and the Rise of Capitalism* (1926) had warned against the destructive social effects of allowing commercialism to become an end in itself. To claim "that the attainment of material riches is the supreme object of human endeavour and the final criterion of human success" was to negate "any system of thought or morals which can ... be described as Christian" (p. 4). Vindication of Tawney, he said, could be found in the city of Los Angeles, as described by Lewis Herber, with its 3.9m cars for a population of 7 m, and its psychological, economic and biological breakdown.[41] Congestion, drug addiction and mental illness were proof that "to pursue efficiency as a primary object will produce such inefficiencies as to destroy efficiency itself" (p. 5). To neglect non-economic, human criteria was to invite periodic human revolt.

It was necessary to distinguish between healthy and unhealthy growth, he said. Do those benefitting from growth care for the fellow-men? "Do they care for God-given Nature or do they think of it as a quarry for exploitation?" (ibid). Christians had a duty to prevent idols from being made of contingent things, such as science, power or economic growth. Signs of impatience and violence were to be seen in agriculture as reported in Rachel Carson's *Silent Spring* (1962) and Ruth Harrison's *Animal Machines* (1964). The near-criminal baseness of factory-farming showed that man was in "a wrongful relationship with God's creation" (p. 7). As Herber (Bookchin) put it, there was "a growing need to restore the normal, balanced, and manageable rhythms of human life" (ibid). Similar signs were also visible in modern industry, where the restoration of human scale was imperative; and in natural resources, where the pillaging of non-renewable fuels showed that we "do not have the patience to be conservationists" (p. 8).

At this time, Schumacher was coping with various conflicting forces in his life. Not only did he find himself defending the coal industry against the encroachments of imported oil, but, by the late 1960s, he was involved in the Coal Board's integration of heavy machinery into the mines. While this lightened the physical burden of the miner, it did so at the cost of greater monotony, heat and dust underground. Throughout, the coal industry remained dangerous and highly polluting, with accidents, deaths and a great deal of waste. A particularly extreme event occurred in October 1966, when a huge spoil-tip became unstable, cascading down a hillside in Aberfan, Wales, engulfing the local school and killing 144 people, mainly children. All of this was a far cry from the work of Schumacher's Intermediate Technology Development Group, which he had set up earlier that year for the propagation of relatively simple tools and machines in the developing world. As aware as ever of his "double-life", Schumacher wished to leave the Coal Board by the mid-sixties, but could not: Robens wanted him, and, remarried, he had to provide for a still-growing family.[42]

Nonetheless, he continued to champ at the bit, allying himself with critical, marginal voices, leagues removed from the Coal Board. One such constituency was that of *Resurgence Magazine*, founded by renegade Church of England minister, peace activist and critic of gigantism, the Rev. John Papworth (1921–2020). *Resurgence* presented itself as a "peace publication", opposed to nuclear weapons, critical of the impact on life of science, technology and "bigness", and preferring radical decentralism. Interestingly, given Schumacher's Labour background, it insisted that, at a sufficiently large scale, *all* power, whether held by communists, capitalists or social democrats, tended to become oligarchic, and to give rise to irrationality and war. "A civilisation that genuinely reflects all that human beings long for and aspire to cannot be prefabricated either by Fabians, Commissars or capitalists; it can only be created on the basis of each person's freely acknowledged power to decide on each of the many questions that affect his life".[43]

Looking back in 1977, Papworth remembered his first meeting with Schumacher a decade earlier: "I saw a tall man in a dark pin-stripe suit, black shoes, a black homburg hat and carrying a black brief case and a carefully rolled black umbrella. He looked the absolute epitome of a senior English civil servant (which in fact is what he was), and I thought, well, that can't be the author of 'Buddhist Economics'. But it was" (1977, p. 4). While Papworth leaves no doubt that he regarded Schumacher, along with Leopold Kohr, as his great editorial "find", his recollection of the man is refreshingly candid: "his conversation over lunch, which ranged from a furious denunciation of Teilhard de Chardin (a fraud and imposter) to a serious enquiry about my 'sign' (he was a great one for astrology), with an admiring disquisition on the work of the Church of England's Mens' Brigade and some knowledgeable talk about wines, had me playing the part of a one-man audience. Much of his conversation was in monologue form, seldom asked questions (and he seldom heard them either) and he always conveyed a sense of absolute certainty on whatever subject engaged his talk" (ibid).

Schumacher's first article for *Resurgence*, appearing in its second issue, was a reprint of the paper with which he had scandalised the economists at Cambridge two years earlier, and he quickly followed it up with a denunciation of "Industrial Society", similar to his Church of England talk.[44] Once again invoking Tawney, he said that spiritual discernment was required in order to avoid unhealthy economic growth, "but the economic calculus has not spiritual discernment" (p. 13). No doubt alluding to his own dilemmas at the Coal Board, he wrote that: "Christians in industry find themselves in an almost hopeless position. They struggle on as best they can, without help or guidance from any source outside their own conscience ... Yet they know perfectly well that every important action they take may have the most far-reaching effects on the soul or spirit of many people, most of whom [they] do not even know" (ibid). At a time when work was being transformed by mechanisation and automation, what was most needed was a philosophy of *work*. It was essential to distinguish wholesome from degrading work, and to resist the temptation to passively let technological development determine the evolution of labour.

Although he never quite paid him due credit, a key influence here on Schumacher was the remarkable Richard B. Gregg (1885–1974), American disciple of Gandhi and later pioneer of the American back-to-the-land

movement, alongside Helen and Scott Nearing. A Harvard law graduate, Gregg spent several years working in the troubled field of labour law
and industrial relations before dropping it all in 1925 to be with Gandhi
in India. There he spent four years, living in Gandhi's ashram, becoming
actively involved in his campaign of *Satyagraha*, or non-violent resistance,
and writing and teaching. Gregg's 1935 pamphlet *The Power of Non-Violence*
would later influence Martin Luther's approach to the civil rights movement, and his 1936 *The Value of Voluntary Simplicity* introduced the latter
term to the reading public. Among his books are *Economics of Khaddar* (1928);
Gandhi's Satyagraha or Non-violent Resistance (1930); *Which Way Lies Hope?
An Examination of Capitalism, Communism, Socialism and Gandhiji's Programme*
(1952); and *A Philosophy of Indian Economic Development* (1958), which contains
an appendix of several of Gandhi's articles from 1926, including his "Value of
Small-Scale Organization".[45] Schumacher read the latter two books, which
contain many of the ideas he later espoused on the philosophy of work in
relation to machinery; the limitation of mechanised mass production; and the
virtues of political and economic decentralisation. Gregg's influence became
evident in "Buddhist Economics", the 1965 reworking of the Burma essay,
where Schumacher even preserves Gregg's misspelling of the name of French
political philosopher, Bertrand de Jouvenel.[46]

In "The New Economics", (*Resurgence*, 1968), Schumacher continued his
critique of the "dismal science", which blindly promoted automation and
ever-larger production units, and remained oblivious to the human benefits of living and producing in "small comprehensible groups" (p. 54). "If
[economics] cannot get beyond its vast abstractions, the national income, the
rate of growth, capital/output ratio, input-output analysis, labour mobility,
capital accumulation, if it cannot get beyond all this and make contact with
the human realities of poverty, frustration, alienation, despair, breakdown,
crime, escapism, stress, congestion, ugliness and spiritual death, then let us
scrap economics and start afresh" (ibid). Striking words, from the chief economist of the National Coal Board.[47]

Still in *Resurgence*, in "The Economics of Permanence", in 1970, the year
of his retirement, he focused more closely on energy supplies and environmental matters. The growth in fuel consumption of the richest countries
presented a clear threat to the availability of energy to the poorest. The use
of nuclear power posed a huge biological threat and terrorist risk, and even
in the improbable event that fossil fuels were to become immediately available, there would be a "problem of thermal pollution on quite a different
scale from anything encountered hitherto" (p. 25). The materialistic attitude
to life "contains within itself no limiting principle, while the environment
in which it is placed is strictly limited" (ibid), and, once more, Keynes was
impugned for his active cultivation of greed when he cautioned that the pursuit of money would be necessary for another century before the so-called
"economic problem" could be solved and leisure attained. Such sentiments
underlay the modern economy's indulgence in an unsustainable "frenzy of

greed and ... orgy of envy", whereas the key concept of wisdom was "permanence". The latter demanded a re-orientation of science towards "the organic, the gentle, the non-violent, the elegant and beautiful" (p. 29).

For what would be the remaining seven years of his life, Schumacher continued to contribute to *Resurgence*.[48] There he found kindred spirits in fellow-contributors such as Satish Kumar (b. 1936), the Indian-born peace activist and Narayan collaborator, who became editor in 1973; Leopold Kohr (1909–1994), decentralist critic of excessive scale and author of *The Breakdown of Nations* (1957); and John Seymour (1914–2004), whose *The Fat of the Land* (1961) and, especially, *Self-Sufficiency* (1973) made him an icon in the British "back-to-the-land" movement.[49] When Narayan, by then an associate editor of *Resurgence*, was arrested by Indira Gandhi in 1975, Kumar organised a *Sarvodaya* conference in London, which featured Schumacher, Kohr, Seymour, Lanza del Vasto, Edward Goldsmith and Thich Nhat Hanh. The magazine was also close to the Welsh independence movement, with Seymour already living in Wales and Kumar taking the magazine there in 1976.[50] Ahead of all that, however, at the invitation of his old wartime colleague, Joan Robinson, Schumacher took one last public crack at the economists.

By 1972, he was two years in retirement, two years within the Catholic Church, and devoting himself completely to his personal causes. Besides *Resurgence* and the Intermediate Technology Development Group, there was the Soil Association, dedicated to the promotion of organic agriculture, which he had joined in 1950 and of which he was now President.[51] Energised by these interests, and no longer constrained by his old employer, he was now freer than ever to speak his mind.

Robinson knew what she was doing by inviting him. During the Coal Board years, she had kept an eye on him at a distance, as it were, thanks to the occasional visit by him to Cambridge, and via mutual friends, such as Manchester development economist and Marxist, Kurt *Martin* – as their wartime colleague Kurt Mandelbaum had become. She knew that Schumacher had undergone a kind of conversion: had "given up the idea of efficiency at all costs [in order] to take a wider view ... You cannot decide things on the basis of costs. Decisions you take are in terms of people and things. The money is just the post mortem. He had a very original approach. An approach based on real common sense, and not on conventions". While "Keynes was opposed to orthodox economics on one point", after Burma and Buddhism, "Fritz became opposed on the whole view of life" (ibid).[52]

Besides Schumacher and herself – "What has become of the Keynesian Revolution?" – Robinson's speakers were Elizabeth Johnson, co-editor of the collected works of Keynes, who spoke about "John Maynard Keynes: Scientist or Politician?"; F. T. Blackaby on "Incomes and Inflation"; M. C. Kennedy on "Employment Policy: What Went Wrong?"; and Thomas Wilson on "Pensions, Inflation and Growth".[53] Her last "guest", however, the up-and-coming monetary economist David Laidler (b. 1938), had been foisted upon her, as it were, by Harry Johnson, husband of the aforementioned

Elizabeth. As President of the British Association, it was Johnson's privilege to choose the Lister lecturer. Many years later, Laidler still recalled his rude mauling at the hands of Robinson.[54]

Schumacher addressed the mixed audience of academics, journalists and students that was typical of Section F. Economics students, he said, were typically told that they could expect to learn about the meaning of various technical terms and concepts; how the economy functions – "how a Smithian order emerges even though millions of people do as they please"; and how to make the economy work better, i.e., "the art of social engineering". But were such pedagogical promises justified?, he asked.

The "statements or theorems" put forward by economists, he said, fell into seven groups:

1 **definitions** and explanations of terms
2 certain logical and mathematical **tautologies,** e.g., world exports equal world imports
3 **psychological generalisations,** e.g., Adam Smith's claim that people desire to better their condition or to best place their capital
4 **psychological generalisation** about human behaviour **within a given social system,** e.g., generalisations made by modern economists
5 **statements** relating to geographical, geological, physiological, tech-nological, organisational and other facts or situations in the "outside world", e.g., the supply of a certain commodity will increase in response to an increase in demand
6 **conditional sentences**, if x is the case, then y will occur (often to get around unknowns in the previous category)
7 **normative statements**, e.g., what people or the government ought to do. (Economists try to avoid such statements.)

The economist was competent in respect of 1, 2 and 6, said Schumacher, but what about 3, 4, 5 and 7? "[A]re economists really competent to pronounce on the immutable structure of human nature (class 3), or on human behaviour in a given society (class 4) or on geological, technological and innumerable other relevant facts of the 'outside world' (class 5) or, finally, on what *ought to be* the goals or man or society?" (p. 29). Given that they are not, he said, "It follows that the competence of economics to explain how the economy actu-ally functions is admitted to be extremely fragmentary and limited" (ibid).

When economics was taught, he continued, there was a "gradual progression – often so gradual as to be almost imperceptible – through four stages: Generalisation; Assumption; Assertion; and Norm" (p. 29). For example, in microeconomics, on the question of "motivation", there was the **generalisa-tion**: "In general and most of the time the individual strives naturally for the accumulation of money and riches as ends in themselves" (ibid). Exceptions could then be got rid of by turning the generalisation into an **assumption**: "Let us assume that individuals invariably strive for the accumulation of money and riches as ends in themselves" (ibid). Used in theory, the assumption could then be subtly turned into an **assertion**: "If we take action A the result will be B, *because* individuals invariably strive for the accumulation of money and riches as ends in themselves" (p. 30). Finally, the assertion could then become a **norm** by suggesting that those who do not comply with it were uneducated or lacked character. To strive for money and riches as ends in themselves "is the only rational mode of behaviour" (ibid).

Similarly, in macroeconomics: "Laissez-faire at the human level ... produces the semblance of order only to the extent that men make no use of their power of freedom and behave as if their natures were fixed and immutable" (p. 31). That is to say, they have "no common aims and aspirations, no social goals, no desire for justice, and no idea of the Common Good. The semblance of order produced by laissez-faire therefore emerges only if men refuse to be men and insist on acting without freedom, like atoms" (ibid).

The economists provided a justification for laissez-faire by "making certain assumptions about free competition, perfect knowledge on the part of producers and consumers alike, and a few other things as well" (ibid). When the laissez-faire system did not work satisfactorily, the situation had to be regarded as an exception, which could be done by turning the first generalisation into a conditional sentence. Hence, "If certain conditions are fulfilled, the laissez-faire system works perfectly" (ibid). The assumption that these conditions are being or can be fulfilled could easily be turned into an assertion: "The laissez-faire system is the most perfect system conceivable". Once again, laissez-faire soon becomes the norm and it is claimed that any interference with free market forces is "irrational, wasteful, uneconomic, and, finally, immoral" (ibid). When this stage has been reached, says Schumacher, there is no more room in economics for such ideas as "justice and the common good, not to mention notions of the Good, the True, and the Beautiful" (ibid). Such notions belong outside economics: we must order our lives first of all exclusively in accordance with economic principles; any concern for "non–economic values" can only be considered afterwards – if we can afford such irrationalities.[55]

The same progression from generalisation to assumption to assertion to norm, he said, could also be observed in the way in which economists had dealt with natural resources and the environment. The generalisation that "natural resources would always be adequate to sustain man's economic activities, no matter how much the latter might expand" (p. 32) quickly became an assertion concerning the ability of science and progress to overcome any temporary limitations. As a result, economics paid little attention to the distinction between renewable and non-renewable primary goods and disregarded the idea of conservation: "If oil was easier to get out of the ground, and therefore cheaper, than coal, why not abandon the collieries? Oil was plentiful and would always remain so" (ibid). The belief that the environment was, and would always be, sufficient to meet any human demands was so powerful as to constitute a norm, with detractors and critics being regarded as eccentric. Were economists, *qua* economists, qualified to study resource limitation, ecological breakdown or human revolt? He didn't think so.

The discipline, he said, had ignored environmental questions, opting instead for "ever increasing concentration of 'internal' analysis and subtlety. The mental efforts that are being devoted to the construction of logical and often mathematical models, designed to 'optimise' the functioning of highly artificial and totally isolated 'systems' is fantastic, but all these 'systems' are erected on assumptions which are almost totally irrelevant" (p. 32). This can hardly have ingratiated him to Laidler whose special lecture, "The Current Inflation – The Problem of Explanation and the Problem of Policy", offered a sophisticated model of wage- and price setting, based on expectations, and used that to argue for a policy of demand management, rather than price controls.

Schumacher then turned on E. H. Phelps Brown, recently retired from the L.S.E., whose 1971 Presidential Address to the Royal Economic Society on "The Underdevelopment of Economics" had just appeared in the *Economic Journal*.[56] There, Phelps Brown suggested that economics had contributed little to such problems as overseas development, inflation, environmental protection, quality of life and urbanism. Schumacher retorted by suggesting that it was more a matter of the *overdevelopment* of economics, for its practitioners had become absorbed in "logical, mathematical, and econometric subtleties" to the neglect of "those determining 'external' factors upon which the meaningfulness of their exercises utterly depends". If economists wished to rejuvenate their subject, they needed to turn their attention to questions that lay *outside* their immediate discipline, namely to "'meta-economics'" (p. 33), i.e.,: first, "a metaphysical 'critique' of economics itself"; then the "study of the physical factors ... which economic reasoning has to respect"; and, third, the "study of man in his wholeness, not simply of 'economic man', a bloodless abstraction" (p. 33).

The metaphysical critique, he said, involved not only his earlier analysis of the theorems and statements of economists, but also the relationship between quantity and quality: "What are we doing when we are pushing economics ever more in the direction of a purely quantitative science, econometric, mathematical, model building, *as if* the actions of people were essentially the same as the behaviour of atoms?". Phelps Brown had approvingly quoted Oskar Morgenstern on the inadequacy of known economic facts, the implication being that, with adequate factual knowledge, economics could become a mathematical science. To believe this, said Schumacher, was to believe that economic facts were "*in their essential nature*" similar to the facts of physics, and that humans were similar to atoms. Such a belief amounted to a "total denial of human freedom, and therewith of human responsibility, creativeness, purpose, and any meaning of human existence" (p. 34). Putting it bluntly, Schumacher said that economists had no idea of what they were really teaching and how it was related to the truth.

As for physical factors, there was an *essential* distinction between renewable and non-renewable raw materials, whereas economics treated them as if they were the same, all bearing a price, all contributing to Gross National Product. Little attention was paid to whether the components of national product were "good or bad, healthy or unhealthy, life-sustaining or life-destroying" (p. 34).[57] To the economist, customers were price-hunters only, and "price" conveyed nothing about whether goods were "home produced or imported renewable or non-renewable, the product of sweated labour or fair dealing" (ibid). Economists had a responsibility to understand "fundamental, qualitative differences between 'goods', differences which the market obliterates" (p. 35). They needed to cooperate with experts in "various important aspects of the physical world – with geologists, ecologists, physicists, technologists, and many others" (ibid).

The third and, to Schumacher's mind, most important aspect, concerned the "picture of Man", where the progression from generalisation through to norm was "most dangerous and, in fact, destructive of civilisation" (ibid). As emphasised by Tawney, Man, from being a spiritual being, who engaged in commerce in order to survive, had gone on to give himself over entirely to economic life. As a result, the secular and religious spheres had become "parallel and independent provinces, governed by different laws, judged by different standards, and amenable to different authorities". Commerce had grown indifferent to religion. While the economists were not primarily responsible for such a development, said Schumacher, they had done little to resist it. Their use of econometric models involved a "ruthless and extreme simplification of the picture of man". He was seen "either as a mechanical robot, whose reactions are ascertainable and predictable like those of mindless matter, or as a 'rational' *homo oeconomicus* solely concerned with material self-enrichment". Neither picture bore the marks of *humanity*, and the intensive study of such a discipline did considerably more harm than good. "For every man, in the course of his life, becomes what he thinks, is formed by his thoughts. If what he thinks is narrow and unreal, he himself becomes narrow and unreal" (p. 36).

Closing, he said that the modern world currently faced three crises at once: a "'crisis of confidence' in the future availability of essential raw material supplies, primarily supplies of *fossil fuels*" (p. 36); a "crisis of the environment, of *living nature* around us, which seems to groan and shudder and to tell us that it cannot survive if we continuously intensify our assaults upon it"; and a "crisis in the reactions of *human nature* to our economic way of life which worships giantism and threatens to submerge the human person ... Giantism in organisation as in technology may occasionally give them a feeling of elation, but it makes them unhappy. All modern literature is full of this unhappiness, and so is modern art" (ibid). The factors responsible for these crises were metaphysical, "lying outside the narrow confines of economics but irresistibly determining its validity. I claim, therefore, that if economists wish to become really helpful they must now most seriously and diligently embark on a systematic exploration of meta–economics" (ibid).

As indicated by the remarks quoted at the beginning of this chapter, Schumacher's talk provoked a great hullabaloo, evidently to Robinson's delight. He had "attacked the model-builders", she said, "who have tried to reduce economics once more to a mechanical system". On the other hand, she said, David Laidler's talk was "a clear illustration of the extent to which Keynes has been smothered in academic teaching ... This lecture is also a remarkably neat illustration of the progression from Generalisation to Assumption to Assertion to Norm, described by Schumacher" (1973, pp. ix–x). Not a word, though, about the inconvenient truth of Schumacher's own smothering of Keynes.[58]

Epilogue

The year after Leicester, bringing articles from the *Observer* and *Resurgence* together with some new chapters, Schumacher published *Small is Beautiful: A Study of Economics as if People Mattered*. He expected little to come of it, but, thanks to its success in America, he soon found himself propelled on to the world stage, and accepting a punishing schedule of international talks. After years of relative obscurity, he was now in the public glare, and his name would remain indelibly associated with his popular book. Notwithstanding its success, however, this was not the work he regarded as his *magnum opus*. That accolade he reserved for *A Guide for the Perplexed*, the book he had begun writing in the mid-fifties, not long after Burma. Finally published just before his unexpected death in 1977, this philosophical guide to life drew on his religious and mythical reading of twenty-five years.

Given that it was precisely such influences that had exorcised him of the spirit of *homo oeconomicus*, it is not surprising that the book says little about the "dismal science". However, Schumacher's allusive remarks about his own pilgrimage provide a capstone for the story we have told in his paper. Thus, in Chapter 6, "The Four Fields of Knowledge – Field One", he describes the "grossly impoverished" picture of man provided by scientific observation. It has little to say, in particular, about self-knowledge, the edict to "know thyself", which was central to all forms of traditional philosophy and spirituality – including Plato, Plotinus, Paracelsus, Indian, Islamic, Buddhist and Chinese thought, Shakespeare and, more recently, the traditional psychological teachings of P. D. Ouspensky. Traditional, as distinct from modern, psychology saw the person as a "pilgrim" or *homo viator*, on a path towards some form of supernormal enlightenment or salvation.

> It is the pilgrim's task to undertake a journey into the interior, which demands a degree of heroism and in any case a readiness occasionally to turn one's back on the petty occupations of everyday life. As Joseph

Campbell shows in his wonderful study of *The Hero with a Thousand Faces*, the traditional teachings, most of which are in the form of mythology, do 'not hold as [their] greatest hero merely the virtuous man. Virtue is but the pedagogical prelude to the culminating insight, which goes beyond all pairs of opposites'.

(p. 78)

Like Campbell, Schumacher points to the *Divina Comedia* of Dante, whose spiritual crisis – *nel mezzo del cammin di nostra vita* – had been his own: "at the height of his powers and outward success, [he] suddenly realises that he is not at the height at all but, on the contrary, 'in a dark wood, where the right way was lost'". Hence, the plunge into the Surrey garden; the "Work" of Gurdjieff-Ouspensky; yoga; Buddhist meditation in Rangoon; and on to Christianity. It was this journey that carried him away from the economic mindset.

All traditional wisdom, of which both Dante and Shakespeare are outstanding representatives, transcends ordinary, calculating logic and defines 'The Good' as that which helps us to become truly human by developing our higher faculties – which are conditional on, and also part of, self-awareness. Without them, there is no humanity ... and the question of what is 'The Good' reduces itself to Darwinian questions of adaptation and survival and the utilitarianism of 'the greatest happiness of the greatest number', where happiness rarely implies anything more than comfort and excitement.

(p. 146)

As if speaking of himself, he asks: "What then is the 'true progress' of a human being"? His first task is to "learn from society and 'tradition' and to find his temporary happiness in receiving directions from outside". The second task is the sorting and sifting of knowledge thus acquired: "'individuation', becoming self-directed". Only then can he turn to the third task, which is to relinquish one's egocentricity: only then has he gained freedom, or become "God-directed" (p. 149).

Faced with the *Inferno* of the modern world, he says, many believed in the likelihood and effectiveness of "technological fixes", but a growing number were realizing that the "modern experiment", which began with the Cartesian revolution, had failed. It was not possible to live without religion, i.e., without "systematic work to keep in contact with and develop towards Higher Levels than those of 'ordinary life'". Given the failure of modernity, the task of the "post-modern" was to achieve a change of heart or attitude, a *metanoia*, and see the world in a new light. Enough was known about ecology to keep the earth healthy, and the same earth was generous enough to feed everyone and to provide adequate shelter, all without recourse to violent technologies. It was unnecessary for anyone to live in misery. The so-called "economic problem", he says, in an allusion to Keynes, was a convergent one, and, in fact, had been solved already. There remained, however, a moral problem, which, being divergent, was of a different order and had to be, not solved, but understood and transcended.

By the time this book was reaching its comparatively small readership, Schumacher himself had been buried in the churchyard at Caterham, Surrey. That his gravestone is devoid of crucifix or any religious symbol might be regarded as curious, given his earlier conversion to Catholicism and the huge funeral ceremony at Westminster Cathedral, but less so, perhaps, when one considers the panoply of esoteric influences along his path. Instead, it reads simply "Ernst Friedrich Schumacher, 1911–1977. A guide for the perplexed".

Notes

1. I am grateful to an anonymous referee and to Abhay Ghiara for comments on an earlier draft. For access to the Schumacher family papers in London and the archives at the Schumacher Center for a New Economics, I thank Barbara Wood and Susan Witt, respectively. For permission to quote from the archival material, I am grateful to Vreni Schumacher. Finally, I thank the Social Science and Humanities Research Council of Canada (Grant No. 435–2021–0893) for their financial support.
2. See Schumacher (1973a).
3. See "Full Employment Conference at The Royal Hotel, Upper Woburn Place, London, W.C.1, Saturday, May 22–Sunday, May 23, 1943", Gillingham-Schumacher Box, Unnamed Folder, Schumacher Papers, Schumacher Centre for a New Economics, Great Barrington, Massachusetts (hereafter SPGB).
4. See Schumacher (1973b).
5. From Robinson interview by Barbara Wood, tape transcript, no date, SPGB.
6. See Sam Essame interview by Barbara Wood, tape transcript, no date, SPGB. There appears to have been little love lost between Schumacher and Bronowski. The latter left the Coal Board in 1964 for the Salk Institute, later going on to make the popular 1973 BBC series, *The Ascent of Man*. That programme's celebration of the human mastery of science and technology stood in contrast with Schumacher's more pessimistic assessment.
7. For a detailed account of the lives and influence of Gurdjieff and Ouspensky, see Webb (1980), *The Harmonious Circle*.
8. Gurdjieff visited Lloyd Wright at Taliesin in 1934, on one of his fund-raising ("sheep-shearing") visits to the United States. In turn, in the 1950s, Lloyd Wright would visit John Bennett's Surrey home where he had built a temple-like *Djamechoonatra*, the architecture of which was inspired by Gurdjieff's nine-pointed Enneagram. See Webb, op. cit.; Lloyd Wright (1934); and Bennett's (1962) autobiography, *Witness: The Story of a Search*.
9. In time, he would also read *The Fourth Way* (1957).
10. Nicoll's *Commentaries* were published by Vincent Stuart, a well-known small London publisher of books on metaphysical subjects. Interestingly, Stuart was also the publisher of not only the Gurdjieffian Rodney Collin's *The Theory of Celestial Influence* (1954) and *The Theory of Eternal Life* (1956) but also *The Pattern of Health* (1961) by Aubrey Westlake, a founder of the Soil Association; Arthur Guirdham (1960) *Man: Divine or Social*; and Ruth Harrison's (1964) *Animal Machines: The New Factory Farming Industry*, all of which Schumacher read. Like Westlake, Guirdham was a proponent of "alternative" medicine. Stuart himself was involved in Gurdjieff's "Work" and would go on to write a book on the subject, *Changing Mind* (1981).

11. See Pogson (1961) and (1975). Schumacher was deeply immersed in this literature, reading the writings of many Work followers, including Orage; Kenneth Walker, the Harley St. urologist, whom he appears to have known personally; Claude Bragdon, American architect and translator of Ouspensky; and Margaret Anderson and Kathryn Hulme, both of whom were American members of *The Rope*, a group of women Gurjieffian disciples in France, close to Gertrude Stein.

12. On Coombe Springs, see Bennett, op. cit. Also, Leonard (2019) and the references therein. Followers of the Work were, if not quite sworn to secrecy, certainly discouraged from talking about their involvement. It was something of an event, therefore, when Schumacher and his Coal Board colleague, Sam Essame, discovered each other as G-O disciples. See Essame interview cited above.

13. At this point, Schumacher's older sister, Edith, visiting from Germany, was also involved in the "Work", and trying to make a new beginning in life. Schumacher and the indefatigable Edith were close, maintaining an energetic correspondence for their entire lives. If he also wrote to his own wife, Anna Maria, it was because of her frequent absence in Reinbek, near Hamburg, home of her family. Her attachment to Germany, and reluctance to settle in England, was a matter of concern for the couple throughout the 1950s.

14. Schumacher was also influenced significantly by another German expatriate in London Edward Conze (1904–1979), a Marxist philosopher-turned-Buddhist scholar and translator. Conze was familiar with not only Buddhism but also the Traditionalist literature in time read by Schumacher.

15. Schumacher was also aware of the Island Hermitage of Ceylon, a Buddhist community established in 1911 by *Nyanatiloka Mahathera* (1878–1957), who was born Anton Gueth in Wiesbaden and later converted to Buddhism. His noted pupil was *Nyanaponika Thera* (1901–1994), a German-Jewish convert, born Siegmund Feniger. Schumacher read a number of the writings of these authors, including Nyanatiloka's 1922 5-volume translation of the *Anguttara Nykaya*, and Nyanaponika's *Satipatthana: The Heart of Buddhist Meditation* (1954). Both monks were also involved in the preparations of the massive Sixth Buddhist Council, held in Rangoon while Schumacher was there and witnessed by him. They were also involved in a campaign, beginning in 1953, to promote Buddhism in post-war Germany, in the light of the catastrophic events of World War II. See Nyanatusita and Hecker (2008).

16. See Schumacher (1977b).

17. "Outline" (4pp.) in bundle of notes titled "Very early beginnings of a 'A Guide' 1956–1959", SPGB.

18. On Guénon, see Sedgwick (2009) and Accart (2005).

19. See Sedgwick, op. cit.

20. On Coomaraswamy, see Lipsey (1977) and Pal (2020).

21. Note that Schumacher was the brother-in-law of German atomic physicist, Werner Heisenberg (1901–1976), who had married Schumacher's younger sister Elisabeth in 1937.

22. Schumacher's words; emphasis in original – in "Guénon", in "Very early beginnings", SPGB.

23. SPGB, Box 5, Folder 1, "Coal". Schumacher appears to have submitted this draft to the *Review of Economics and Statistics*, edited by P. W. S. Andrews. A reference letter from American Charles Hitch, formerly at Oxford and by then at the RAND Corporation, found the central part of the paper to be worthy of publication. See letter Hitch to Andrews, 21 January, 1959, loc. cit.

24. It is noteworthy that this draft also marked Schumacher's continued distancing from Keynes. In an earlier BBC broadcast, in 1955, he had suggested that Keynes, were he still alive, would no doubt be attentive to the matter of non-renewable resources and would not be an advocate of the heedless expansion of consumption

and waste. In the present "coal paper", he cites the *General Theory* of Keynes as "an excellent example of success attained by a ruthless 'reduction to quantity'" (p. 4) Within a year, as we shall see, he would be unambiguous in his criticism of Keynes on ethical grounds.

25. Lecture notebooks in Gillingham-Schumacher Box 2, SPGB.

26. See Ruskin (1907).

27. Schumacher's assessment of Communism was informed by his reading of the religious, anti-Communist, Russian-émigré philosopher, Nikolai Berdyaev (1874–1948). His library contains annotated copies of *The Beginning and the End* (1952), *The Realm of the Spirit and the Realm of Caesar* (1952) and *Truth and Revelation* (1953).

28. See McRobie and Porter interviews by Barbara Wood, tape transcripts, no date, SPGB.

29. See Wood (1984), pp. 286–288. Dante became quite important for Schumacher at this time, and he read quite deeply on the subject. For example, Charles Williams' *The Figure of Beatrice* (1943) which provided a mystical interpretation of the allegory, and Dorothy P. Sayers' (1954) *Introductory Papers on Dante* and (1957) *Further Papers on Dante*. Novelist Sayers was of particular importance insofar as she also wrote in defence of Christianity against the pressures of commercial society and about the importance of meaningful work: see *The Mind of the Maker* (1941) and *Creed or Chaos* (1947). Sayers was a significant influence upon Schumacher, who viewed her as one of the most important critics of modern society. She was also read by authors close to the Soil Association, such as H. J. Massingham. See, for example, his *The Tree of Life* (1943).

30. These appeared as (1962) "Roots of Economic Growth". Narayan had already noticed Schumacher's Burma paper "Economics in a Buddhist Country", publishing it as an appendix in his (1959) *A Plea for the Restoration of Indian Polity*, alongside an extract from Erich Fromm's (1956) *The Sane Society*.

31. See "Economic Development & the Search for Peace", in Gillingham-Schumacher Box 2, SPGB.

32. See Robens interview by Barbara Wood, tape transcript, no date, SPGB.

33. This paper, first published as Schumacher (1964), was reprinted several times, most prominently as Schumacher (1971a).

34. See Roy Hodson (1964), "Do-It-Yourself Industrialisation", *The Statist*, 25 September, pp. 833–834.

35. Robinson, op. cit. p. 4.

36. See Kaldor interview by Barbara Wood, tape transcript, no date, SPGB.

37. See "Asia Broadcast, 1965", Box 5, Folder 10, SPGB.

38. For an example of his popular wartime economic writings advocating the development of international trade and transport, see Schumacher (1942) and (1945).

39. Coomaraswamy was *the* celebrant of Indian craft, with books such as (1909) *The Indian Craftsman* (London: Probsthain & Co., 1909) and *Art and Swadeshi* (Madras: Ganesh & Co., 1912). On the cultural splendour of pre-colonial India, the key reference among Gandhians and Traditionalists is George Birdwood (1880) *The Industrial Arts of India* (London: Chapman & Hall).

40. "Christian Men in Industry – A Talk to the Church of England Men's Society", typewritten draft, September 8, 1966, Box 5, Folder 6, Spirituality, SPGB.

41. The book by Herber, *alias* Murray Bookchin, was his 1962 *Our Synthetic Environment*.

42. Schumacher had married Verena Rosenberger in 1962, with whom he went on to have a further four children.

43. See the editor's "Statement of Intent" in *Resurgence*, Vol. I, No. I, May/June 1966, pp. 2–3.

44. See Schumacher (1964) and (1966a), respectively. By the time of his death, ten years later, he had written some thirty-five contributions to *Resurgence*.

45. Gregg was also connected to the Traditionalist movement insofar as he knew Ananda Coomaraswamy in Boston and contributed an article on "The Value of Indian Handcrafts in the Industrial Era" to the 1947 *Festschrift* for the latter (See Gregg (1947)). On Gregg, see the recent biography by J. Wooding (2021).
46. Schumacher (1976a) offers some, though in my opinion, inadequate, acknowledgement of Gregg's influence.
47. Reviewing Gunnar Myrdal's (1968) *Asian Drama*, Schumacher was lukewarm about the author's obsession with methodology, an "exceedingly tedious subject", but agreed with his judgement that Western science and technology were causing more harm than good in developing countries. Underwhelmed by Myrdal's two-thousand pages, he suggested that he write a 100-page summary of his main findings. See Schumacher (1969c).
48. Amongst his further contributions, for example, his "The Economics of Intermediate Technology" (1966b),"Man need not Starve (1967), "Industry and Morals" (1969a), "Healthy Development" (1969b), "Modern Industry in the Light of the Gospel" (1971b), "Christian Responsibility in the present Economic and Inflationary Crisis" (1971c), "Conscious Culture of Poverty" (1975), and "The Turn of the Tree" (1976a) and "Asia Undermined" (1976b).
49. For Kohr's and Seymour's tributes to Schumacher after his death in 1977, see Kohr (1977) and Seymour (1977).
50. Kumar moved to Pentre Ifan, a farm owned by Peggy Hemming, Oxford graduate, Treasury economist and occasional *Resurgence* contributor. See Kumar's (2011) *No Destination: Autobiography of an Earth Pilgrim.*
51. Although Schumacher himself found it difficult to maintain his gardening activity at Caterham, he did insist on making home-made bread with home-milledsey flour – the latter using wheat grown by Sam Mayall, a Soil Association stalwart, and a hand-mill of the kind promoted as Intermediate Technology. After the appearance of his book, Schumacher would write some *Resurgence*-type articles in the newsletter of the Soil Association. See (1976c) and (1977a).
52. From Robinson interview by Barbara Wood, tape transcript, no date, SPGB. Though none bears evidence of careful reading, Schumacher had a number of Robinson's books in his library, including her *Letters from a Visitor to China* (1954); *Economic Philosophy* (1968 [1962]) and *Freedom and Necessity* (1970).
53. See Robinson (ed.) (1973).
54. See Laidler (1973). Remembering the event, Laidler recalled her abusing the chair in order to criticize his talk through misrepresentation, leaving no time for discussion from the floor. He felt that his inclusion had been engineered by Johnson in order to provide some balance to Robinson's choice of speakers (D. Laidler, E-mail to the author, Nov. 20, 2014). See also Laidler (1997). The proceedings of Robinson's session were published in Part I of *After Keynes*. Coincidentally, given Schumacher's interests, the rest of the book contains the proceedings of a joint symposium with Section D on environmental quality, as well as the latter section's presidential address, by K. Mellanby on the biological effects of pollution.
55. Here, Schumacher quotes witheringly Sicco Mansholt, who, as European Commissioner of Agriculture, had been the architect of the Mansholt Plan for the modernisation of agriculture, and, with that, the elimination of the many "uneconomic" family-farms: "For nobody can afford the luxury of not acting economically" (ibid). Similarly to how he regarded Eugene Black of the World Bank, Schumacher saw Mansholt as a enemy of traditional practices and communities, motivated only by considerations of production and efficiency.
56. See Phelps Brown (1972).
57. Schumacher makes no mention of E.J. Mishan's (1967) *The Costs of Economic Growth*, which, at some point, he read and annotated. Whether he did so before or after 1972 is unclear.

58. The sole academic review of the book I have been able to find is by David Worswick, who was also a Beveridge Plan colleague of Schumacher and Robinson. Curiously, it does not even mention Schumacher's contribution. See Worswick (1974).

References

Accart, Xavier (2005), *René Guénon ou le Renversement des Clartés: Influence d'un Métaphysicien sur la Vie intellectuelle française*, Milan: Arche.

Bennett, John G. (1962), *Witness: The Story of a Search*, London: Hodder & Stoughton.

Birdwood, George (1880), *The Industrial Arts of India*, London: Chapman & Hall

Carson, Rachel (1962), *Silent Spring*, Boston, MA: Houghton Mifflin.

Coomaraswamy, Ananda (1909), *The Indian Craftsman*, London: Probsthain & Co.

——— (1912), *Art and Swadeshi*, Madras: Ganesh & Co.

Fromm, Erich (1956), *The Sane Society*, London: Routledge & Kegan Paul

Gregg, Richard B. (1947), "The Validity of Industrial Handcrafts in this Industrial Era", in Iyer, K. Bharatha (ed.) *Art and Thought*, London: Luzac & Co., pp. 95–100.

Harrison, Ruth (1964), *Animal Machines: The New Factory Farming Industry*, with a foreword by Rachel Carson, London: Vincent Stuart.

Hodson, Roy (1964), "Do-It-Yourself Industrialisation", *The Statist*, 25 September, pp. 833–834

Kohr, Leopold (1977), "Tribute to Schumacher", *Resurgence*, Vol. 8, No. 6 (Nov. – Dec.) pp. 5–6.

Kumar, Satish (2011 [1992]), *No Destination: Autobiography of an Earth Pilgrim*, Totnes: Green Books.

Laidler, David (1973), "The Current Inflation – The Problem of Explanation and the Problem of Policy", (Lister Lecture) in Robinson (ed.) *After Keynes*, pp. 37–54.

——— (1997), *Money and Macroeconomics: The Selected Essays of David Laidler*, Cheltenham: Edward Elgar.

——— (2014), E-mail to the author.

Leonard, Robert (2019), "E. F. Schumacher and the Making of 'Buddhist Economics', 1950 – 1973", *Journal of the History of Economic Thought*, Vol. 41, No. 2, (June), pp. 159–186

Lipsey, Roger (1977), *Coomaraswamy: His Life and Work*, Princeton: Princeton University Press.

Lloyd Wright, Frank (1934), "Gurdjeef [sic] at Taliesin", *Capitol Times* (Madison, Wisconsin) August 26th.

Mishan, E. J. (1967), *The Costs of Economic Growth*, London: Staples Press

Myrdal, Gunnar (1968), *Asian Drama: An Inquiry into the Poverty of Nations, Vols. I, II and III*, New York: Pantheon

Nicoll, Maurice (1998 [1940]), *Simple Explanation of Work Ideas*, Utrecht: Eureka Editions.

Nyanatusita, Bhikku and Hellmuth Hecker (2008), *The Life of Nyanatiloka Thera: The Biography of a Western Buddhist Pioneer*, Kandy: Buddhist Publication Society.

Pal, Pratapaditya (2020), *Quest for Coomaraswamy: A Life in the Arts*, Calgary: Bayeux Arts.

Papworth, John (1977), "Dr. E. F. Schumacher", *Resurgence*, Vol. 8, No. 6, (Nov.–Dec.), p. 4.

Phelps Brown, E. H. (1972), "The Underdevelopment of Economics", *Economic Journal*, Vol. 82, No. 325, (March), pp. 1–10

Pogson, Beryl (1961), *Maurice Nicoll: A Portrait*, London: Vincent Stuart.

———— (1975), *The Work Life: Talks at Dorton House and Nutley Terrace, based on the teachings of Gurdjieff, Ouspensky and Nicoll*, privately printed, Belfast.

Robinson, Joan (ed.) (1973), *After Keynes*, Oxford: Basil Blackwell.

Robinson, Ronald (ed.) (1971), *Developing the Third World: the Experience of the Nineteen-Sixties*, Cambridge: Cambridge, UK: Cambridge University Press.

Ruskin, John (1907), *Unto this Last and Other Essays*, London: J. M. Dent.

Sayers, Dorothy P. (1954), *Introductory Papers on Dante*, London: Methuen.

———— (1957), *Further Papers on Dante*, London: Methuen.

Schumacher, E. F. (1942), "A Plan for International Trade", World Review, October, pp. 28–31.

———— (1945), "Hands Wanted: A Survey of Britain's Economic Prospects", Current Affairs (Army Bureau of Current Affairs), No. 106 (A), October 20th, 19pp.

———— (1959), "Economics in a Buddhist Country", in Jaya Prakash Narayan, *A Plea for Reconstruction of Indian Polity*, Varanasi, Wardha: A. B. Sarva Seva Sangh, Appendix A, pp. 81–88.

———— (1962), *The Roots of Economic Growth*, Varanasi: Gandhian Institute of Studies.

———— (1964), "Industrialisation through 'Intermediate Technology'", Cambridge Conference on Development report 1964, reprinted in *Resurgence*, Vol. 1, No. 2, July–Aug., 1966; in Robinson (ed.) (1971), pp. 85–93, and in Schumacher (1997), pp. 130–142.

———— (1966a), "Industrial Society", *Resurgence*, Vol. 1, No. 3, (Sept.–Oct.), pp. 12–16.

———— (1966b), "The Economics of Intermediate Technology", *Resurgence*, Vol. 1, No. 2, (Jul.–Aug.), pp. 8–10.

———— (1967), "Man need not Starve", *Resurgence*, Vol. 1, No. 10, (Nov.–Dec.), pp. 143–158, reprinted in *This I Believe*, pp. 143–158.

———— (1968), "The New Economics", *Resurgence*, Vol. 2, No. 3, (Sept.–Oct.), pp. 8–11, reprinted in *This I Believe*, pp. 44–54.

———— (1969a), "Industry & Morals", *Resurgence*, Vol. 2, No. 5, (Jan.–Feb.), pp. 7–10, reprinted in This I Believe, pp. 87–96.

———— (1969b), "Healthy Development", *Resurgence*, Vol. 2, No. 8/9, (Jul.–Oct.), reprinted in This I Believe, pp. 119–129.

———— (1969c), Review of Gunnar Myrdal (1968) *Asian Drama: An Inquiry into the Poverty of Nations, Vols. I, II and III*, New York, NY: Pantheon, 2284pp., in *International Affairs*, Vol. 45, No. 1, pp. 169–170.

———— (1970), "The Economics of Permanence", *Resurgence*, Vol. 3, No. 1, (May–Jun.), reprinted in *Small is Beautiful* as "Peace and Permanence", pp. 19–35.

———— (1971a), "Industrialisation through 'Intermediate Technology'", in Robinson (ed.) (1971), pp. 85–93

———— (1971b), "Modern Industry in the Light of the Gospel", *Resurgence*, Vol. 3, No. 6, (Mar.–Apr.), pp. 8–11.

———— (1971c), "Christian Responsibility in the present Economic and Inflationary Crisis", *Resurgence*, Vol. 3, No. 7, (May–Jun.), pp. 16–17.

———— (1973a), "Does Economics Help? An Exploration of Meta-economics", in Robinson (ed.) *After Keynes*, pp. 26–36.

———— (1973b), *Small is Beautiful: A Study of Economics as if People Mattered*, London: Blonde & Briggs.

———— (1975), "Conscious Culture of Poverty", *Resurgence*, Vol. 6, No. 1, (Mar.–Apr.), pp. 10–11.

———— (1976a), "The Turn of the Tree", *Resurgence*, Vol. 7, No. 2, (May–Jun.), p. 23.

_____ (1976b), "Asia Undermined", *Resurgence*, Vol. 7, No.3 (July – Aug.), pp. 15–18.

_____ (1976c), "The Generosity of Nature", *The Soil Association, Quarterly Review*, Vol. 2, No. 4, (Dec.), pp. 1–2.

_____ (1977a), "The Next Thirty Years", *The Soil Association, Quarterly Review*, Vol. 3, No. 4, (Dec.), pp. 1–2.

_____ (1977b), *A Guide for the Perplexed*, London: Jonathan Cape.

Schuon, Fritjhof (2007, [1953]), *Spiritual Perspectives and Human Facts. A New Translation with Selected Letters*, edited by James Cutsinger, Bloomington, IN: World Wisdom (Version in Schumacher's library: 1954, Faber).

Sedgwick, Mark (2009), *Against the Modern World: Traditionalism and the Secret Intellectual History of the Twentieth Century*, Oxford: Oxford U.P.

Seymour, John (1977), "Lost Leader", *Resurgence*, Vol. 8, No. 6, (Nov. – Dec.), p. 5.

Stuart, Vincent G. (1981), *Changing Mind*, Middlesex: Penguin.

Webb, James (1980), *The Harmonious Circle: The Lives and Work of G. I. Gurdjieff, P. D. Ouspensky and Their Followers*, London: Thames & Hudson, 608pp.

Williams, Charles (1943), *The Figure of Beatrice*, London: Faber.

Wood, Barbara (1984), *E. F. Schumacher: His Life and Thought*, New York: Harper & Row

Wooding, John (2021), *The Power of Non-Violence. The Enduring Legacy of Richard Gregg*, Lowell, MA: Loom Press.

Worswick, G. D. N. (1974), Review of Robinson, Joan (ed.) (1973) *After Keynes,*(Oxford: Basil Blackwell), in Economica, *New Series*, Vol. 41, No. 164 (Nov.), pp. 454–455.

Part IV

Behavioral economics

10 Hands on Nudging

Daniel M. Hausman

Wade Hands has written so much on so many subject matters that I cannot imagine anything short of a book that would do justice to his writings. Moreover, any appreciation of his contributions to economics and economic methodology can hardly confine itself to his writings, given his extensive history as an editor and mentor. What I propose to do instead is to focus on a single recent article that exemplifies the virtues of his work, even as I shall offer the perverse flattery of criticism, which is appreciated only by those, like Hands, who are true philosophers.

Hands on general equilibrium

First a personal digression. I've known Wade for 40 years, although it was only after a few years corresponding that we met in person. The oldest letter from him that I can find is dated June 30, 1981, and it's pretty amazing. Here is a portion:

> GE is unique in that it is not empirical in any traditional sense, yet it is more than merely mathematics. For instance – a model which allows for complementarities between goods is preferred to one which only allows substitution – simply because we know that some goods are complements in any actual economy. Yet this preference for "realism" is somewhat trite, since no GE model is falsifiable, complementarities or not. I think the important thing is that there is something like a criteria of progress within GE. The editors of *Econometrica* know whether a certain result is "progressive" or not, but the criterion employed is nothing like "more confirmed," "more potentially falsifiable," or even a "theoretically progressive problemshift," and yet the criteria are not like the standards used for determining what goes into a literature (or even a philosophy) journal. Progress in GE is quasi-empirical and yet fundamentally different from what satisfies any criteria proposed for natural science. What is this criterion? What makes GE progressive? I don't know, but I feel it has something to do with the growth of knowledge in "possible world" systems. I think you are on a similar track (and further along).

DOI: 10.4324/9781003266051-15

This is vintage Hands (and not merely owing to its age). He is focused on the economics, which he knows inside and out. (Other parts of the letter criticize me for focusing on issues concerning the existence of general equilibrium, which he rightly regards as by then superseded by other issues.) At the same time, there is an easy familiarity with state-of-the-art philosophy of science. With utter clarity, he lays out the central question: "What constitutes progress in general equilibrium theory?" and he resists plumping for any facile answer. At the same time that he asks big questions, he ties them to concrete issues. He ends this passage with characteristic generosity.

Nudging and steering

One can see this same intellect equipped with the same clarity, forthrightness, and precision at work in Wade's recent essay, "Libertarian Paternalism: Taking Econs Seriously" (2020). As readers know, unless they have been trekking in the wilderness for the last few decades, there has been a surge of empirical investigation by economists and psychologists which has identified systematic ways in which choice behavior diverges from models of self-interested rational choice. Rather than carrying around with them an all-purpose complete and transitive preference ranking, people tend to generate on the fly their preferences among the immediate objects of choice. Of course, there are constraints. Maryanne, who has been a vegetarian for years, is unlikely suddenly to choose meatballs from the menu at an Italian restaurant rather than eggplant parmesan. But among the unfamiliar vegetarian entrées at a Japanese restaurant, she may make up her rankings, which might have been different at another time of the day or in different company. In a different context or with a different prompt, many of the preferences individuals express or reveal in their behavior will differ, and even within a single context, their preferences may be gappy and intransitive. Choice behavior is sensitive to a wide variety of contextual factors, psychological foibles and heuristics that lead individuals to act in ways that they themselves may regard as mistakes.

Although it takes no great acumen to recognize that individuals sometimes make stupid choices (just think honestly about oneself!), economists before this surge of behavioral investigation could pretend that mistaken choices were uncommon and unsystematic. But with the identification of systematic violations of economic rationality, economists could no longer pretend that, as a good first approximation, individuals always choose whatever is best for themselves. That means that the specter of paternalism cannot be exorcized as an impossibility, on the grounds that individuals are already doing whatever is best for themselves. One reaction has been to embrace paternalism ("oh, the horror, the horror!"), but to lessen the sting by avoiding coercion.

In their influential book, *Nudge* (2008), Richard Thaler and Cass Sunstein discuss the possibilities of influencing people's choices without coercing them by improving the "architecture" of their choices. If customers have to retrieve their bank card from an ATM machine before it gives out any cash, then it takes a great deal less attention and care from bank customers to avoid leaving their cards in the machine. Thaler and Sunstein point out that governments can get people to make better choices *without limiting their freedom*, by structuring intelligently the circumstances in which they make their choices.

Thaler and Sunstein define a nudge as "any aspect of the choice architecture that alters people's behavior in a predictable way without forbidding any options or significantly changing their economic incentives" (Thaler and Sunstein 2008, p. 6). In more recent work, Sunstein elaborates on this characterization of nudges as follows:

> Nudges are interventions that steer people in particular directions but that also allow them to go their own way. A reminder is a nudge; so is a warning. A GPS nudges; a default rule nudges. To qualify as a nudge, an intervention must not impose significant material incentives (including disincentives). A subsidy is not a nudge; a tax is not a nudge; a fine or a jail sentence is not a nudge. To count as such, a nudge must fully preserve freedom of choice.... Some nudges work because they inform people; other nudges work because they make certain choices easier; still other nudges work because of the power of inertia and procrastination.
>
> (Sunstein 2015, p. 417)

As Thaler and Sunstein define nudges, they consist of any way of influencing choices that preserves freedom of choice. So defined, nudges could include, at one extreme, slipping some valium into one's rich and stingy uncle's dinner before asking for a loan, or, at the opposite extreme, offering a group of voters a course in decision theory.

As these examples show, actions that aim to shape choices non-coercively are an extremely heterogeneous grouping, and it is questionable whether much can be said about them all, other than that they are not coercive, and they aim to influence behavior. Consider the following twelve methods of shaping choices[1]:

1 *Encouraging or discouraging*: Providing weak or non-material incentives, such as issuing a plea to the public during a pandemic not to gather in large groups.
2 *Informing*: Providing relevant information, such as studies showing the reduction in transmission of Covid-19 when individuals wear masks, and rational arguments concerning the implications of the information.
3 *Authoritative direction*: Legitimate, credible, and trustworthy institutions and experts can issue directions for the public to follow at its discretion, which are potent because of the respect and trust accorded to those institutions and individuals, without need of sanctions.
4 *Social influencing and modeling*: Describing what other people do, or providing models of behavior, as exemplified both positively and negatively by recent administrations in the U.S.

5 *Activating or inciting:* Stimulating emotions to motivate individuals, such as calling obligatory shut downs or mask mandates "tyranny" or "fascism."
6 *Rewarding:* Giving people an additional incentive. For example, people might be entered in lotteries in exchange for being vaccinated. Thaler and Sunstein might want to exclude this method, on the grounds that one is changing the material incentives. But a lottery ticket with a modest cash value is not coercive, and the rewards offered need not be financial.
7 *Training or educating:* Influencing the deliberative capacities.[2] There isn't much that government can do to enhance deliberative capacities, but it seems that political leaders can undermine rational deliberation by means of sloppy and dishonest political speeches.
8 *Deceiving:* Providing false information. Arguably this can cross the line to coercion. Someone who makes a choice on the basis of misinformation provided by a competitor or enemy is arguably not choosing freely. But not just any false belief undermines voluntary choice.
9 *Cooling off:* Calming emotions and encouraging patient deliberation. Given the incentives on the media to provide excitement, this method is more often available at a local level.
10 *Confusing:* Employing fallacious arguments. Arguments in general seem to have a lesser role in the political fray than unargued assertions.
11 *Framing:* Shifting the *meaning* of actions, rather than changing the options among which people are choosing. For example, not wearing a mask can be conceptualized as a political statement, as a matter of self-protection, or as an altruistic effort to protect others.
12 *Nudging* (in a narrow sense): Changing the choice circumstances to neutralize or to exploit deliberative foibles. For example, designing parking ramps so that the exit gate will not open until drivers have retrieved their credit cards makes it difficult for them to leave their cards accidentally.

Note that nudges need not be employed paternalistically. They are devices for influencing behavior without coercion, regardless of the purposes. However, for the rest of the paper, I shall, like Hands, focus on shaping behavior for paternalistic purposes – that is, on so-called "libertarian paternalism," (LP). Except where noted, when I speak of nudges, I shall be referring exclusively to nudges that are paternalistic in intent.

Nudging narrowly conceived

The methods of influencing behavior listed above obviously differ, and, as far as I can tell, all can be employed toward admirable or despicable ends. Thaler and Sunstein would call all of these "nudges," except perhaps deception and reward. Rather than using "nudging" to refer both to non-coercive persuasion in general and to the use of choice architecture, I call non-coercive influencing "steering," to avoid conflating it with nudging in the narrow sense, which I take to be one method of steering people.

Like Hands, I shall use the term, "nudge," only to refer to influencing choices by modifying the circumstances of choice, because that notion fits the central examples that Thaler and Sunstein give and, moreover, it is only in that notion that there is any novelty in Thaler and Sunstein's work. Changing the default on a retirement plan so that employees are automatically enrolled unless they opt out is not informing, educating, deceiving, rewarding, or inciting them. What Thaler and Sunstein' are concerned with, and what makes their work original and important is not the recognition that it is possible to persuade people without coercing them. Long before Henry V declared to his small band at Agincourt, "We would not die in that man's company that fears his fellowship to die with us," leaders were well aware that they could to some extent control people's actions, by exhorting them, informing them, deceiving them, or inciting them. What make Thaler's and Sunstein's *Nudge* noteworthy is its recognition that the heuristics and flaws that behavioral economics have identified in human decision-making constitute not only problems but also opportunities for public policy. Thaler and Sunstein's contribution rests on what they have to say about nudges in the narrow sense. In placing healthy foods prominently in a cafeteria line, Thaler and Sunstein's "choice architect," Caroline, is not encouraging or discouraging, informing, inciting, training, or deceiving individuals. She is instead nudging them.

What is at issue is the importance of distinguishing among the many ways to influence choices, not which of these one calls "nudges." What makes this taxonomic discussion worthwhile is its reminder of the enormous differences among ways of influencing choices and hence of the variety of techniques that governments may employ for purposes such as improving adherence to tiresome current public-health guidelines or overcoming vaccine hesitancy. The different ways of influencing behavior raise distinct questions concerning the feasibility and permissibility of non-coercive influences. For example, in his 2015 essay, Sunstein asks whether "nudges" (by which he means, roughly, any non-coercive methods of influencing behavior) promote or undermine welfare, autonomy, and dignity (p. 413). But there is no reason to suppose that the same answer should be given for each of the different methods or whether Sunstein's question makes sense without specifying which method one is asking about. Providing information or cooling people down does not threaten autonomy. Deception and confusion do.

Sunstein seems implicitly to concede the criticism when he writes, for example, that whether "nudges intrude on autonomy" "depends on what kind of nudge is involved" (2015, p. 437). But when confronted with criticisms of one method of influencing behavior that falls under the broad rubric of what he regards as nudges, he responds by pointing out that the criticism fails with respect to other methods. So, for example, when addressing the criticism that nudges (in the narrow sense) exploit rather than improve cognitive flaws (Conly 2012, p. 30), Sunstein replies that her criticism "is not fairly leveled against most kinds of nudges. Recall that many nudges are educative" (2015, p. 446). Only through equivocating on the concept of a nudge can the fact that informing people does not play on people's cognitive foibles count as a defense against the charge that choice architecture does.

Imposing rigor on libertarian paternalism

Nudging is supposed to address mistakes that humans make. Thaler and Sunstein declare emphatically that their aim is "to make people better off *as judged by themselves*" (2008, p. 5). But if individuals judge that they are better off eating the fruit for dessert, why do they choose the cake when they are not nudged? One answer, which Infante, Lecouteux, and Sugden (2016a) defend, is that individuals contain an "inner rational agent," with rational preferences that are context independent, and provide the standard of what makes people better off "as judged by themselves." "The normative criterion is the satisfaction of each individual's latent (or 'purified') preferences" (2016b, p. 33). The inner rational agent is the self, once one strips away the psychological muck that is responsible for the irrationality one finds in ordinary behavior.

Hands accepts this interpretation without hesitation and links it to the contrast Thaler and Sunstein draw between humans and "Econs," who have rational, context independent preferences, whose choices will be unaffected by (paternalistic) nudges:

> Like the agents in traditional economics textbooks, Econs are endowed with stable well-ordered preferences that (along with beliefs and constraints) are causally responsible for, and/or can systematically rationalize, the choices of individual Econs. *But it also follows that Humans have Econs deep inside*—an inner rational agent (Infante *et al.* 2016a, p. 14)— but that inner Econ is seldom responsible for, and/or rationalizes, Human choices, because that inner rational agent is surrounded by a psychological shell of heuristics, biases, frames, and other factors which systematically prevent Humans from manifesting the preferences of their inner rational agent.
>
> (2020, p. 422; italics added).

It is not clear how the definition of an Econ or the need for a criterion to determine what is better for individuals as judged by themselves implies the existence of an inner rational agent. Postulating such an agent gives a clear sense of how it can be that x is better for person A than y, as judged by A, even though A chooses y over x (at least prior to being nudged). In sympathy with Hands and Infante, Lecouteux, and Sugden (ILS), one might ask how else one can make sense of Thaler and Sunstein's mild paternalism, which insists on heeding the ends of agents, whatever they may be. I will return to this question later in the "Reconstructing libertarian paternalism" section.

Hands takes the concept of an Econ and the relationship between the Econs within and the Humans they inhabit very seriously. Although consonant with most of what ILS have to say about LP, the precision with which Hands lays out the issues permits him to derive more clear-cut implications. First of all, he argues that Econs and Humans do not exhaust the choice behaviors found in humans (lower case), who are not necessarily "faulty Econs," and whose choices need not derive (with psychological distortions) from the "purified" preferences possessed by an inner Econ.

> For example, actual humans may make the choices they do because their behavior is a result of the simple conditioned responses of early behaviorism; or because they are nothing but robotic survival machines being propelled by the replication of their selfish genes ...; or perhaps behavior is structurally and culturally determined as with the *homo sociologicus* of traditional social theory; or perhaps it is because of the boundedly rational, but not preference-based, mechanisms of fast-and-frugal ecological rationality...; and there are of course many other possibilities.
>
> (2020, p. 423)

I think that Hands has missed another possibility here. All of the explanatory factors that Hands cites can be located in the psychological "shell" that blocks the manifestation of the Econ's preferences in the Human's choices. Of course, factors such as bounded rationality deny that Econs are possible, but one can bracket that concern or regard bounded rationality as refuting the Econ idealization rather than limiting its scope.

If one takes Thaler and Sunstein literally, as Hands sets out to do, one should conceive of Econs as the idealized agents depicted in mainstream economic theory, such as consumer choice theory. So, Hands argues,

> Econs solve this [consumer choice] problem perfectly while Humans have the utility function $U(x)$, but fail to solve the problem correctly; they make mistakes. In the fully optimizing case these demand functions will satisfy certain potentially observable comparative statics conditions ... and making mistakes means that either the consumer does not have demand functions or their demand functions are missing some of these properties....
>
> So given this, what does a LP [libertarian paternalist] nudge do? They nudge Humans into optimal behavior and thus onto the demand functions that they would have if they were Econs.... The problem to be solved by nudging is a mistake (i.e., in the decision-making process) and not the irrationality or instability of the agent's preferences.
>
> (2020, p. 429)

As ILS note, the result is ironic. The context dependence and instability in preferences behavioral economists have identified (Lichtenstein and Slovic

2006) and the fact that individuals often construct their preferences on the fly with many violations of rationality conditions turn out to cloak a perfect *homo economicus* who would stand before us like the golden and jeweled Maltese Falcon, once we strip off its black coating.

> The mistakes of Humans do not come from having something wrong with their preferences, but rather from their outer psychological shell that leads them to the wrong choices, given their preferences....
>
>   if Econ is the normative standard and defined by textbook homo economicus, then it is a given that Econ has fixed well-behaved preferences—as does the inner rational agent of Humans—and thus neither type of agent could have constructed preferences. Real people may well have constructed preferences—or no preferences whatsoever—but such people are not Econ and they cannot be nudged into being Econ, because there is no coherent way of talking about mistakes in rational decision making unless there are stable well-ordered preferences to serve as the normative reference point.
>
> (2020, p. 433)

Hands' logic is trenchant and relentless. To be a Human (a faulty Econ), an individual must have an Econ's preferences (which may mean that there are no Humans). Since nudging only removes mistakes in implementing fixed preferences, those without an Econ within cannot be successfully nudged, because there is no fixed preference ranking in terms of which nudging improves the outcome from the agent's perspective. Starting from essentially ILS's position, Hands winds up with conclusions that are consonant with theirs but in their precision, they are more devastating to Thaler and Sunstein and others who rely on an inner rational agent: "LP's commitment to Econs as the proper normative baseline means that constructed preferences play no role in LP theory or practice" (2020, p. 433). "It [LP] is weak in part because even if it were entirely effective, it only deals with an extremely small set of ways that the behavior of agents could deviate from the rationality of Econ" (2020, p. 436).

   Although Hands is here – as always – polite, he has apparently eviscerated Thaler and Sunstein's LP. LP has a non-existent scope (unless one believes, contrary to the findings of behavioral economics, that humans are Humans, who walk around with stable, rational, context independent latent preferences). Nudges appear to be of value only insofar as they are confused with other positions (2020, p. 438).

Reconstructing libertarian paternalism

Things have gone so badly wrong that perhaps we should take a step back and see whether there is some other way of understanding nudges and LP that is more interesting and defensible. The view I shall sketch on behalf of Thaler and Sunstein (2003, 2008) and Camerer *et al.* (2003) will not be faithful to everything they write, but it leads to a coherent account of nudges that explains how they can be useful and consistent with the findings of behavioral economics.

The first step in formulating a valuable form of LP, or (paternalistic) nudges, is to be clear about what mechanism(s) LP uses to influence choices. There are many possibilities listed above, including especially framing and social influencing, but I shall focus on choice architecture or nudging – changing the structure or context of individual choices. If one can believe other findings of behavioral economics, what happens is that when faced with choices among retirement plans, some individuals have relatively fixed preferences, and their choice of whether to enroll or not is not influenced by whether enrollment is the default. Those who have such stable preferences concerning retirement do not necessarily have stable preferences between cake and fruit in the cafeteria. What makes nudging potent is that many individuals do not have fixed preferences among retirement plans and instead construct their preferences among them or their preferences among desserts "on the fly." If the default is not to enroll, many people, through laziness or some heuristic or other, do not enroll, even though with a different default they would have constructed other preferences. When asked, they will construct rationalizations for their choices. Regarding nudges as influencing preference formation rather than as enabling latent preferences to show themselves is both intuitively more plausible than is the story of Econs and Humans and in far better accord with the findings of behavioral economics.

However, this account appears to undermine the criterion upon which nudges are assessed. What sense can we make of the view that nudges are successful if they "make people better off *as judged by themselves*" (Thaler and Sunstein 2008, p. 8), when the preferences that ground those judgments may be made up on the spot?

Let us then consider this criterion with some care. First, unlike Cartwright and Hight (2020), I interpret the object of the judgment that one is better off to be the outcome of the nudge, not the experience of having been nudged itself, which individuals in some cases, may not even be aware of. Second, does the condition that people be better off "as judged by themselves" mean that individuals are in fact better off and they also judge correctly that they are, or does it mean merely that individuals believe that they are better off? When Thaler and Sunstein first introduce the objective of making individuals better off "as judged by themselves," they write, "we argue for self-conscious efforts … to steer people's choices in directions that will improve their lives" (2008, p. 5). The ambition is to make people better off, not merely to make them believe that they are better off. Yet, the first interpretation is apparently ruled out by Thaler and Sunstein's insistence that they are not committed to any view of which is the better choice, full stop. They insist that they have no ambition of telling people how to behave. When they assert that "some changes in the choice architecture could make their lives go better" they immediately add, "(as judged by their own preferences, not those of some bureaucrat)" (pp. 9–10). They claim to rely entirely on the values of the agents themselves. Hence, all they can mean when they say that LP policies "make people better off *as judged by themselves*" is that people believe that successful nudges make them better off.

Whether a successfully nudged individual believes she is better off does not require an authoritative interior oracle. To be sure, if choice architecture determines preferences and not just how preferences display themselves in choices, it is possible that individuals may be just as satisfied with their choices regardless of which way they are nudged. In that case, there would be little basis for the conclusion that nudging makes people better off. But, if all that one cares about is that people judge that they are better off, what is the problem? There is no reason to invoke an inner rational agent, unless one wants to make people better off and needs the judgments of an inner rational agent to provide a criterion for success.

Of course, those who enroll in a retirement plan because enrollment is the default are unlikely to have any belief about how much better off they are than if they had not enrolled – probably not for decades in any case (Cartwright and Hight 2020). If they do think they are better off, it may be due to cognitive dissonance, which would have led them to be just as satisfied with the opposite choice. To the extent that the question ever occurs to Harry, Beatrice, and others of whether the fruit last Tuesday made them better off than the cake they usually take, they are bound to have a variety of views. How large a consensus is needed? Does the justifiability of the nudge depend on such an opinion poll?

The way out of this morass and at the same time to respond to ILS's and Hands' criticisms of LP is to give up the pretense that LP functions without any normative premises other than that it is good if people are better off "as judged by themselves." It is good if people are better off "as judged by themselves" provides a criterion by which to judge the success of nudging only if being better off "as judged by themselves" has some relationship to being better off, full stop. Thaler and Sunstein clearly assume that there is some relationship, since they aim to "steer people's choices in directions that will improve their lives" (2008, p. 5)

In recent work, Sunstein addresses this point more explicitly. He writes, "Many nudges are designed to make people better off, as judged by themselves. This criterion, *meant to ensure that nudges will increase people's welfare,* contains some ambiguity" (2018, p. 1 [italics added]). If one assumes that whenever nudges help people to satisfy fixed antecedent preferences, those who are nudged believe correctly that they are better off, then there is no difficulty in regarding nudges as increasing welfare whenever people believe that they are better off. However, prompted by Sugden's criticisms (2017), Sunstein recognizes that it may be the case that, nudged toward x, Nancy would judge x as better for her than y, while nudged toward y, she would judge y as better for her than x. In such a case, her judgment does not determine which enhances her welfare.

Sunstein responds:

> Social planners—or in our terminology, choice architects—might well have their own ideas about what would make choosers better off, but in our view, the lodestar is people's own judgments. To be a bit more specific: The lodestar is welfare, and under the appropriate conditions, people's own judgments are a good (if sometimes imperfect) way to test the question whether nudges are increasing their welfare.
>
> (2018, p. 2)

The first sentence sounds as if it reaffirms the insistence on deferring to the judgments of those who are nudged, but the second sentence takes that back. It implies that the objective is to make people better off, *regardless of their judgment*, which is only "a good (if sometimes imperfect) way to test the question whether nudges are increasing their welfare." The views of the nudged are only evidence concerning what increases people's welfare. The approval of the nudged is no proof of an improvement in welfare, even in the easy cases in which nudges merely facilitate the satisfaction of antecedent preferences. This is, in my view, a perfectly satisfactory conclusion; however, uncomfortable it may make Thaler and Sunstein and other economists who would prefer to delegate normative judgments to someone else.

Recognizing that approval of the nudged is not decisive means that Thaler and Sunstein should concede that they rely on substantive generalizations concerning what choices make people better off. Policy makers are, of course, in no position to know whether Harry is better off with the cake or the fruit or whether Beatrice will be unable to pursue some important expensive goal because of mistakenly enrolling in a retirement plan – though policy makers are not in a much better position to know whether Harry thinks he's better off with the fruit than whether he is actually better off. What policy makers can judge – fallibly, of course – is that fruit is a better dessert for most people and that people generally save too little for retirement.[3] Such rough generalizations, that are moreover only weakly confirmed, would be an extremely precarious basis for coercive policies, but they are arguably sufficient to justify the more prominent placement of fruit and setting the default in a retirement plan, since it is easy for those who want the cake rather than the fruit or present consumption rather than saving for retirement to do as they please.

The existence of these generalizations concerning prudent choices makes it possible to judge whether nudges are wise or inadvisable without reference to latent preference rankings that individuals may be made to confess to after sufficient "purification" of their manifest preferences. Rather than justifying nudging people not to smoke by supposing that down deep smokers share their inner Econ's preferences not to smoke, generalizations such as "smoking is on average harmful to individuals" can do the job of justifying nudging people not to smoke.

Thaler and Sunstein may not be happy with my call to them to come out into the open not only as paternalists, which they already confess to, but also as paternalists who are prepared to nudge individuals toward choices that are generally prudent, whether or not the agents see it that way. What is especially attractive about nudges is that policy makers can institute policies that they believe to be generally prudent with relatively low risk, since nudges are weak, and agents are free to go their own way. What justifies an apparently successful nudge, such as painting "Look right" and "Look left" at street corners in London is whether the warnings avert accidents (given the assumption that fewer accidents make people better off), not a survey of whether people believe that these warnings have made them better off.

Conclusion: away with the ghostly nudge judge

Having jettisoned the "as judged by themselves" criterion for successful nudging, there is no need to invoke Econs within to serve as the judges of nudges. It is time to exorcize those ghosts. Whether invoking a notion of well-being that is independent of the beliefs of the nudged or relying exclusively on the beliefs of the nudged, there is no need to invoke an inner rational agent to appraise nudges, and very good reason not to. The conflicts with the findings of behavioral economics thereby dissolve. LP aims to use choice architecture to make real individuals – humans, not Humans, in Hand's terminology – better off. That aim is fully consistent with a recognition that people's preferences are often constructed on the fly, that they are incomplete, context independent, and often intransitive. How much good nudges can do is uncertain, but LP is not committed to an inner rational agent.

Notes

1. There are other methods of influencing choices that cannot be used by democratic governments, such as drugging individuals or brain washing them with subliminal messages. There are also dozens and dozens of very specific ways that in everyday encounters people attempt to influence the behavior of others. For example, to encourage behavior, we cajole, praise, exhort, urge, or goad one another, and to discourage behavior, we criticize, shame, embarrass, dishonor, or humiliate each other. The extent to which it is feasible or proper for public officials to employ such means requires a long discussion, which I shall not provide here.
2. Grüne-Yanoff and Hertwig (2016) call this "boosting" rather than training. I prefer "training," because it avoids implying that changes induced in people's deliberation are necessarily positive.
3. One sees such judgments in *Nudge* itself, despite Thaler and Sunstein's claim to defer to the judgments of the nudged. "With respect to diet, smoking, and drinking, people's current choices cannot reasonably be claimed to be the best means of promoting their well-being" (Thaler and Sunstein 2008, p. 7).

References

Camerer C., S. Issacharoff, G. Loewenstein, T. O'Donoghue, and M. Rabin. 2003. "Regulation for Conservatives: Behavioral Economics and the Case for 'Asymmetric Paternalism'." *University of Pennsylvania Law Review* 151:1211–1254.

Cartwright, A. and M. Hight. 2020. "'Better Off as Judged by Themselves': A Critical Analysis of the Conceptual Foundations of Nudging." *Cambridge Journal of Economics* 44:33–54. https://doi.org/10.1093/cje/bez012

Conly, S. 2012. *Against Autonomy: Justifying Coercive Paternalism.* Cambridge: Cambridge University Press.

Grüne-Yanoff, T. and R. Hertwig. 2016. "Nudge Versus Boost: How Coherent are Policy and Theory?" *Minds and Machines* 26:149–183.

Hands, D. Wade. 2020. "Libertarian Paternalism: Taking Econs Seriously." *International Review of Economics* 67:419–441.

Infante, G., G. Lecouteux, and R. Sugden. 2016a. "Preference Purification and the Inner Rational Agent: A Critique of the Conventional Wisdom of Behavioural Welfare Economics." *Journal of Economic Methodology* 23:1–25.

———. 2016b. "On the Econ within': A Reply to Daniel Hausman." *Journal of Economic Methodology* 23:33–37.

Lichtenstein, S. and P. Slovic. 2006. The Construction of Preference: An Overview. In: Lichtenstein, S. and P. Slovic, eds. *The Construction of Preference.* New York, NY: Cambridge University Press, pp. 1–40.

Sugden, R. 2017. "Do People Really Want to be Nudged towards Healthy Lifestyles?" *International Review of Economics* 64:113–23.

———. 2018. "'Better Off, as Judged by Themselves': A Reply to Cass Sunstein." *International Review of Economics* 65:9–13.

Sunstein, C. 2015. "The Ethics of Nudging." *Yale Journal on Regulation* 32:413–450.

———. 2018. "'Better Off, as Judged by Themselves': A Comment on Evaluating Nudges." *International Review of Economics* 65:1–8.

Thaler, R. and C. Sunstein. 2003. "Behavioral Economics, Public Policy, and Paternalism." *American Economic Review* 93:175–179.

———. 2008. *Nudge.* New Haven, CT: Yale University Press.

11 Does the Inclusion of Social Preferences in Economic Models Challenge the Positive-Normative Distinction?[1]

Jack Vromen

Introduction

Wade Hands has written several commendable papers on the positive – normative distinction in economics (see, for example, Hands 2008, 2012, 2013a,b, 2020). I hold them in high esteem because they display a thorough understanding of the relevant literatures in both economics (and its history) and philosophy (and its history). This combination of expertise is not only rare, but it is also necessary especially in the case of the positive – normative distinction, as economists and philosophers seem to understand "positive" and "normative" in different ways. I learned a lot from reading Wade's papers and I also mostly agree with what he argues. There might be one exception, though. Hands (2008) argues that the inclusion of social preferences in economic analyses not only increases the normative content of economics but also challenges the positive-normative distinction in economics. This paper explores these two claims.

In doing so, I bring together two issues. The first issue is about whether welfare economics, which to many is normative economics *par excellence*, can instead be seen as a part of positive economics. Several economists have argued this, but it seems they have very different senses in which welfare economics can be positive in mind. Engaging with this issue obviously implies having a closer look at what positive and normative mean (or might mean) in economics. The second issue is about what repercussions, if any, the recognition of social preferences has for the welfare criteria to be invoked in welfare economics. I argue that this is an issue warranting more attention and discussion in the nascent field of Behavioral Welfare Economics (BWE) than it has hitherto received. Both issues are complex and multi-faceted. They need more and deeper analysis than I can offer here. All I hope to do is that in scratching the surface I am able to highlight interesting and important issues that will inspire further research.

Social preferences in "positive" behavioral economics (BE)

This paper is triggered by a remark in Hands (2008) that puzzles me. Hands discusses several arguments for increasing the normative content of positive economic science. One such argument, Hands argues, is provided by findings

DOI: 10.4324/9781003266051-16

in the experimental literature suggesting that moral beliefs, such beliefs about what is fair, matter to decision-making. According to Hands, such findings challenge the profession's traditional view on the positive and the normative: "Instead of ethical norms interfering with the scientific investigation, these are cases where including ethical beliefs in the analysis improves the theory's descriptive accuracy" (p. 9).

I agree with Hands that in the literature he is discussing, bringing in ethical beliefs in the analysis is meant to improve the theory's descriptive accuracy. What I find puzzling, though, is why this would increase the normative content of positive economics, and also why this would challenge the profession's traditional view on the positive and the normative. Hands is clearly referring here to the social preference models developed in behavioral economics (BE). In social preference models, social preferences, such as a preference for fairness (Fehr and Schmidt 1999), or for social efficiency (Charness and Rabin 2002) and reciprocity (Rabin 1993, Dufwenberg and Kirchsteiger 2004), are included as separate arguments in the utility functions of agents. This is done to account for choice anomalies, observed patterns of behavior that systematically deviate from the behavior predicted by (what is called) the standard self-interest model. Assuming, as Hands and most behavioral economists do, that moral beliefs and values of agents underlie these social preferences, this does indeed imply, as Hands argues, that moral beliefs apparently matter to decision-making. So Hands is right in arguing that including moral beliefs in economic models is claimed to improve the model's descriptive accuracy.

But how does this challenge the profession's traditional view on the positive and the normative? And how does the inclusion of moral beliefs in economic models increase their normative content? Aren't the ethical beliefs of individuals treated as facts here so that social preference models safely stay within the bounds of positive economics? I take it that the traditional view on the positive and the normative in economics is roughly the following.[2] Positive economics is in the business of explanation and prediction and pursues descriptive accuracy in its "is-statements" (i.e., getting the facts right). Normative economics is in the business of prescriptions, recommendations and advice and produces "ought-statements" to that extent. Ought-statements are supposed to express or reflect ideals or states of affairs that are deemed desirable and that one wants to attain. And these ideals or desired states of affairs are in turn assumed to reflect values. Whereas it is fine (and perhaps even inevitable) that moral values permeate normative economics, they should be left out in positive economics. Positive economics should stick to the facts and should not be colored by the economist's values.

If this is indeed approximately the profession's traditional view on the difference between positive and normative analysis, then it is hard to see how it is challenged in social preference models in BE. Social preference models are developed in BE to improve on the explanatory and predictive power of "self-interest only" models in standard economics. Social preference models are not in the business of prescriptions, recommendations and advice and do not produce "ought-statements". Insofar as the social preferences in those models reflect moral values and beliefs, these moral values and beliefs are taken to be facts about the economic agents; facts that are believed to be relevant for better explaining and predicting their behaviors. The central claim of social preference models is that without assuming the existence and causal efficacy of social preferences in our models, large chunks of observed behaviors cannot be properly explained and predicted. The moral values and beliefs of agents are not taken to reflect ideals that public policy should help attain.

Should we then simply conclude that Hands is wrong in arguing that social preference models increase the normative content of positive economic analysis? I think that conclusion would be premature. Proponents of social preference models in BE often do not leave it with just treating the moral values and beliefs that people actually have as relevant matters of fact for explaining and predicting behavior. Proponents often express their approval of the existence of social preferences and the sorts of prosocial behaviors that they give rise to (see, e.g., Capraro et al. 2019). A concern for fairness, for example, and the prosocial sharing behavior they might lead to is treated favorably. The same holds for reciprocity and the sustenance of cooperation it leads to (Fehr and Gächter 2000). By contrast, antisocial preferences leading to the punishment of cooperators are treated unfavorably (Herrmann et al. 2008). In making these sorts of evaluations, proponents of social preference models seem to attach a positive value to both social preferences and prosocial behavior.

Here, it seems behavioral economists allow their own moral values to enter their analyses. It also looks as if their own values enter their analyses already at an earlier stage of their analyses. It seems most work in "positive" BE start with *choice anomalies*; observations of systematic deviations in behavior from the behavior predicted by "the standard economic model". It is always observations of such non-standard patterns of behaviors that behavioral economists think call for explanations and predictions in terms of non-standard models. This does not only hold for social preference models, but also for the numerous cognitive biases in decision-making that behavioral economists have unearthed. In all cases, observed patterns of behavior are evaluated against the backdrop of the predictions made by the standard economic model. In the case of social preference, it is the "self-interest only" part of this model that is challenged. In the case of cognitive biases, it is the "full rationality" part of this model that is challenged. In this sense, the standard "self-interest-only-*cum*-full rationality" economic model provides the undisputed normative benchmark for most of positive BE.

In short, most analyses in "positive" BE start with evaluations of observed behaviors for which the standard "self-interest-only-*cum*-full rationality" model provides the normative benchmark. In case deviations from the predictions of this model are observed, behavioral economists think non-standard models are called for. A striking difference between the social preferences branch and the cognitive biases branch is that deviations spotted in the former

branch tend to be treated favorably by behavioral economists, whereas deviations in the latter tend to be treated unfavorably by behavioral economists.
In the cognitive biases branch, the normative appeal of the standard full
rationality model is unchallenged. Deviations due to cognitive biases can
only signify rationality failures and it is believed that these failures tend to go
at the expense of the individual's own well-being. By contrast, deviations due
to social preferences are typically not treated as failures, shortcomings or limitations of one kind or another, but are welcomed and cherished. Here, in the
social preferences branch of "positive" BE, it seems the normative appeal of
the "self-interest-only" model does seem to be challenged, even though acting on social preferences is (like actions affected by cognitive biases) assumed
to be detrimental to the individual's own well-being (or at least to their
material payoffs).

Now why is that? It is not easy to find explicit answers to this question
in the literature. Sometimes behavioral economists working in this branch
simply seem to take it for granted (or as obvious) that we all believe it is good
when people have social preferences and act on them so that there is more
prosocial behavior. Sometimes they seem to think it is sufficient to recognize
we are talking here about our nobler (or nice, or kind) instincts (and not our
nastier instincts as in the case of antisocial preferences).[3] Only occasionally
they do not leave it at this. Only sometimes explicit arguments are given for
why social preferences and prosocial behavior are to be welcomed. These
arguments refer to standard social welfare considerations: more social preferences (or, rather, more actions based on social preferences) and more prosocial
behavior are *social welfare*-enhancing. Even though they go at the cost of the
individual well-being of the prosocially behaving agent, the leading idea
seems to be that prosocial behavior has positive externalities for others (so
that the net effect on social welfare is positive; see, e.g., Chetty et al. 2014).
Fehr and Gächter (2000) show, for example, that strong reciprocity helps in
flattening the (otherwise steep) decline in social efficiency over time in public
goods games.

What the latter shows is that, appearances notwithstanding, the standard
welfare criteria are accepted also in the social preference branch of "positive"
BE (see also Angner 2015). It might have seemed at first that whereas behavioral economists working in the cognitive biases branch, who stress that any
deviation from the standard economic model signifies a rationality failure,
accept the normative benchmark of the standard economic model, behavioral
economists working in the social preferences branch, who stress that deviations from the standard model do not signify any failure or shortcoming,
reject the normative benchmark of the standard economic model. But on
closer inspection also the latter accept what are taken to be criteria for social
welfare in standard welfare economics.

Where does this leave us with the positive – normative distinction? I
have argued that behavioral economists working in "positive" BE routinely
engage in evaluations of observed patterns of behavior. Indeed, it can be

argued that most work in "positive" BE start with such evaluations. I have furthermore argued that the normative benchmark for such evaluations is provided by standard economics, be it the standard full rationality model or standard welfare economics. Thus, "positive" behavioral economists do not shy away from valuing behavior. Does this make "positive" BE a normative undertaking? In the next section, I argue that on a refined understanding of what economists mean by "normative" this is not necessarily the case.

Can evaluations be purely positive?

We saw that the received view in economics is that positive economics pursues explanations and predictions and that normative economics pursues prescriptions and policy advice. We also saw that evaluations are central to "positive" BE. Evaluations seem to differ from both explanations and predictions on the one hand and prescriptions and policy advice on the other. Evaluations can be seen as a mixture of positive and normative elements (Alexandrova 2018). Evaluations can only be correct and informative if they get the (relevant) facts right. But it is equally true that evaluations inevitably invoke a normative standard (or criterion, or benchmark) against which the facts are compared. Thus, making a decision about what normative standard to invoke seems to be indispensable in evaluations. This characterization of evaluations seems to imply that it cannot be denied that evaluations are at least in part normative. Yet, several economists (and also some philosophers) have vehemently denied this. They argue that making evaluations is (or at least can be) an altogether "positive" affair.

Several reasons have been put forward to support the view that making evaluations is not (or at least need not be) normative. One is that the normative standard invoked in evaluations need not be moral in kind (or do not need to reflect moral values, such as a concern for a fair distribution of income and wealth, or a concern for the general interest). The normative standard invoked might reflect cognitive or epistemic values only, such as empirical adequacy, explanatory and predictive power and simplicity. Consider empirical research. The empirical testing of hypotheses, to determine the degree to which they are confirmed by the available evidence, for example, inevitably involves a normative standard. Yet (ideally at least) the normative standard invoked does not reflect moral values of the empirical investigator. For many philosophers, this reason reflects an unduly restrictive or narrow view on normativity (Putnam 2004). But on a broader view on normativity, insofar as the values at stake are purely cognitive or epistemic, nobody would find the normativity at stake problematic (in the sense that it threatens the impartiality, objectivity or value-neutrality of the research being done).[4]

Quite a different reason for maintaining that evaluations can be purely positive is the following. We have seen that "normativity" in economics is tied up with giving prescriptions and policy advice. Evaluations do not need to result (or "issue in") prescriptions and also do not necessarily imply prescriptions. This is how Gul and Pesendorfer (2008) defend their view that welfare economics is a part of positive economics. Gul and Pesendorfer contrast what they take to be the purpose of "standard welfare analysis" with the "therapeutic" (or ameliorative) purpose of what they call "neuroeconomic welfare analysis". They argue that if some prevailing institution is found to be inefficient, the purpose of standard welfare analysis is not, as neuroeconomic welfare analysis argues it should, to find alternative, more efficient institutions, but to explain why the prevailing institution persists despite its inefficiency (ibid., p. 25). So Gul and Pesendorfer argue here that the evaluation in welfare economics that some institution is inefficient need not, does not and also should not issue in prescriptions and policy advice, but rather in better positive models of the institution in question.[5]

One could object here that what Gul and Pesendorfer argue here is not so much that evaluations themselves are not (or at least need not be) normative, but that there are no necessary links between evaluations and prescriptions. In fact, Gul and Pesendorfer do not deny but rather affirm that evaluations such as "the prevailing institution is inefficient" are normative statements. To them, as to many philosophers, the fact that with the notion of Pareto efficiency, welfare economics provides a normative benchmark for evaluations seems already enough to warrant the conclusion that welfare economics always starts with normative statements (ibid., p. 5). Yet there also are economists and philosophers who also deny the latter. The altogether different reasons that they give, and to which I will turn now, is that economists need not and should not allow their own moral values to influence their own research. If economists succeed in leaving out their own moral values, not only in their factual analyses of the degree to which states meet some normative benchmark, but also in the selection of the normative benchmark, they engage in positive, not normative analysis.

In a way, this is the Weberian ideal of *Wertfreiheit* (value-neutrality) applied to evaluations. The idea is that in their evaluations, scientists can invoke normative benchmarks without making any further commitment to the desirability of undesirability of attaining the benchmarks in reality. Such evaluations are what Nagel (1961) calls *characterizing value judgments*. Nagel gives the example of anemia. Biologists can determine purely on factual grounds the degree to which some animal is anemic without taking any stand on the issue of whether anemia is an undesirable condition. Nagel contrasts characterizing value judgments with *appraising value judgments*, in which approval or disapproval of some state of affairs (indicated by the normative benchmark) by the person uttering the judgments is expressed. The point of drawing the contrast is that whereas appraising value judgments obviously express values of the person making the judgments, characterizing value judgments can (at least in principle) be made in a value-free way.

As Nagel himself suggests, characterizing value judgments can be conceived of as *conditional* assertions. Instead of expressing categorical or absolute evaluations, characterizing value judgments tell you what is or isn't lacking in some actual or imagined state *if* some particular normative benchmark is invoked. As Alexandrova (2018) argues, this conditionalization of hypotheses (or claims) can in principle be used to arrive at a sensible notion of impartiality.[6] The idea is to neatly contain in the antecedent of the conditional hypothesis all the non-cognitive values that go into the choice of the normative benchmark so that non-cognitive values do not play any further role in affecting the decision whether or not to accept the conditional hypothesis. Once the normative benchmark is determined, only the facts together with cognitive values ought to "impartially" determine whether or not the conditional hypothesis is to be accepted.

On this view, the roles of non-cognitive moral values on the one hand and facts and cognitive values on the other hand are neatly separated. All non-cognitive moral values should find their places only in the determination (or selection) of the normative benchmark. And once the normative benchmark is set, only facts and cognitive values are allowed to play a role in the assessment of the acceptability of the evaluation. In principle, this leaves open the possibility that the non-cognitive moral values of economists (or scientists, or theorists in general) decide what normative benchmark is invoked in evaluations. But if this happens, characterizing value judgments are effectively turned into appraising value judgments and the ensuing analysis is no longer "positive" and value-free. This is in accordance with what Mongin (2006) calls the *authoritative criterion* in economics: "... a statement made by an economist counts as *normative* if it is paired with a value judgment made by *that* economist (not somebody else), and as *positive* otherwise (in particular, it may bear on somebody else's value judgments)" (p. 259). Thus, if the normative benchmark invoked reflects the non-cognitive moral values of others and if the economist refrains from committing or subscribing to it, evaluations made by economists can stay within the domain of "positive economics".

In short, on this view on evaluations as the outcomes of purely positive analyses, it is not denied that evaluations inevitably involve the use of some normative benchmark. It is not denied either that non-cognitive moral values might be involved in the choice of the normative benchmark. The only thing that is denied is that economists cannot leave out their own non-cognitive moral values in the choice of the normative benchmark. Economists can and also should leave out their own moral values and if they succeed in doing so, they have not left the domain of positive analysis. We could call this the PUMA (Positive analysis as analysis Unaffected by the Moral values of the Analyst) notion of positive analysis.

Turning back to "positive" BE now, it is easy to see that on the view on "positive" analysis just discussed, evaluations of systematic deviations from the predictions of "the standard economic model" as forms of irrational behavior, or as errors or mistakes, do not necessarily make these evaluations normative. For it is not necessarily the case that behavioral economists subscribe to the standard full rationality model in economics as the normatively adequate theory of rationality. All they might be claiming is that *if* the standard full rationality model in economics is accepted as the normatively adequate theory of rationality, then the observed systematic deviations in behavior represent less-than-fully rational behavior. And if this is indeed all they are claiming, then their evaluations are within the domain of positive economics.

Welfare economics as conducting positive analyses

What about welfare economics? Welfare economics is seen by many as normative economics *par excellence*. And indeed it cannot be denied that welfare economists often engage in policy advice and prescriptions. Gul and Pesendorfer (2008) rightly argue that (what they call) normative statements (such as "The prevailing institution is inefficient") need not issue in advice about how to improve efficiency and can be understood as a quest for better positive models. But for many welfare economists, it cannot be denied that they do have ameliorative aspirations. If they spot inefficiencies, their impulse is to look out for "something better" (Schelling 1981). Just think of the vast literature on market failures and on how to avoid or cure them.

But Gul and Pesendorfer are right that, regardless of whether welfare economists have explanatory or ameliorative ambitions, welfare economics starts with evaluations. As Mongin (2005) puts it, "… normative economics is primarily concerned with evaluations, and only secondarily with recommendations or prescriptions" (p. 1). If we concentrate now on the sorts of evaluations typically made in welfare economics, can these evaluations be called "positive" in the PUMA sense discussed before?

Archibald (1959) argues they can, if the relevant requirement is met: in their analyses, welfare economists should leave out their own moral values. Archibald furthermore argues that welfare economists can leave out their own moral values completely in conducting their analyses; in particular, they can conduct their analyses without morally judging the preferences (or wants or ends) of the individuals whose welfare is at stake. The crux of the matter for Archibald is that "welfare" is defined in welfare economics as the satisfaction of preferences (and these in turn as the choices individuals would make if they were in the position to choose) and that welfare economists can simply take the latter as given. There is no need for welfare economists to morally judge these preferences for them to conduct their analyses: "If we enquire into the efficiency of alternative arrangements for satisfying given wants, why is a judgment about these wants a necessary foundation for the theorems we discover?" (Archibald 1959, p. 317). If the hallmark of positive economics is as Robbins (1932/1935) characterized it, namely the study of how the attainment of the given ends that people actually have is conditioned by the scarcity of means, then the analyses conducted by welfare economists can fall squarely within the domain of positive economics.

We can reconstruct what Archibald is arguing here in the terms in which I analyzed evaluations in general before. I argued that evaluations always involve both the use of some normative benchmark and a comparison of some actual or hypothesized state with this benchmark. Both elements recur in the evaluations made in welfare economics.[7] Welfare economics first of all can be said to be involved in the selection of acceptable (or appropriate, or suitable) welfare criteria (as the relevant normative benchmarks in welfare economics) and second, in the determination of the degree to which some given state or institution (or arrangement, or policy proposal) meets the welfare criteria. Now, what Archibald argues is that welfare economists can leave out their own moral values not only in the second part (which is relatively uncontroversial), but also in the first part (which is more controversial), in the selection of welfare criteria. All welfare economists need to do for this is to treat the preferences of individuals as given and to withhold judgment of these. If they succeed in doing the latter, we could say they conduct positive analyses in the PUMA sense.

Archibald made clear he was talking only about "new Paretean welfare economics", in which criteria involving interpersonal comparisons of utility (or well-being) are avoided. Accordingly, Archibald discusses Pareto efficiency as the only sensible social welfare criterion.[8] But it remains to be seen whether Archibald's argument cannot be generalized to the additional (or other) social welfare criteria that can be invoked if instead we adopt a social welfare function (SWF) approach and allow for interpersonal comparisons of utility.[9] In the SWF approach pioneered by Bergson (1938) and Samuelson (1947), social welfare is conceived of as a mathematical function of the welfares (or well-beings) of the individuals involved. Social states are evaluated in terms of the degree to which they (fail to) maximize the SWF. Thus, the SWF is meant to specify acceptable social welfare criteria. The SWF framework leaves open a vast array of possible SWFs; SWFs might take many different functional forms. The strong Pareto principle, stating that social state B has higher social welfare than social state A if there is at least one individual better off (has higher individual well-being) in B than in A and no one is worse off in B than in A, is but one criterion or axiom that can be imposed (as a reasonable constraint) on the functional form of the SWF. There are other possible criteria that can be imposed on the functional form of the SWF, such as the Dalton-Pigou criterion, expressing a greater distributional concern for the well-beings of worse-off persons than for the well-beings of persons that are better off (Adler 2019).

A crucial issue raised by the SWF approach is: who is to decide about what axioms to impose on the functional form of the SWF, or more generally, who is to decide about what social welfare criteria are acceptable?[10] There is a long-standing tradition in welfare economics holding that, ideally, the social welfare criteria ought to reflect the moral values of the individuals involved (Graaff 1957, p. 10). In particular, they ought to reflect what objectives individuals think public policy should attend to. In line with the general idea put forward by Archibald (1959), we can ask ourselves whether we can defer to preferences of individuals to identify social welfare criteria. In particular, and this is the issue that I will turn to in the next section, can the social preferences of individuals identified in social preference models be deferred to in order to define or select acceptable social welfare criteria?

Social preferences in behavioral welfare economics (BWE)

BWE is often seen as the normative branch of BE. BWE is the systematic inquiry into how standard social welfare criteria should be modified (if at all) if we take the insights and findings of "positive" BE seriously (Bernheim and Rangel 2007, McQuillin and Sugden 2012,). Standard social welfare criteria are the criteria used in standard welfare economics: social welfare is seen as a SWF of individual well-beings, the functional form of the SWF should at a minimum respect the Strong Pareto Principle, and individual well-beings in turn are understood in terms of the degrees to which the actual preferences (as revealed in their choices) are satisfied.[11] The insights and findings of positive BE that are treated as most relevant in this regard are that there are several *choice anomalies* observed, patterns of behavior that systematically deviate from what standard economic theory predicts, and that actual preferences (as revealed in actual choice behavior) are often incoherent and inconsistent (they exhibit great context-dependence, e.g.). It is clear that these insights and findings call the social welfare criteria (and in particular, it seems, the individual welfare criterium in it) in question. What is less clear is what modifications of the criteria are needed, and especially how radical the modifications should be. McQuillin and Sugden (2012) dub this the *reconciliation problem*.

Above I already noted that evaluations are crucial also already in "positive" BE. It is not just that the standard economic model provides the benchmark for dubbing observed patterns of behavior that systematically deviate from the standard economic model's predictions "irrational", or as errors or mistakes. It is also often maintained that such behaviors, supposedly stemming from cognitive biases, go at the expense of the individuals' own well-being. With respect to social preferences, behavioral economists often do not leave it with proposing social preference models that allegedly better explain observed patterns of prosocial behavior than standard "self-interest-only" models in economics. We saw that social preference model proponents also often welcome and value prosocial behavior. And to the extent that they provide an explicit justification for this, they seem to incur standard social welfare criteria such as notably Pareto efficiency.

On the PUMA notion of "positive economics" that I discussed in this chapter, the fact that behavioral economists often make such evaluations does not necessarily mean that they, supposedly working in "positive economics", crossed the line with normative economics. For they do not necessarily subscribe to and commit to the normative benchmarks they invoke. They might simply treat the benchmarks invoked in standard economics as given (or accept them "for the sake of argument") and only research how much observed patterns of behavior deviate from them. Or they might be inclined to argue that the benchmarks invoked reflect the individuals' own under-standing of, and views on, individual well-being and social welfare. Note that in both cases this would make their analyses positive, as insofar as the choice of the benchmarks reflects moral values, these are the moral values of others, not those they have themselves.

The issue I want to address now is to what extent the social preferences identified in social preference models warrant or even necessitate a modi-fication of standard welfare criteria. In contrast to the implications of the identification of a host of cognitive biases for welfare economics, which has taken center stage in BWE, to this date very little attention has been paid in BWE to this issue.[12] And to the extent that social preferences are discussed at all in BWE, the issue has invariably been whether the satisfaction of social preferences contributes to the *individual* well-being of those acting on their social preferences. If by acting on their social preferences individuals satisfy these preferences, is their individual well-being thereby enhanced? Or is their individual well-being thereby rather diminished, or unaffected?

Opinions about this seem to differ. Roughly, the issue at stake here is whether the satisfaction of social preferences contributes to the individual well-being of the individual having the social preferences. Opinions about this issue seem to differ. On the one side, we have scholars such as Bernheim and Rangel (2008), Posner and Sunstein (2017) and Kaplow and Shavell (2003) who seem to give an affirmative answer: if individuals with social preferences really care about the payoffs of others (and if these preferences are not ill-informed or ill-conceived in other ways), then the satisfaction of these social preferences contribute to the well-beings of these individuals. Note that this view differs from the standard individual well-being criterion as it is often specified in practice, but not from how the standard individual well-being criterion is understood in theory. True, on this view, not only the individual's own payoffs matter to the individual's well-being, and but also in this sense, it deviates from how the standard individual well-being criterion is often specified in practice. But the standard individual well-being criterion as it is understood in theory does not rule out "non-standard preferences" as legitimate contributors to individual well-being.

On the other side, we have scholars such as Dworkin (1977), Harsanyi (1982) and Hausman (2012) who insist that satisfying non-self-interested social preferences might contribute to the individual well-beings of bene-ficiaries but do not contribute to the individual's own well-being. Thus in a sense, they subscribe to the standard individual well-being criterion as it is often specified in practice: only the satisfaction of self-interested (or self-regarding) preferences contribute to an individual's well-being. One reason for doing so seems to be straightforward. If we allow the satisfaction of all sorts of preferences to contribute to someone's well-being, we cannot make sense of self-sacrifice (Overvold 1984). Suppose Jacob is a pure altruist, willing to give up everything to contribute to Jill's well-being. Shouldn't we say then that in satisfying his social preference, Jacob is contributing to Jill's well-being rather than to his own well-being? Furthermore, if we were to include someone's concern for the payoffs of others in that individual's well-being, this can lead to faulty *double-counting* of the others' well-beings. Suppose we have a mini-society of two persons, Jacob and Jill. If Jacob is a pure altruist, caring only about Jill's payoffs, and Jill is a pure egoist, caring only about her own payoffs, then if we accept Jacob's social preference as a complete measure of his individual well-being, then it seems the consequence of this is that the interest of Jill is counted twice and the interest of Jacob counts for nothing.[13]

From the perspective of BE, given its focus on individual decision-making, it is understandable that the discussion concentrates on individual well-being. But from the perspective of welfare economics, it is a bit strange. After all, we have seen that there is a long-standing tradition in welfare economics suggesting that the social welfare criteria rather than the individual well-being criteria should reflect the moral views and values of individuals. And the social preferences posited in social preference models are often seen as expressions of the moral views and values of the individuals. Fairness as inequity-aversion, for example, is often seen as an expression of the moral view that undeserved inequality in payoffs received by individuals is unfair (Fehr and Schmidt 1999). Social efficiency, making the sum total of the payoffs all individuals receive as large as possible, is often seen as a moral concern for the general or common good (Engelmann and Strobel 2004). And strong reciprocity is believed to express the moral view that cooperators and contributors ought to be rewarded for their good deeds and defectors, cheaters and free-riders ought to be punished for their bad deeds (Bowles and Gintis 2011). From the perspective of welfare economics, then, if social preferences indeed express the moral views and values of the individuals acting on social preferences, it seems social preferences should be reflected in social welfare criteria, not in individual well-being criteria.[14]

This is indeed what some welfare economists think should be done. Moral values should find their way into social welfare criteria, not individual welfare criteria. Hammond (2008), for example, argues that "The main role of altruism in welfare economics is to help determine ethical views, not to determine individual welfare. Concepts of Pareto efficiency which include altruism in individual welfare have little normative significance" (Hammond 2008, p. 4; see also Diamond 2006). Hammond's twofold reasons for believing so must by now sound familiar. First, a real altruist cares about the well-beings of others, whereas it is only the self-regarding preferences that should find a place in individual well-beings in the SWF framework; and, second, nonetheless, including altruism in the altruist's individual well-being leads to undesirable double counting. Assuming now that the individuals' "ethical views" (such as altruism) should be reflected in the functional form of the SWF, the following "sorting device" picture emerges: the self-regarding preferences of individuals should be reflected in their individual well-beings, and the social preferences of individuals, expressing the moral views of individuals, should be reflected in their individual SWFs. These individual SWFs then should be deferred to in order to derive acceptable social welfare criteria.

What to think of this picture? There are many issues at stake here. All I can do here is to sort them out a bit and briefly comment on each of them. A rather obvious issue is that there seems to be great heterogeneity in the social preferences that individuals have. It is not only that some individuals seem to have a fairness-as-inequity-aversion preference, for example, whereas others seem to have a social efficiency preference. It is also that some individuals are assumed to have no social preferences at all. Should the latter then have no say in what social welfare criteria are acceptable? That seems outrageous. Anyway, it is clear that heterogeneity in social preferences greatly complicates finding social welfare criteria that are acceptable to all. Another issue is that it might be hard to draw a sharp line between self-regarding preferences and social preferences. Is an inclination to help someone in need because the sight or idea of someone being in need makes one feel miserable self-regarding or other-regarding, for example?

But let me bracket these complications for the time being. Even if we were to find a satisfying solution for these complications, there is the more fundamental issue of whether the social preferences, as they are identified in the social preference models proposed by behavioral economists, provide us with the sort of information we are after. What we are ultimately after is what objectives individuals think public policy should attend to. Their ideas and beliefs about this matter are assumed to reflect their moral values. Do they think that public policy should aim at maximizing collective welfare (or social efficiency), for example, or do they also care about how equally the economic pie is distributed? What we get in social preference models is information about how observed patterns of behavior, including prosocial behavior, can be explained. Observed patterns of behavior are rationalized by assuming that individuals maximize utility functions in which next to a concern for their own material payoff a concern for the material payoffs of others (or for how nice or kind others are) are included as separate arguments. So the explanatory purpose for which social preferences are introduced in social preference models is very different than the purpose for which we want to elicit the individuals' moral values: to find an acceptable social welfare criterion.

It might nevertheless be tempting to assume that these different concerns imputed to individuals correspond exactly to the sorts of things we are after. That is, the concern for their own material payoff corresponds with self-interested preferences that are indicative of their own individual well-being, and the concern for the material payoffs of others corresponds with what objectives individuals think public policy ought to attend to. Although I do not deny there might be some correspondence here, there are several reasons to believe that the correspondence is rather crude at best.

The first reason for doubt is that the social preferences imputed to individuals in social preference models might not identify real psychological

mechanisms actually producing their behaviors. They might rather be theoretical construct partly imposed by the "constrained maximization"
framework (Vromen 2021). Rather than identifying intrinsic concerns that
are stable across contexts, they might reflect the existence and efficacy of
context-sensitive social norms, for example.[15] Or, contrary to the full rationality assumed, they might reflect (partly at least) mistaken beliefs (Miettinen
et al. 2020). Or, they might reflect a narrow opportunity set of individuals
rather than genuine intrinsic concerns. To repeat, what we are ultimately
after is what objectives individuals think public policy ought to attend to.
Individuals are supposed to imagine what they would decide if they were in
the position to decide this. But individuals of course never are in the position
of an "impartial benevolent dictator" who can decide this. So how are we
to elicit such beliefs and preferences? How people actually behave in experimental settings, in which they are faced with very different situations and
issues, might be a poor indicator for this.

Although many commentators do not shy away from attributing particular
motivations to people acting on social preferences, this is quite problematic.
Hammond (2008) briefly discusses the case of a rich person experiencing revulsion when confronted with extreme poverty. He calls the revulsion the rich
person feels selfish and suggests that, unlike altruism, this is a welfare-relevant
externality that should be reflected in the rich person's individual well-being.[16] But if the type of motivation provides the relevant dividing line, we can
ask whether the concern for the material payoffs by others posited in social
preference models always has the right type of motivation. Think, for example, of Sen's sympathy or Andreoni's impure "warm glow" altruism, which
could underlie a concern for the material payoffs by others. In both cases, the
underlying motivation would be selfish and they wouldn't qualify as "ethical
views" that should go into the choice of an acceptable social welfare criterion.

There are good reasons to assume that the mapping between a particular
type of motivation and a particular social preference is not one-to-one, as some
seem to assume, but rather many-to-one. Consider fairness-as-inequity-aversion (Fehr and Schmidt 1999). Fairness sounds as a distinctly "unselfish" moral
consideration that can unproblematically go into the choice of an acceptable social welfare criterion. But several commentators have argued that the
disadvantageous part of inequity-aversion (that is, when individuals receive
lower payoffs than others), which is assumed to be stronger than the advanta-
geous part of it in Fehr and Schmidt's model, is driven by envy (Engelmann
and Strobel 2004). Envy is similar to Hammond's revulsion in that it is an
unpleasant feeling for the person experiencing it. If individuals exhibit inequity-aversion by taking actions to lower the payoffs of others receiving higher
payoffs than they receive themselves just to satisfy their "envy preference",
isn't this as "selfish" as when people are poverty-averse because they cannot
stand the confrontation with extreme poverty?

To sum up, there are several reasons to doubt that the social preferences
identified in social preference models accurately reflect the sort of moral

values determining what objectives the individuals, allegedly having the social preferences, think public policy ought to attend to. It seems this makes social preferences a poor, unreliable indicator of what social welfare criteria individuals deem acceptable. If so, social preferences do not provide a reliable source of information for "positive" BWE ("positive" in the PUMA sense, discussed before). Other sources of information might be more reliable. If such sources are found, in principle a "positive" BWE could be implemented. That is, behavioral welfare economists could in principle leave out their own moral views also in the choice of acceptable welfare criteria and still conduct welfare analyses. But do they actually leave out their own moral values in this? And is it a good idea for behavioral welfare economists to do so? Thus, far I explored only the possibility of a purely positive BWE. I now turn to a preliminary discussion of its actuality and desirability.

Do welfare economists *de facto* leave out their moral values? And is it desirable that they do so?

Thus, far I inquired about the possibility of having a positive BWE (in the PUMA sense), in which social preferences of individuals (as they are identified in BE's social preference models) are deferred to as indicators of acceptable social welfare criteria. Although I questioned that social preferences can be treated as reliable indicators for this purpose, the idea that the moral values of practitioners of BWE can (at least in principle) be completely left out in the determination of acceptable social welfare criteria was not called in question. For there can be other ways for practitioners of BWE to observe relevant values and beliefs of individuals (that are reliable indicators of what the individuals deem acceptable welfare criteria) that are not influenced by their own moral values. So the upshot is that at least in principle practitioners of BWE can leave out their own moral values in the determination of acceptable social welfare criteria. But this does not settle the issues of, first, whether welfare economists do in fact leave out their own moral values in determining acceptable social welfare criteria and, second, whether it is a good idea for them to do so.

Let me first tackle the issue of whether welfare economists do in fact leave out their own moral values in determining acceptable social welfare criteria. This is hard to tell.[17] From the way in which welfare economists discuss acceptable social welfare criteria, it seems we cannot infer whether they themselves concur with the social welfare criteria discussed and also how important that is for their discussion. If they disagree with a set of stated social welfare criteria, do they think they are not worth discussing? Or do they simply treat them as "given", as Archibald (1959) suggests they should do?

In the spirit of Archibald (1959), welfare economists often argue that the determination of welfare criteria is best left to others. They say they do not see it as their task and responsibility and also not as part of their expertise to determine what welfare criteria are acceptable or appropriate. What they do see as belonging to their tasks, responsibilities and expertise is to find out whether some state, institution or policy is efficient given the welfare criteria set by others, and if not, whether some other feasible state, institution or policy is more efficient. And they often claim that in their efforts to find this out, they can and should stick to the facts. Their assessments and renderings of the facts should not be tainted by their own moral values.

Schelling (1981/1984) talks of the "somewhat ethically evasive character" of economics, by which he means that economists tend to shy away from telling others what objectives they should pursue. What economics can offer is something else: "... economic reasoning is better at helping to choose among ways to accomplish a distributional objective than at helping to choose objectives" (p. 18). In other words, economists can help in finding more efficient allocations of resources to accomplish some given objective. Or, as Schelling himself prefers to put it (since he dislikes the "engineering" associations of "efficiency"), economists constantly follow the "something better approach". Whatever it is that individuals pursue, economists can help them in realizing their objectives to a fuller extent (or to the same extent, but with lower costs).

What this suggests is that economists are not wedded to any particular set of objectives, but that they are wedded to promoting and, if possible, enhancing efficiency. As Schelling suggests, the idea is that regardless of what preferences individuals want to satisfy, it is always better for them to find and implement more efficient arrangements for doing so. Social efficiency, in terms of Pareto efficiency, invariably is seen as one of the central, if not the only defensible, social welfare criteria in welfare economics. Surely then, Pareto efficiency is a normative criterion welfare economists are committed to?

One way to escape drawing this conclusion is suggested by Archibald (1959). Archibald suggests that the only thing welfare economists are doing is fleshing out how welfare economists understand "welfare". Once this understanding is accepted, the Strong Pareto Principle *ipso facto* is accepted also. As discussed above, Archibald argues that for welfare economics "welfare" simply means what individuals prefer (or what individuals would choose if they were provided with the relevant choice options). Now, all the Strong Pareto Principle states seems to be implied by this: if there is a social state B in which the preferences of at least one individual are satisfied to a larger degree than in social state A and if there are no individuals whose preferences are satisfied to a lesser degree in B than in A, then the individuals prefer B to A.[18] Insofar as the preferences of individuals reflect moral values, these are the moral values of individuals and not those of the welfare economist. On Mongin's authoritative criterion, this would count as positive. No normative commitment of welfare economists to the Strong Pareto Principle would be implied over and above their commitment to a particular understanding of "welfare".

This reasoning might seem unassailable, but in fact it is not. The reason why it is not is foreshadowed in our discussion of social preferences. The Strong Pareto principle links preferences about individual welfare (or well-beings) to preferences about social welfare. As we have seen, individuals need not care only about their own individual welfares, they might also care about social welfare. The considerations that go into their personal social welfare rankings need not coincide with the considerations that go into their individual welfare rankings. For that reason, not all individuals need to prefer B to A even if some prefer B to A and no one prefers A to B with respect to their individual welfares. Thus, the fact that B is more conducive to the individual welfares of some than A (while B is not less conducive to the individual welfares of others) does not imply that all individuals prefer (or ought to prefer) B to A.[19]

Interestingly, although he puts himself in the same tradition as Archibald (1959), Hennipman (1992) develops a slightly different argument to buttress his claim that welfare economists are not committed to the desirability of efficiency. Hennipman argues that welfare economists are well aware that efficiency improvements are not always desirable. He gives the following example to bring home his point: "… it is not always true that efficiency is 'more desirable' than inefficiency. In general its moral value obviously depends on the ends, means and ways of action. One may very well prefer an inefficient to an efficient Gestapo" (p. 422). Hennipman here sensibly makes the desirability of efficiency contingent and conditional on the desirability of ends, means and ways of action. But, and this makes his argument somewhat different than Archibald's, he seems to leave open the possibility that it is the welfare economist's own moral values, not those of the individuals involved, that can (and perhaps should) decide over the desirability of ends, means and ways of action. After all, the "inconvenient truth" is that the objectives of the Gestapo seem to have reflected the moral views and values of many Germans at the time about what objectives public policy should attend to. If so, according to the moral values of many Germans at the time, an efficient Gestapo would have been preferable to an inefficient Gestapo.

This finally brings me to the intricate issue of whether welfare economists should leave out their own moral values in determining acceptable social welfare criteria. Hennipman's example of the preferability of an inefficient to an efficient Gestapo highlights the dangers of relying uncritically on the moral values of the individuals whose welfare is at stake. From a critical, detached ethical point of view, the moral values actually held by individuals might at times appear as cruel and horrifying. In other words, the normative authority of the moral views actually held by individuals at times might and perhaps should be challenged by welfare economists (see also Adler 2019). Deferring to the moral values of individuals rather than those of welfare economists in determining social welfare criteria might sound attractive, as it avoids "imposition" of the criteria by welfare economists. But simply accepting the moral values of individuals as being normatively authoritative might also not be the way to go. By simply accepting the moral values as being normatively authoritative and looking out for the most efficient ways to facilitate them, welfare economists make themselves complicit in realizing them. In doing so, it seems they escape their own responsibility. It seems welfare economists have to steer here between the Scylla of authoritarian imposition of their own moral values and the Charybdis of uncritically relying on the moral values of the individuals whose welfares are at stake.[20]

Conclusions

Including social preferences in "positive" BE need not increase the normative content of positive economics. And it need not call the positive – normative distinction as it is commonly understood in economics in question either. It is not only that it is a genuine option for behavioral economists to refrain from making judgments about the desirability of social preferences. It is also that in the sort of evaluations of behaviors routinely made by behavioral economists, which provide the points of departure for most if not all the work done in "positive" BE, the normative benchmarks invoked do not necessarily reflect the behavioral economists' own moral values. On a popular understanding of "positive" and "normative" in economics, if the normative benchmarks invoked reflect the moral values of others, these evaluations qualify as positive.

I furthermore argued, following Archibald (1959), that welfare economics, which to many is clearly normative economics, can in principle be practiced as positive analysis in the same PUMA sense: Positive analysis as analysis Unaffected by the Moral values of the Analyst. The welfare economist can take the ideas of others about what are acceptable welfare criteria as given, refraining from making any moral judgment about their desirability. I then explored whether the social preferences ascribed to individuals in social preference models can be deferred to in order to identify what social welfare criteria the individuals find acceptable. Although I expressed several doubts as to whether social preferences provide reliable indicators for this, it is in principle possible for welfare economists to empirically find out what social welfare criteria individuals find acceptable, and in doing so to completely leave out their own moral values. Whether welfare economists actually do leave out their own moral values in their analyses and whether it is desirable that they do so are different matters needing further discussion.

Notes

1. Part of this chapter has been written while I was enjoying a NIAS-fellowship (from August 2020–February 2021).
2. I will refine this rough-and-ready discussion of "positive" and "normative" in economics in the next section. Much has been written about this distinction (see, e.g., the Putnam–Dasgupta debate; Putnam 2003, Dasgupta 2009; see also Davis 2016) and some also argue for the need to distinguish "art" as a separate third branch (Su and Colander 2013, Colander and Su 2015).
3. This is tricky. It is not obvious that social preferences reflect our nobler instincts. I will get back to this later in the chapter.
4. In the rest of this chapter, I will simply assume that cognitive and non-cognitive values can be neatly separated and that moral values are non-cognitive values.

5. Note that this is similar to how I described common practice in "positive" BE: starting with observations of behaviors that systematically deviate from the "standard economic model", develop new models to explain these systematic deviations.

6. Although Alexandrova thinks this indicates a sensible notion of impartiality, she is not in favor of it because she thinks the notion does not help resolve the problems of "imposition" and "inattention".

7. I realize there are different renderings possible of what welfare economics is and what it aims to do. Sugden (2021) contains a short, but helpful discussion of these.

8. An interesting issue here is whether Pareto efficiency is a criterion welfare economists value and are committed to, or whether this is a criterion they are not necessarily committed to. In line with Archibald (1959), Hennipman (1992) argues for the latter: welfare economists are not even committed to (Pareto) efficiency. Blaug (1980) disagrees. This is a controversial issue to which I will return later.

9. I cannot go deeply into this now, but all Robbins' (in)famous ban on making interpersonal utility (or well-being) comparisons seems to be based on is the, by itself, correct observation that making interpersonal utility comparisons inevitably involves moral value judgments (see also Adler 2019). But the important insight for our purpose here is that these need not be the moral value judgments of the welfare economist.

10. It is important to note that all individuals, whose welfares are at stake, might have their own personal SWF and thus also their own preferred social welfare criteria (reflecting their moral views on what objectives public policy ought to attend to).

11. "Standard welfare criteria" is ambiguous. It can refer to the abstract, unspecified SWF framework adopted in standard welfare economics (Dasgupta 2009). But it can also refer to a particular specification of the SWF standardly accepted in public economics (Fleurbaey and Mongin 2005): one in which individual well-beings are the only arguments in the SWF and in which the SWF has an utilitarian functional form (meaning that all individual well-beings are being weighted equally). The latter SWF satisfies the Strong Pareto principle (or axiom; see Adler 2019). In what follows I assume that "positive" BE does not call the SWF framework in question, but might call in question the specific utilitarian specification of the SWF accepted in public economics.

12. This is remarkable, as Truc (2021) finds (in a bibliometric study) that since the 1990s, more work has been done in BE on social preferences than on any other subject (including cognitive biases).

13. Note that with the discussion of fallacious double counting, we in fact shifted from discussing individual welfare criteria to discussing social welfare criteria. For a discussion of double counting presupposes that we have a prior understanding of how we think the well-beings or interests of individuals ought to weighted (Hart 1979).

14. But see Vromen (2012, 2017) for in-depth analyses questioning that moral values necessarily underlie "strong reciprocity".

15. It is unclear whether social norms differ from social preferences (Binmore 2010), or whether social preferences are rather expressions of the existence and efficacy of social norms (Kimbrough and Vostroknutov 2016, Buyalskaya et al. 2021).

16. But what if the rich person "perversely" were to feel delight rather than revulsion when confronted with extreme poverty? Should that also be treated as a welfare-relevant externality that should be taken into account?

17. Evidence seems to be mounting that economists do not succeed in leaving out their own moral values (and ideologies) in their "positive" analyses, for example, in evaluating how well certain institutions and policies meet given welfare criteria (Randazzo and Haidt 2015, Van Dalen 2019). Leaving out their own moral values completely might be logically possible but is perhaps not psychologically possible.

18. There seem to be several economists believing that meeting the Strong Pareto Principle commands unanimous consent by all (see, for example, Milgrom 1993). This

might also explain why some economists seem to treat Pareto efficiency as unobjectionable (Feldstein 2005, Mankiw 2013). As I argue below, this is unfounded.
19. Mongin (2006, p. 260) makes a similar point: in accepting Pareto efficiency, welfare economists in fact add a separable value judgment to observations of preference orderings of individuals.
20. Perhaps organizing mini-publics (Fishkin 2018) and citizen panels (Brown 2006) provide a promising compromise.

References

Adler, M. (2019). *Measuring Social Welfare: An Introduction.* New York, NY: Oxford University Press.

Alexandrova, A. (2018). Can the science of well-being be objective? *British Journal for the Philosophy of Science* 69(2), 421–445. https://doi.org/10.1093/bjps/axw027

Angner, E. (2015). Well-being and economics. In Fletcher, G. (ed.). *The Routledge Handbook of Philosophy of Well-Being* (pp. 492–503). Routledge. https://www.routledgehandbooks.com/doi/10.4324/9781315682266.ch40

Archibald, G.C. (1959). Welfare economics, ethics, and essentialism. *Economica* 26(104), 316–327.

Bergson [Burk] A. (1938). A reformulation of certain aspects of welfare economics. *Quarterly Journal of Economics* 52: 310–334.

Bernheim, D & Rangel, A. (2007). Toward choice-theoretic foundations for behavioral welfare economics. *American Economic Review,* 97(2), 464-470.

Binmore, K. (2010). Social norms or social preferences? *Mind & Society* 9, 139157. DOI:10.1007/s11299-010-0073-2

Blaug, M. (1980). *The Methodology of Economics: Or How Economists Explain.* Cambridge: Cambridge University Press.

Bowles, S., & Gintis, H. (2011). *A Cooperative Species: Human Reciprocity and Its Evolution.* Princeton and Oxford: Princeton University Press.

Brown, M.B. (2006). Survey article: Citizen panels and the concept of representation. *Journal of Political Philosophy* 14(2), 203–225.

Buyalskaya, A., Gallo, M., & Camerer, C.F. (2021). The golden age of social science. *PNAS 2021: Perspective.* DOI: 10.1073/pnas.2002923118

Capraro, V., Jagfeld, G., Klein, R., Mul, M., & van de Pol, I. (2019). Increasing altruistic and cooperative behaviour with simple moral nudges. *Scientific Reports* 9(1), 11880. https://doi.org/10.1038/s41598-019-48094-4

Charness, G., & Rabin, M. (2002). Understanding social preferences with simple tests. *The Quarterly Journal of Economics* 117(3), 817–869. https://doi.org/10.1162/003355302760193904

Chetty, R., Saez, E., & Sándor, L. (2014). What policies increase prosocial behavior? An experiment with referees at *The Journal of Public Economics. Journal of Economic Perspectives* 28(3), 169–188.

Colander, D., & Su, H-C (2015) Making sense of economists' positive-normative distinction. *Journal of Economic Methodology* 22(2), 157–170, DOI:10.1080/1350178X.2015.1024877

Dasgupta, P. (2009). Facts and values in economics. In Kincaid, H. & Ross, D. (eds.). *The Oxford Handbook of Philosophy of Economics.* Oxford University Press. DOI:10.1093/oxfordhb/9780195189254.003.0022

Davis, J. (2016). Economists' odd stand on the positive-normative distinction: A behavioral economics view. In DeMartino, G. & McCloskey, D. (eds.). Oxford: *Oxford University Press Handbook on Professional Economic Ethics: Views from the Economics Profession and Beyond* (pp. 200–218). Oxford: Oxford University Press.

Diamond, P. (2006). Optimal tax treatment of private contributions to public goods with and without warm glow preferences. *Journal of Public Economics* 90, 897–919. https://doi.org/10.1016/j.jpubeco.2005.06.001

Dufwenberg, M., & Kirchsteiger, G. (2004). A theory of sequential reciprocity. *Games and Economic Behavior* 47(2), 268–298. https://doi.org/10.1016/j.geb.2003.06.003

Dworkin, R. (1977). *Taking Rights Seriously*. Cambridge, MA: Harvard University Press.

Engelmann, D., & Strobel, M. (2004). Inequality aversion, efficiency, and maximin preferences in simple distribution experiments. *American Economic Review* 94(4), 857–869.

Fehr, E., & Schmidt, K.M. (1999). A theory of fairness, competition, and cooperation. *The Quarterly Journal of Economics* 114(3), 817–868. https://doi.org/10.1162/003355399556151

Fehr, E., & Gächter, S. (2000). Cooperation and punishment in public goods experiments. *American Economic Review* 90(4), 980–994. https://doi.org/10.1257/aer.90.4.980

Feldstein, M. (2005). Rethinking social insurance. *The American Economic Review* 95(1), 1–24.

Fishkin, J.S. (2018). *Democracy When the People Are Thinking: Revitalizing Our Politics Through Public Deliberation* (1st ed.). Oxford: Oxford University Press.

Fleurbaey, M., & Mongin, P. (2005). The news of the death of welfare economics is greatly exaggerated. *Social Choice and Welfare* 25, 381–418.

Graaff, J. de V. (1957). *Theoretical Welfare Economics*. Cambridge: Cambridge University Press.

Gul, F., & Pesendorfer, W. (2008). The case for mindless economics. In Caplin, A. & Schotter, A. (eds.). *The Foundations of Positive and Normative Economics: A Handbook*. New York, NY: Oxford University Press.

Hammond, P.J. (2008). Altruism. In *The New Palgrave Dictionary of Economics*. DOI:10.1057/978-1-349-95121-5_470-1

Hands, D.W. (2008). Philosophy and economics. In Durlauf, S.N. & Blume, L.E. (eds.). *The New Palgrave Dictionary of Economics* (2nd ed., pp. 410–420). London: Palgrave Macmillan. On line at www.dictionaryofeconomics.com.

Hands, D.W. (2012). The positive-normative dichotomy and economics. In Mäki, U. (ed.). *Philosophy of Economics* (pp. 219–239), Vol. 13 of D. Gabbay, P. Thagard & J. Woods (eds.), Handbook of the Philosophy of Science. Amsterdam: Elsevier.

Hands, D.W. (2013a). Mark Blaug on the normativity of welfare economics. *Erasmus Journal for Philosophy and Economics* 6, 1–25.

Hands, D.W. (2013b). GP08 is the new F53: Gul and Pesendorfer's methodological essay from the viewpoint of Blaug's popperian methodology. In Boumans, M. & Klaes M. (eds.). *Mark Blaug: Rebel With Many Causes* (pp. 245–265). Cheltenham: Edward Elgar.

Hands, D.W. (2020). Libertarian paternalism: Taking Econs seriously. *International Review of Economics* 67, 419–441. https://doi.org/10.1007/s12232-020-00349-7

Harsanyi, J. (1982). Morality and the theory of rational behaviour. In A. Sen & B. Williams (eds.). *Utilitarianism and Beyond* (1st ed., pp. 39–62). Cambridge University Press. https://doi.org/10.1017/CBO9780511611964.004

Hart, H.L.A. (1979). Between utility and rights. *Columbia Law Review* 79(5), 828–846.

Hausman, D.M. (2012). *Preference, Value, Choice, and Welfare*. New York, NY: Cambridge University Press.

Hennipman, P. (1992). The reasoning of a great methodologist: Mark Blaug on the nature of Paretian welfare economics. *De Economist* 140(4), 413–445.

Herrmann, B., Thoni, C., & Gachter, S. (2008). Antisocial punishment across societies. *Science* 319(5868), 1362–1367. https://doi.org/10.1126/science.1153808

Kaplow, L., & Shavell, S. (2003). Fairness versus welfare: Notes on the Pareto principle, preferences, and distributive justice. *The Journal of Legal Studies* 32(1), 331–362.

Kimbrough, E.O., & Vostroknutov, A. (2016). Norms make preferences social. *Journal of the European Economic Association* 14(3), 608–638.

Mankiw, N.G. (2013). Defending the one percent. *Journal of Economic Perspectives* 27(3), 21–34.

McQuillin, B., & Sugden, R. (2012). Reconciling normative and behavioural economics: The problems to be solved. *Social Choice and Welfare* 38, 553–567.

Miettinen, T., Kosfeld, M., Fehr, E., & Weibull, J.W. (2020). *Revealed Preferences in a Sequential Prisoners' Dilemma: A Horse-Race between Six Utility Functions.* CESifo Working Paper Series No. 6358. https://papers.ssrn.com/sol3/papers.cfm?abstract_id=2939010

Milgrom, P. (1993). Is sympathy an economic value? Philosophy, economics, and the contingent valuation method. In Hausman, J.A. (ed.). *Contingent Valuation: A Critical Assessment* (pp. 417–435). Amsterdam: Elsevier.

Mongin, P. (2005). A concept of progress for normative economics. hal-00242961 (A concept of progress for normative economics – Archive ouverte HAL (archives-ouvertes.fr)

Mongin, P. (2006). Value judgments and value neutrality in economics. *Economica* 73, 257–286.

Nagel, E. (1961). *The Structure of Science. Problems in the Logic of Scientific Explanation.* London: Routledge & Kegan Paul.

Overvold, M. (1984). Morality, self-interest, and the reasons for being moral. *Philosophy and Phenomenological Research* 44, 493–507.

Posner, E.A., & Sunstein, C.R. (2017). Moral commitments in cost-benefit analysis. *Virginia Law Review* 103, 1809–1860.

Putnam, H. (2004). *The Collapse of the Fact/Value Dichotomy and Other Essays.* Cambridge, MA: Harvard University Press.

Putnam, H. (2003). For ethics and economics without the dichotomies. *Review of Political Economy* 15, 395–412. DOI:10.1080/09538250308432

Rabin, M. (1993). Incorporating fairness into game theory and economics. *The American Economic Review* 83(5), 1281–1302.

Randazzo, A., & Haidt, J. (2015). *Are Economists Influenced by Their Moral Worldviews? Evidence from the Moral Foundations of Economists Questionnaire.* Working Paper; SSRN-id2700889%20(1).pdf.

Robbins, L. (1932/1935). *The Nature and Significance of Economic Science* (2nd ed.). London: The MacMillan Press.

Samuelson P.A. (1947). *Foundations of Economic Analysis.* Cambridge, MA: Harvard University Press.

Schelling, T.C. (1981/1984). Economic reasoning and the ethics of policy. *The Public Interest* 63, 37–61 (reprinted in Schelling, T.C. 1984. *Choice and Consequence: Perspectives of an Errant Economist.* Harvard University Press.

Su, H., & Colander, D. (2013). A failure to communicate: The fact/value divide and the Putnam/Dasgupta debate. *Erasmus Journal for Philosophy and Economics* 6(2), 1–23.

Sugden, R. (2021). Normative economics without preferences. *International Review of Economics* 68, 5–19. https://doi.org/10.1007/s12232-020-00356-8

Truc, A. (2021). Interdisciplinary influences in behavioral economics: a bibliometric analysis of cross-disciplinary citations. *The Journal of Economic Methodology.* https://doi-org.eur.idm.oclc.org/10.1080/1350178X.2021.2011374

Van Dalen, H. (2019). Values of economists matter in the art and science of economics. *Kyklos* 72(3), 472–499.

Vromen, J. (2012). Human cooperation and reciprocity. In K. Binmore & S. Okasha (eds.). *Evolution and Rationality* (pp. 158–184). Cambridge University Press. https://doi.org/10.1017/CBO9780511792601.009

Vromen, J. (2017). Ultimate and proximate explanations of strong reciprocity. *History and Philosophy of the Life Sciences* 39(3), 25. https://doi.org/10.1007/s40656-017-0151-4

Vromen, J. (2021). *As if* social preference models. Inn Heilmann, C. & Reiss, J. (eds.). *The Routledge Handbook of Philosophy of Economics,* London: Routledge, pp. 125–137.

Index

Printed in the United States
by Baker & Taylor Publisher Services